THE END OF THE THIRD WORLD

Also by Guy Arnold

AID AND THE THIRD WORLD
AID IN AFRICA
BRAINWASH: The Cover-up Society
BRITAIN SINCE 1945
BRITAIN'S OIL
DOWN THE DANUBE
ECONOMIC COOPERATION IN THE COMMONWEALTH
HELD FAST FOR ENGLAND
JOURNEY ROUND TURKEY
KENYATTA AND THE POLITICS OF KENYA
THE LAST BUNKER
LONGHOUSE AND JUNGLE
MODERN KENYA
MODERN NIGERIA
*SOUTH AFRICA: Crossing the Rubicon
STRATEGIC HIGHWAYS OF AFRICA (*with Ruth Weiss*)
THE THIRD WORLD HANDBOOK
TOWARDS PEACE AND A MULTIRACIAL
  COMMONWEALTH
THE UNIONS
WARS IN THE THIRD WORLD SINCE 1945

From the same publishers

The End of the Third World

Guy Arnold

St. Martin's Press

First published in Great Britain 1993 by
THE MACMILLAN PRESS LTD
Houndmills, Basingstoke, Hampshire RG21 2XS
and London
Companies and representatives
throughout the world

A catalogue record for this book is available
from the British Library.

ISBN 0-333-59379-0

Printed in Great Britain by
Ipswich Book Co Ltd
Ipswich, Suffolk

First published in the United States of America 1993 by
Scholarly and Reference Division,
ST. MARTIN'S PRESS, INC.,
175 Fifth Avenue,
New York, N.Y. 10010

ISBN 0-312-10092-2

Library of Congress Cataloging-in-Publication Data
Arnold, Guy.
The end of the Third World / Guy Arnold.
p.   cm.
Includes index.
ISBN 0-312-10092-2
1. Developing countries—Economic conditions.   I. Title.
HC59.7.A8335   1993
330.91721'4—dc20   93-15803
                                          CIP

Contents

Preface		vii
1	Introduction	1
2	Origins and history	13
3	Aid	27
4	The Poor of the World	43
5	Pressures on the Third World	57
6	Special Cases	71
7	The Question of Debt	89
8	Resources	103
9	The Turn to the East	121
10	Western Racism	139
11	The Politics of Contentment	155
12	Policing the South	171
13	The United Nations Alternative	189
14	The New Imperialism	201
Notes and References		217
Index		223

Preface

The Third World was the creation of the Cold War; it arose out of the determination of the newly independent countries of Asia, led by Pandit Nehru of India, not to be drawn into the ideological confrontation of the two superpowers and their allies and for a time the Third World and the Non-Aligned Movement were to be synonymous. However, the Nehru idea of standing apart from, or even holding the balance between, the two sides in the Cold War foundered on the simple question of power, or lack of it. During the course of the Cold War the Third World grew in numbers until more than 100 nations could claim to belong, and though its members did not possess much power they did control sufficient of the world's resources, or occupy such strategically vital areas, as to make it worthwhile for both sides in the Cold War to woo them. Aid became the symbol of this relationship but by the 1980s, as Soviet power declined and it became increasingly apparent that it was losing the economic confrontation, so western attitudes towards the Third World hardened and the message from the rich nations, the aid donors whose assistance had become essential to the economic survival of Third World countries, was 'do as we say – accept IMF prescriptions and its "seal of approval", privatise, democratise and improve your humanitarian records – or there will be no more aid'. The process gathered momentum through the 1980s and by the time the Cold War finally came to an end at the beginning of the 1990s the attitude of the rich nations towards the poor nations of the South had fundamentally changed : no longer was it a question of helping the countries of the Third World make the essential breakthroughs to development that had been a theme of the 1960s; nor was the concept of partnership, which had been a vogue word at the time of the 1980 Brandt Report, any longer in use. Instead, President Bush had proclaimed a 'new world order' which implied a world controlled by the North that in its turn was led by a United States no longer constrained by its confrontation with the Soviet Union. There was no place for a Third World in this new dispensation, only a dominant North and a dependent South. This is not to argue that the problems of the Third World, above all its overwhelming poverty, have been resolved, for if anything they have become more difficult; rather, it is to suggest that the rules governing the relations between North and South have fundamentally changed. This change was signalled for some time before the end of the Cold War by a growing indifference in the North to the plight of the South and by the replacement of 'partnership', though the term had never been translated into any meaningful practice, by a developing arrogance whose most obvious manifestations were encapsulated in the new morality: 'do as we say and you may receive some help; defy us and you risk disciplinary action'. The balance of the twentieth century is likely to prove an even more difficult and challenging time for the South – the old Third World – than has been the case through the near half-century of the Cold War.

GUY ARNOLD

1   Introduction

When, in 1974, India exploded her first nuclear device she provoked much anger in the West: in part this was because a leading nation of the Non-Aligned Movement should both want and prove capable of creating a nuclear arsenal of her own; still more, the moral indignation which ensued was in reality outrage that India had dared to break the monopoly of the leading nuclear powers and was not prepared to behave according to the dictates of the North which saw itself then (and even more today) as the power-broker of the world. Most of the relationships existing between the North and the South or the Third World are, more or less overtly, relationships of neo-colonialism: aid is the most obvious example of this relationship but so too are the EC's Lomé Conventions which link the African, Caribbean and Pacific (ACP) countries unwillingly to the European economic juggernaut, or the arms selling business. Given the current and growing indifference of the North to the problems of the South and the huge indebtedness of the latter to the former (debt being a cardinal instrument of control) the relationship between North and South gives every indication of becoming even more neo-colonial in the future than it is already. Indeed, the most likely development to arise out of the end of the Cold War will also be the disappearance of any independent capacity to bargain on the part of the old Third World on the one hand, and a growth of neo-colonial controls exercised by the North on the other.

Once it had become obvious that the end of the Cold War also meant an end to the world-wide confrontations of the superpowers and their allies the Third World began to realise what had already been emerging during the brutal, recession-dominated 1980s: that it was largely expendable. From about the middle of 1989 Third World leaders expressed increasing

1

fears that their case – for aid, for better trade conditions, for a more equitable world order – would go by default as a triumphalist West turned its attention to the new and vastly more satisfying problem of reincorporating Eastern Europe, including the successor states to the Soviet Union, into the western capitalist system. Just as the concept of a Third World (originally, in fact, of a Third Force) emerged during the 1950s when newly independent countries led by India's Nehru determined not to be absorbed by one or other side in the Cold War, so the end of the Cold War meant that the Third World suddenly had nowhere to go. It has become an anachronism of history and what now happens to the countries of the South remains one of the great question marks over the final years of the twentieth century. Despite protestations to the contrary, western concern with the new possibilities in the east, led by a united Germany that is really beginning to feel its strength again, means that a majority of Third World countries which were already becoming marginal to the interests of the North in the 1980s will find themselves becoming even more marginal during the 1990s.

A new pattern had begun to emerge even before Gorbachev's *perestroika* had brought an end to the old confrontations, for it had already become clear that except for a few special cases such as Angola the USSR had largely opted out of the aid game, leaving the field to the rich donors of the West. And once this had been realised in Europe and North America new and irresistible pressures came to be exerted upon the countries of the South: to privatise, to accept the *diktats* of the IMF and World Bank with their Economic Recovery Programmes (ERPs) and Structural Adjustment Programmes (SAPs) while, at the same time, the North discovered a new morality of its own and began to make aid dependent upon human rights and a return to democracy. During the 1980s almost every international meeting – at the UN, UNCTAD, the IMF, World Bank, the Non-Aligned Movement (NAM) or the Commonwealth – resolved itself into a confrontation, less and less between West and East and more and more between North and South. The unwillingness of the North to help the South was highlighted in the 1992 *Human Development Report* of the UNDP (itself an unusual and brave document to come from the UN stable) which contrasted the unwillingness of the West to write off Africa's debts with its readiness to reduce the debts of Poland by 50% despite the fact that Poland's per capita income was five times that of the average for Africa. The contrast in approach was striking. By the time that UNDP report was published in mid-1992 most Third World leaders had come to realise that they faced the grim prospect of a period of neglect; in a time of deepening world recession their calls for a more equitable world system would fall upon increasingly deaf ears as the interest of the West became almost totally absorbed in the problems of the newly enfranchised ex-communist world. By the beginning of the 1990s, indeed, whatever the genesis of the term 'Third World', it had by then come largely to mean the end of the poverty line. Even more alarming for the old Third World was the emergence of a new set of western attitudes and 'guidelines' towards the South: a readiness to act as the policeman of the South; growing racism, which was expressed as fear of incoming immigrants and led to a tightening of controls; and a determination to prescribe political patterns of behaviour as the prerequisite for any fresh aid. These new approaches, moreover, have been accompanied by an obvious and rapidly diminishing interest in even attempting to solve some of the most glaring problems of the South. This new attitude (or part of it) was again highlighted by the UNDP *Human Development Report* when it pointed out that while the United States was not prepared to increase its contributions to either the World Bank or the IMF it was also reluctant that others, and particularly Japan, should do so either, since that would alter the voting powers in such institutions to the detriment of US influence and control, and it is control rather than solutions which Washington seeks through its membership of such bodies.

1992, indeed, turned out to be a most instructive year, with concern for the environment – real or feigned – well to the fore.

A wide range of international pressures had at least ensured
that environmental issues would be aired and discussed at the
UN Conference on Environment and Development (UNCED)
at Rio de Janeiro in Brazil; predictably, North–South lines
were drawn up well in advance and included some fresh
arguments which had not been previously aired. Scientists
representing western, highly industrialised interests countered
'Green' arguments with a broad thesis that because we have
done things in the past we can continue to do them in the
future, while both sides seemed more interested in faulting the
arguments of the other than coming up with sensible solutions
to what after all are global problems. The extent of the divide
between the two sides was emphasised at Rio de Janeiro by
Governor Gilberto Mestrinho from Brazil's state of Amazonas,
who told journalists at the Global Forum: 'You chopped down
your forests and now you don't want us to cut down a single
tree because it will affect the climate in Norway or somewhere.'
Coming closer to the nub of the problem, he made the
accusation that: 'The developed world sold $200bn of products
based on molecules from the tropical forest(s) last year, yet not
one cent came to the Amazon region.'[1] A crude accusation to
make, perhaps, yet it accurately reflects the response to what is
seen as an increasingly crude and ruthless attitude of dominant
acquisitiveness on the part of the rich North.

And yet western triumphalism at the collapse of communism
has not been matched by any equivalent readiness to help the
former Soviet Empire. From 1989, as the East Europeans
struggled to move back into the market economy, most help
from the West was reluctant; this was especially the case with
the United States, with advice being freely offered unsupported as a rule by financial help. Possibly even more
depressing for North and South alike was the manifest
disarray in western ranks in relation to the aftermath of the
Gulf War and what to do about Saddam Hussein, or the
West's still more disastrous and disoriented policies in the
former Yugoslavia, where interference solely on humanitarian
grounds threatened to turn a brutal civil war into an even

worse catastrophe. But perhaps nothing underlined more clearly the moral bankruptcy and narrowly selfish objectives of the North on the one hand, and the growing gap between North and South on almost all important issues on the other, than the Rio Earth Summit.

The Earth Summit was held in June 1992 and most of the preceding six months were taken up with complicated manoeuvring by the two sides, so that long before the delegates met the meeting had developed into a confrontation between North and South over money. The summit had two broad aims: to ensure that development in the Third World is carried out in environmentally sustainable ways; and to see that urgent measures are taken by the industrialised countries to reduce damage to the global ecology from pollution and the over-use of non-renewable resources. Just to state these two aims is to provide a measure of the potential for conflict. Heads of government of every UN member were invited to take part. According to Maurice Strong, the Canadian secretary-general of the conference, the Third World countries will require $125bn a year in aid if they are to develop without adding to the damage already done to the environment by the industrialised world. He gave this calculation at a time when total aid to the Third World came to only $50bn a year and when all the signs also pointed to a lessening rather than to any increase in aid commitments by the North to the South.[2] While Mr Strong was making his calculations President Bush announced, in February 1992, that he would attend the summit only if it produced a treaty serving US interests. 'The definition of a productive meeting is whether it's in the best interests of the United States', a senior White House official said[3] and what soon became clear was American concern over a treaty on global warming that would limit emissions of carbon dioxide levels in the year 2000 to those of 1990. President Bush did not wish or intend to endorse a treaty that limited such emissions on the grounds that it would impose added stress on a US economy which was already in trouble. The United States is the world's most prolific burner of the fossil fuels responsible for global warming; it was obvious that if the United States was going to baulk at any controls it would be unrealistic to suppose that other nations would submit to them except in token ways. This was hardly an inspiring augury for the summit.

As the Rio summit drew nearer, it became obvious during the first half of 1992 that few if any meaningful commitments would be made, and talk by optimists of Rio's unique historic importance was replaced by more realistic suggestions that it might be the start of a gradual process or a 'useful green consciousness-raising exercise'. Third World countries saw the Rio Summit as providing a chance to win concessions on debt relief, to obtain promises of greater aid and better terms of trade, in return for which they would be prepared to moderate their worst environmental excesses. Such a bargaining approach was bound to heighten the suspicions between North and South – as it did. As a senior European civil servant put it: 'The poor countries wanted a lot of new money with no strings attached, while the rich ones wanted to give a little money with lots of strings.'[4] Such attitudes had already emerged during the preparatory meetings held in New York during March and early April; certain subjects – in particular population control and consumption – were either treated as though they were totally taboo or were seen as provocative. Then, in mid-April, Prince Charles entered the debate in Britain with a major speech on population in which he argued that no country could hope to prosper while its population growth outstripped its economic expansion. Prince Charles made his speech to the reconvened Brundtland Commission meeting in London (the Brundtland Commission's report *Our Common Future* on the state of the world presented in 1987 was what had led to the Rio summit being called). Prince Charles complained of population being left off the Rio agenda, but also took the rich nations to task for their lack of generosity and failure to curb global pollution: 'We will not slow the birthrate until we address poverty and we will not protect the environment until we address the issues of population growth and poverty in the same breath.'[5]

Comparisons were inevitably made in early 1992 between the state of the world in 1972, when the Stockholm Conference had first advanced the environment as a world issue, and its state in 1992 as UNCED approached. The earth had gained 2bn people, 50mn children in the Third World had died from drinking polluted water, 500mn acres of tropical rainforest had been felled and 500bn tonnes of topsoil (equivalent to the entire crop-land of the United States) had been lost, while the gap between the richest and poorest countries had doubled, the hole in the ozone layer had appeared and the world's climate appeared to have begun heating up. There was no shortage of prophets of doom yet their prophecies, even if believed, made little impression upon politicians from the two sides of the North–South divide as they jockeyed determinedly for position. The United States objected to any references to Western over-consumption, the Vatican and a number of predominantly Catholic countries objected to discussion of population control, the Arab oil producers – anxious to sell more oil – objected to discussion of energy saving, and countries with major forests objected to discussion of the rate at which these were being cut down. As Malaysia's Prime Minister, Mahathir Mohamad, argued, the wealthy nations must be prepared to provide both money and ecologically sound technology to assist poor countries cut back on logging or other activities that damage the environment: 'If the rich North expects the poor to foot the bill for a cleaner environment, Rio would become an exercise in futility.'[6] Unfortunately that did seem to be what the North was expecting. In May, the EC environment commissioner, Ripa di Meana, threatened not to go to Rio and claimed that the draft treaty on global warming had so many loopholes that any serious outcome at Rio would be impossible. Since the rich were busy squabbling among themselves, with the commissioner proposing that members of the EC should impose a carbon tax while Spain furiously opposed this as likely to slow down its development, there did not appear much prospect that any serious agreements could be reached between North and South. However, as is the way with such international conferences, agreement of sorts is usually forthcoming, and in New York during May it did seem that some form of international climate treaty would be agreed, though in such a watered-down form as to be all but meaningless. Even so, the great majority of the OECD countries appeared ready to agree to stabilise their output of carbon dioxide – the most destructive of the 'greenhouse gases' – at 1990 levels by the year 2000, although the United States, which produces more of this gas both in total and per capita than any other nation, declined to accept any cap on its emissions. The principal object of all the preliminary meetings appeared to be the determination of the main participants to water down every proposal that was before them.

The Earth Summit was opened by the UN Secretary-General Boutros Boutros-Ghali on 3 June and by then the negotiations had been broken down under the following subjects: a treaty on global warming; a treaty on biodiversity (protection of plants and animals); a statement of principles relating to conserving or sustainably exploiting forests; a Rio declaration on principles concerning development and environmental protection; Agenda 21 – an action plan for sustainable development in the twenty-first century; money – the need for a Green Fund to finance sustainable development in the developing countries; technology transfer – access by developing countries to cleaner technologies of the North; and finally, what post-summit institutions should be created to monitor its decisions. The possibilities did not look good before the conference and, as Mahathir Mohamad told a pre-Rio meeting of developing country ministers in April: 'There will be no development if the poor countries are not allowed to extract their natural wealth . . . fear by the North of environmental degradation provides the South with the leverage that did not exist before. If it is in the interest of the rich that we do not cut down our trees, then they must compensate us for the loss of income.'[7] There was not much sign that the North, admittedly hard hit by recession, had any such intention. And as the conference took place scientists, predictably, argued that nothing was certain, warning against green fundamentalists who in their turn attacked the market forces so beloved of the North, which they argued posed the greatest threat to the environment. Increasingly, indeed, the proponents of radically opposed approaches to the world's real problems appeared to have less and less in common with one another, and almost no chance of finding common ground outside a few vague statements of principle. What too often appeared to be overlooked was the fact that the conference was about the environment *and* development: after decades of arguing that the poverty of the Third World can only be overcome by development, too many supporters of green policies seemed to have forgotten that development means consuming resources. On the other side, with the United States in the vanguard, a defence of the right to exploit resources seemed to have overborne any sense that such exploitation must be controlled. The stark answer to the central concerns of the Rio summit – environmental degradation – is money: only if the rich provide the funds can the developing countries be expected to break the deadlock between economic growth and environmental degradation.

The most persistent impression coming from almost all the participants from the North was of extreme reluctance to take the problems posed by the conference sufficiently seriously. At base, this reluctance was due to a sound appreciation of what was involved: if global warming really does threaten the long-term future of the world then it will be combated only by a real change of lifestyle in the most industrialised countries – and that means less consumption, the one topic President Bush would not allow to be placed on the agenda. And the United States, which is the world's greatest producer of carbon emissions, sees conservation of energy as likely to deepen its recession. This concern illustrates the greatest difficulty of finding long-term solutions. All politicians – whether of the North or the South – are concerned primarily with immediate problems and political survival while almost all the problems posed at the Rio summit concerned the long-term future (long-term in political if not global terms) and therefore in most cases worthy of little more than lip-service from these politicians. Such unconcern with long-term environmental issues was as true of politicians from the North, who did not want to accept any limitations upon either growth or consumption, as it was of politicians of the South, whose concern was development and how to fund it.

When the conference finally began Boutros Boutros-Ghali produced a most expressive phrase to cover the problems which afflict the relations of North and South when he said that the planet was 'sick with over-and under-development'.[8] Finding a mean between those two extremes is what the North–South divide is all about. Japan, seemingly as intent upon embarrassing the Americans as anything else, sent a huge delegation to Rio and hinted that it was considering doubling its aid to the Third World; were Japan in fact to do this it would have an enormous 'knock-on' effect and force other rich nations to follow suit, or at least make some gestures. The end of the conference appeared as much as anything to be a photo-opportunity for heads of state from the North to assure the world how much they cared. In the end, the summit agreed: a treaty to combat global warming; a treaty to protect wildlife (not signed by the United States); moves towards a treaty to halt the spread of deserts; steps to tackle over-fishing and pollution of seas; Agenda 21 – an 800-page action programme for the next decade; a Rio Declaration of Environmental Principles; the setting up of a Sustainable Development Commission – a new UN body – the setting up of an Earth Council to monitor progress by governments. There was no treaty on forests, although a statement of principles was agreed.

Perhaps, in the end, it was Fidel Castro who encapsulated what the conference was supposed to be about. An anachronistic figure in his olive-green uniform and breast of medals, and very much a survivor from Cold War confrontations as well as one of the more successful Third World leaders, both in terms of improving the lot of his own people and in grimly defying the giant of the North, he began his speech to the conference by saying: 'An important biological species runs the risk of disappearing due to the rapid, progressive liquidation of its natural living conditions: Man.' Speaking before US President Bush, Germany's Chancellor Kohl and Britain's Prime Minister Major, Castro firmly placed the blame for environmental destruction upon the developed world who 'with just 20 per cent of the world's population, [they] consume two-thirds of all its metals and three-quarters of all the energy produced.' Later he said: 'We need less luxury and waste in a few countries so there can be less poverty and hunger in the greater part of the world.'[9] He represented at that moment, *par excellence*, the vanishing Third World to which he so uncompromisingly belonged.

2 Origins and History

When the victorious allies created the United Nations in 1945 they saw it as an instrument to be used to maintain the status quo; they did not expect that it would become the champion of the rights of all people to have a voice in running the world. That, however, is what happened, and the entity of the Third World came to represent the voice of the poorest, the hitherto dispossessed. The Third World emerged out of years of exploitation and, as much as anything, arose out of frustrations with the world's power structures. It was the stark realities of a Cold War confrontation backed by nuclear weapons with all their potentially frightful consequences for mankind that led Pandit Nehru and other leaders to turn to a 'Third Force' concept in the 1950s. The claim of the powerful that they know best how to solve the world's problems is always, ultimately, backed by their capacity to use force to obtain their ends, and though the conventional wisdom condemns such an approach in theory, in reality we have hardly begun to move away from a situation in which the North 'knows' how the world ought to conduct its affairs and is prepared to help the South only on sufferance and only when it behaves as the North requires. The sin of Nehru and other non-aligned or Third World leaders was their refusal to accept this arrogant assumption. Ironically, it was the fear among the leaders of the big powers that India under Nehru (1947–64), Egypt under Nasser (1954–70), or Yugoslavia under Tito (1945–80) would go their own ways that immeasurably strengthened the resolve of such leaders to do just that. And so the Third World was born. Most of the states which came to see themselves as belonging to the Third World were newly independent and the very act of proclaiming their membership of the Third World and the Non-Aligned Movement was an act of independence, and an indication of their determination to assert their rights in a world still dominated

13

by the great powers. Politically the determination to belong to the Third World made a great deal of sense to its members, but as a rule politics alone will not advance a country's interests very far unless these are backed up by economic strength. Economic weakness always meant that Third World initiatives, had, at best, only a marginal chance of success.

There would not have been a Third World without the Cold War, for the very concept of a Third World depended upon a wider world that was already divided between East and West. Only later was the poverty factor to take over and become the overriding consideration in any dialogue between North and South. At first, the dialogue was about the nature of the world political divide which the Cold War had created, and where the Third World countries stood or wished to stand in relation to it. The Third World was in essence thus the creation of the Cold War. It was the determination of the newly independent Asian countries not to be drawn into the Cold War which led them to formulate the principles of Non-Alignment; later, as new nations from Africa and elsewhere joined the group it came increasingly to be referred to as the Third World. All these countries of the Third World – despite huge cultural and economic differences – nonetheless had certain characteristics in common: they suffered from poverty and lack of development; until after 1945 most of them had been colonies of the European powers; and they each wished to stand aside from the confrontations of the Cold War which they saw in a quite different light to the main protaganists. The Third World developed with the Cold War and as the colonial empires were liquidated, and its membership could be divided into six groups: the new nations of Asia; China, which stood on its own; Latin America (most of whose states had enjoyed a century or more of independence); Africa, which was generally the poorest region of all; the Arab states of the Middle East, which possessed most of the world's surplus oil resources; and the small territories scattered through the Caribbean, Asian and Pacific regions, many of which could only just stand on their own feet as independent entities.

The Third World created its own structures: regional structures such as the Organisation of African Unity (OAU), and all-embracing structures of which the Non-Aligned Movement (NAM) was the most important, at least in its ideological purpose, whatever the real outcome of its deliberations. Though at first the two sides in the Cold War tried to play down the very idea that a large group of weak newly independent countries could stand aside from their all-absorbing confrontation, they soon came to realise that the Third World countries, and most especially the larger more influential ones like India, had to be wooed; hence, in its turn, came the phenomenon of the major rich nations offering aid on a scale that had never been seen or envisaged before. But although a great deal of mythology about aid has been created – that it represents part of a 'one world' philosophy – in fact policy is always based upon self-interest, and the North involved itself in the economic problems of the Third World not in order to find solutions to those problems but so as to further its own interests.

China's reassertion of its independence under Mao Zedong following the civil war which brought the Chinese Communist Party to power in 1949 gave enormous impetus to Asian independence and the sense that a new era in world affairs had arrived; at last the time had come, or so it was hoped, to make the Europeans and Americans leave Asia to its own devices. When China's Zhou En-lai visited New Delhi in 1954 he and Nehru agreed the Five Principles of Peaceful Co-existence or *Panchsila*: 'The principles and considerations which govern our mutual relations and the approach of the two countries to each other are as follows: (1) mutual respect for each other's territorial integrity and sovereignty; (2) mutual non-aggression; (3) mutual non-interference in each other's internal affairs; (4) equality and mutual benefit; and (5) peaceful co-existence.'[1] These principles had immediate relevance to Asian relations at that time (and most especially between the two Asian giants, China and India) but the concept of Peaceful Co-existence became the natural starting point for the Non-Aligned Movement to adopt as the basis of its relations with the two sides in the Cold War; a year after the New Delhi meeting *Panchsila* was adopted as its policy by the newly formed Non-Aligned Movement which emerged out of the Bandung meeting of 1955.

The Bandung Conference of April 1955 may be taken as the formal date which signalled the birth of the Non-Aligned Movement whose principal architects were Nehru of India, Sukarno of Indonesia (host to the conference), Nasser of Egypt and Tito of Yugoslavia. The Non-Aligned Movement (or NAM) was a conscious alternative to membership of one or other side in the Cold War; the new nations wished to stand aside from the ideological confrontation of the major powers and concentrate instead upon their own economic development. In its early days NAM was concerned with peace – that is, acting as a Third Force between the two sides in the Cold War; later, however, during the 1960s and afterwards it became increasingly concerned with the problems of development and the poverty of most of its members. An important side effect of the triangular world of East, West and Third World was the extent to which both sides in the Cold War provided aid for the uncommitted in an attempt to woo them away from non-alignment. However, although all members of the Non-Aligned Movement were also members of the Third World not all members of the Third World were members of NAM, with most of the Latin American countries reluctant to join while some Third World countries were clearly and overtly aligned to one or other side in the Cold War: Côte d'Ivoire and Kenya in Africa, for example, were in the western camp just as Cuba was in the Soviet camp and in real terms such countries could not claim to be non-aligned, though they insisted upon membership of NAM on the general grounds that they opposed big power confrontations.

The first summit of the NAM countries was held at Belgrade in 1961, six years after the Bandung Conference. The summit issued a Peace Appeal to the USSR and the United States on 5 September and both Khrushchev of the USSR and Kennedy of the United States responded by welcoming the peace appeal, thereby signalling their acceptance – however reluctant – of the concept of a third group of nations outside the two opposing camps in the Cold War: NAM had come of age. Subsequently NAM held regular summits – Cairo, 1964; Lusaka, 1970; Algiers, 1973; Colombo, 1976; Havana, 1979; New Delhi, 1983; Harare, 1986; and Belgrade again, 1989. By the 1980s, however, the concern of NAM was overwhelmingly economic.

It was perhaps appropriate that the 1992 NAM summit should be held in Indonesia where the organisation was born and where, possibly, it was about to die, for the representatives of its now 110 member states must have been acutely aware of how much they were likely to be adversely affected by the disintegrating structures of the post-Cold War age. Officials, for example, had tried to shelve the issue of Yugoslavia (one of NAM's founder members now disintegrating) but Malaysia and Iran would not allow this to happen and lashed out at Serbian attacks on Moslems in Bosnia. Indonesia, once more the host, tried to refocus attention on the issue of development and how to reduce Third World debts, by then standing at $1.3 trillion. When Malaysia's Prime Minister, Mahathir Mohamad, said that 'The Western attitude towards the daily killings of the Bosnians stands in stark contrast to the response of the alleged killings of the Kurds in Iraq'[2] he was, once more, highlighting the deep suspicions which divide North and South. He went on to claim that the Non-Aligned Movement needed to redefine itself in a changing global environment or face the bullying of the rich and powerful nations in what he said amounted to 'a revival of the old Western colonialism', and he probably voiced the fears of a majority when he said it. But it was President Suharto of Indonesia, in opening the conference, who went to the heart of the South's problem: 'If a country desires development for its people it should strive to bring its own house in order', he said, and continued 'A nation must not depend on others for its own development.'[3] That simple statement sums up all the misgivings of the South ever since Julius Nyerere examined the effects of aid dependence in his

Arusha Declaration of 1967, but to state the problem is not to come up with a solution, although in 1992 it seemed more likely than at any time in the preceding forty years that the South would have to develop on its own simply because the North was so manifestly losing interest. But though many had come to question the relevance of NAM in a post-Cold War age the UN Secretary-General, Boutros Boutros-Ghali, reminded the summit of an old truth when in his message to it he said that 'neither de-colonisation nor the dislocation of blocs has erased the phenomenon of power. The temptation to dominate, either world-wide or regionally, remains.'[4] By the end of this summit it was clear that doubts about NAM's future role had not been resolved. At least during the Cold War, despite all the hypocrisies which attended NAM meetings, it was possible to be genuinely non-aligned and to argue for a clear stand against the ideological confrontation of the North's two superpowers. By 1992, however, only poverty, and the same, repeated demands for debt relief and a more equitable world economic order, had any chance of achieving a consensus among otherwise squabbling and disparate members.

Although, like the other creations of the Cold War such as NATO, the Non-Aligned Movement will no doubt find justifications for its continued existence, it is doubtful that it will do anything except decline in influence and importance, neither of which were ever very great. At least the Bandung meeting of 1955 was the first ever Africa–Asia meeting without western or big power sponsorship; then 29 nations met to consider their role. By 1992 NAM had (with four new members joining) 110 member states representing 2bn people of the world's poorest nations. But, like a law of science, NAM's prospects of acting as an effective entity diminish in proportion as members' economic prospects improve; alternately, the poorest and weakest see themselves and the whole Third World simply being marginalised as a direct result of the end of the Cold War.

'Seek ye first the political kingdom', said Kwame Nkrumah in his heyday, and he was right as far as he went; but the next kingdom after the political one is the economic one, and control of that was all too rarely achieved by newly emancipated Third World countries. Though Third World countries refused to join sides in the Cold War they soon found that economic weakness did not allow them much room in which to manoeuvre or do anything else. Sensing this vulnerability, the North substituted aid for colonialism and the aid age was born. Only when it has escaped from the aid trap will the South begin to be truly independent; whether its members are either capable of escaping from aid dependence, or want to do so, is another matter.

Only once during the years of the Cold War was there any real possibility of the Third World escaping from the dependence trap in which it found itself enmeshed, and that was during the 1970s when the rise of OPEC threatened western economic hegemony and allowed a brief period in which the Third World could bargain with the rich North on something like equal terms. It did not last long. The 13 members of OPEC were all members of the Third World and between them they controlled the greater part of the world's traded oil upon which the western economies were dependent. The phenomenon of the rise and fall of OPEC during the 1970s was crucial to Third World hopes, though in the end these were to be disappointed. Nonetheless, for four or five years OPEC wrested the economic initiative from the leading western economies and was able to act as a vanguard for change, calling for a new international economic order in the process. During the years 1973–5 there was approaching panic in the West as oil prices rose; it was at this time that the concept of North and South was born, while western hesitation in face of OPEC power gave new hope to the Third World that it might at last achieve a more equitable world order. Because all the OPEC member countries came from its ranks it was assumed by the rest of the Third World that they were entirely in sympathy with the wider aspirations of the group as a whole; in consequence, OPEC's successes were regarded as an assertion of all the Third World's rights in confrontation with the North. It did not, of course, work out

that way. Nonetheless, the Third World as a whole had a
vested interest in OPEC even when the huge price increases it
imposed inflicted major economic hardship upon non-oil
producing countries of the South. The need for solidarity was
paramount, and Third World countries lined up behind OPEC
as it took on the major industrial countries of the North.

In March 1975 OPEC leaders met in Algiers where,
presenting themselves as the vanguard of the Third World,
they demanded a New International Economic Order (NIEO).
In June of that year, this time meeting in Gabon, OPEC
demanded that oil should be quoted in SDRs rather than in US
dollars. None of this was palatable to the West (the USSR was
a net exporter of oil and so could sit back to enjoy the spectacle
of the West in trouble). The western response to these OPEC
pressures was to convene the Conference on International
Economic Cooperation and Development (CIEC), which was
held in Paris late in 1975: there 19 representatives of the Third
World met eight representatives of the capitalist West and the
idea of a North–South dialogue was born.[5] In fact that meeting
(to which the West had agreed only with extreme reluctance)
represented the summit of OPEC power; shortly thereafter the
West regained the initiative as both sides realised that huge
currency balances sitting in Riyadh or other OPEC countries
were not of themselves going to do anything to assist development. The OPEC countries had to spend their surpluses and
'buy' development in one form or another, and so the new
jargon word 'recycling' became fashionable. Once the West
realised that OPEC countries had to recycle their funds it
breathed a sigh of collective relief and the temporarily altered
economic power balance tipped back again in favour of the
West. In fact, at Paris the OPEC countries behaved 'respon-
sibly' and thereafter employed their huge surpluses to purchase
western goods and invest heavily in the West either in
companies and real estate or by building up investment
portfolios. Nothing perhaps illustrates better the weakness of
the Third World than the haste with which its richest members
invested in the West, thus propping up the very system which

had exploited them for so long. After a brief display of power OPEC countries behaved like junior partners in the western-dominated economic system rather than as the spearhead of the Third World as a whole, and the hopes it had raised were soon dissipated. Even so, OPEC did briefly demonstrate that solidarity, backed in this case by oil power, meant that there were circumstances in which the Third World could force the North to pay more than lip-service to the problems of the South. By 1980, however, OPEC solidarity was proving a mirage, the idea of a NIEO had been largely shelved and North–South dialogue, when it took place, was acrimonious and unconstructive. The lessons of OPEC power during the 1970s were twofold: that united Third World action when spearheaded by economic power was capable of forcing a change in western policy; and that any hope of long-term Third World solidarity was a myth – those countries that can escape their Third World status will do so just as fast as they are able.

The story of OPEC power in the years 1973–80, and the closely parallel attempt to establish a NIEO are instructive: between them they brought out most clearly the determination of the rich nations of the North to maintain at all costs the old order which they control. Indeed, the concept of a NIEO was a contradiction in terms (as far as the North was concerned) since it could come into being only at the expense of the existing order which the North controlled to its own advantage. Then, and subsequently, it would be true to argue that the North takes 90% of major world decisions, and does so because it controls the world economy. Thus, to ask the North to surrender this power, which in essence was what the demand for a NIEO amounted to, was simply unrealistic. The concept of a NIEO was therefore flawed from the beginning because self-interest does not work towards a one-world community (the idea inherent in NIEO) but, on the contrary, is about individual or regional hegemonies. It is just possible that a NIEO in some form might have been achieved during the years 1973–5, but only provided that OPEC had used the oil weapon relentlessly to force the North to change – and when it came to the point OPEC lacked both the singleness of purpose and solidarity as well as the will to undertake so momentous a task. The concept of NIEO is socialist – an equitable sharing of world economic resources (and therefore power) – with the result that demands for NIEO were going to be met, if at all, only by pressures mounted by OPEC on behalf of the whole Third World. Such solidarity was never attainable and after the first giddy experience of power culminating in the 1975 CIEC conference the principal OPEC countries found other priorities, essentially concerning their own interests, to pursue.

In May 1974 the Sixth Special Session of the United Nations to look at economic questions only was held in Algiers and the principles of what came to be called a NIEO – in essence greater economic equality – were spelled out in the *Charter of Economic Rights and Duties of States* which was subsequently voted upon at the UN General Assembly in November of that year when 120 voted for the Charter, 6 against and 10 abstained (these latter 16 being the 'free' western economies).[6] The Charter was adopted in December 1974; among other things, it stipulated that every nation has the right to exercise *full permanent sovereignty* over its wealth and natural resources. This, however, works two ways. In 1979 the United Nations called for a third special session on economics (a second one had been held in 1975) and this proclaimed the *Third Development Decade* to run during the 1980s with a number of development targets being set for the Third World. Such targets were no doubt worth setting, as was the idea of another Development Decade, but by 1980 the world climate was visibly changing: OPEC was about to pass its peak of influence, recession was beginning to bite in the western economies and the political attitudes of the principal western governments – those of the USA, Britain, and West Germany – had noticeably hardened against aid and even more against a concept such as NIEO. The assumption behind demands for NIEO during the 1970s was that the Third World possessed the resources and that in solidarity it could withhold them, always provided that OPEC, which controlled the most vital resource of all, would act as the spearhead of Third World demands. But OPEC declined the role; it wanted its advantages for itself. A NIEO amounted to calls for a greater Third World say in such institutions as the World Bank or IMF, even though its members would not pay an equivalent extra share of dues. Such demands were resisted absolutely by the North. Only in the short period of maximum OPEC power (1974–6) was there any chance for a NIEO to be launched, but once the principal OPEC demand at the CIEC conference in Paris (that oil prices should match prices for a 'basket' of western exports) had been successfully resisted the North was able to ride out the storm and wait for OPEC members to go their separate ways, which in due course they did. Some concession had to be made, and this came in the form of the Brandt Report. This report, however presented, was in truth a delaying tactic, a gesture of concern by the North to the concept of a NIEO and the demands of the South for greater economic justice; it gave the impression that something was going to be done but nothing came of it, and within two years of its publication in 1980 it had joined all the other reports about a better world gathering dust on library shelves.[7]

The lesson of the 1970s was that only the solidarity of the South could withstand the enormous pressures which the North could bring to bear and that such solidarity was likely, at most, to be transient. By the early 1980s even the term NIEO was largely forgotten; it represented one of the more imaginative and less forlorn attempts of the South to equalise the world order if only a little, but it failed because even a fully united South could bring to bear upon the North only a tithe of the latter's economic power.

Growing awareness of its helplessness in relation to the North's economic power was a feature of various deliberations in the South during the 1970s and at Monrovia in 1979 a seminar of eminent African economists and others produced a document – *Africa 2000* – which spelled out the continent's concerns about its economic dependence. The symposium was preparing recommendations for consideration at the 16th OAU summit to be held later that year also in Monrovia and, as it argued in *Africa 2000*, the prime objective of development has to be the creation of a material and cultural environment that is conducive to self-fulfilment and creative participation. This implies a number of breaks with the past: a break with a number of concepts and habits, starting with *excessive mimicry in every field*. It went on: 'The objective for the year 2000 is to rid the continent of the general approach that currently prevails and which accepts without question the concept and practice of "transfer of technology" – an expression which the Symposium suggests should be stricken from the international vocabulary.' The Symposium had much else to say as, for example, 'The Symposium proposed that the degree of a country's dependence for its food imports should henceforth be considered as one of the most significant indicators of its level of development', but overall its message was much the same as an earlier document out of Africa, the Arusha Declaration of 12 years before: that developing countries would solve their problems only by self-reliance.[8]

The Third World has forced the North to face a series of difficult questions – about aid and its responsibilities towards the South; about a NIEO; about how to respond to the non-aligned; and about the line to take in relation to a North–South dialogue – and though the power and wealth of the North has meant that dialogues have almost always resolved themselves into the Third World acting as supplicants for the North's favours, in fact the North has by no means always won the arguments. Hardly ever able to argue from strength and increasingly weighed down by poverty and debt, the Third World found that by the 1980s almost any dialogue was only about aid and the extent to which the North was prepared to alleviate the economic burdens of the South. The answer, moreover, was not to any great degree, as the North demonstrated, a growing irritation with countries which on the one hand refused any longer to accept its tutelage (as a result of the end of empires), while on the other kept insisting that a one world philosophy demanded more concessions than the North was ever willing to make. But it was not simply a question of an unwilling North resisting demands upon its resources. The North, indeed, both resented and resisted attempts by the South to break its dependence: the demand for self-reliance enshrined in Nyerere's Arusha Declaration[9] was undermined by the clever tactic of kindness and praise – Tanzania was subsequently swamped with aid. The demand for a NIEO was temporarily far more dangerous to the North because it was backed by OPEC power but once the process of recycling had got under way that, too, could be sidestepped as the rich oil producers were, at least temporarily, wooed into a new economic power structure. The extremely dangerous demand of the South for a new world press or media order made through UNESCO was killed when first the USA and then Britain withdrew from the organisation and, more important, took their funding with them.

The emergence of the Third World in the 1950s posed fundamental questions about the existing world order which had long been controlled by the major powers of the North, and since that process of questioning coincided with the end of the European empires it created a deep sense of resentment in the North which quickly surfaces, especially when the fundamental justice of the Third World's demands is apparent. The 1980s was a cruel decade in this respect because world-wide recession, debts which in some cases had become an almost impossible burden, a series of natural disasters especially in Africa and a widening gap between rich and poor each contributed to create a single picture of the Third World that equated it almost entirely with poverty and catastrophe. And though, from time to time, there was a good deal of rhetoric about interdependence (for example in relation to the Lomé III Convention of 1984 between the EC and the ACP countries) in fact the ACP countries were seen increasingly as supplicants for better terms of trade, easier access to European markets, and more aid. The principal problems which surround all North–South issues are not questions of compassion, equity or justice, though each has its place, but questions of power, and by the end of the 1980s when the Cold War had

officially been declared over the deeply troubled powers of the
North saw other problems as far more urgent than the abiding
and apparently growing poverty of the South. These developing attitudes in the North were given enormous impetus by
such events as the Gulf War of 1991, the disintegration of
Yugoslavia or the crisis in Europe over the Maastricht Treaty.
As a North in deepening recession and growing political
disunity faced the 1990s the outlook for the South, and most
especially if it looked to the North for assistance in solving its
problems, appeared more bleak than at any time in the
preceding 40 years.

3 Aid

The history of aid is largely synonymous with the history of the Third World and though a certain amount of aid pre-dated the Cold War era – early British moves to provide development assistance in the Empire (such as the Colonial Development and Welfare Act of 1940) or Marshall Aid for post-war European reconstruction which was originally offered to the USSR as well – aid as it is generally understood consists of the flow of funds (as well as the provision of technical assistance) from North to South to assist development in the poor or less developed regions of the world, as opposed to the contra-flow of funds from South to North in the form of capital repayments, interest and profits on investments. At the height of the aid age, when the concept still retained some of its freshness and popularity, Professor Bauer argued: 'The concept of the Third World or the South and the policy of official aid are inseparable. They are two sides of the same coin. The Third World is the creation of foreign aid: without foreign aid there is no Third World.'[1]

The flow of aid grew quickly through the 1950s while the Suez crisis of 1956 gave it a definitive Cold War *raison d'être*. The Suez crisis (Nasser's nationalisation of the Suez Canal) arose in the first place because the West (the United States, the World Bank and Britain) withdrew their offer of financial assistance for the construction of the Aswan High Dam because Nasser insisted upon accepting military assistance from the Eastern Bloc. Subsequently, the USSR offered to provide finance for the dam (an offer which Nasser accepted) and a pattern of turning to both sides in the Cold War had been clearly established: if one side would not provide aid, the other would; alternately, the mere suggestion sometimes that aid would be sought from the other side was enough to improve an offer.

At the beginning of the 1960s the American economist W. W. Rostow published his book *The Stages of Economic Growth*, which popularised the idea that the right injection of aid into a developing economy would ensure its 'take-off'; Rostow was very much a Cold War warrior and had in mind injections of aid into Third World countries that could be weaned from communism.[2] The high optimism of the early 1960s, when the new Kennedy regime in Washington launched the Peace Corps and most western aid budgets expanded quite rapidly, began to give way at the end of the decade to the first signs of aid-weariness and cynicism as the 'bottomless sink' syndrome (that some aid recipients would absorb whatever aid was on offer indefinitely without this making any difference to their economic performance) became increasingly fashionable as it also became clear that some aid recipients at least were going to be clients for aid more or less for ever. The end of that decade saw a determined attempt to give the aid concept new life with the publication in 1969 of the Pearson Report (named after Lester Pearson, the former Canadian Liberal prime minister) which first set the UN target of 0.7% of GNP in aid from rich countries. Then came the OPEC and NIEO upheavals of the mid-1970s (see Chapter 2 above) by which time the Third World had come to realise how little economic power it had and how long a haul it faced if ever it was to achieve real economic breakthrough. The Brandt Report of 1980 was the equivalent of a Royal Commission on aid and North–South relations which, by showing concern, relieved the North of pressures for action. By the 1980s aid had – apparently – become a permanent feature of North-South relations; few observers any longer believed it would achieve much more than to help the poorest keep their heads above water – references to economic take-off had long been forgotten – while attitudes to aid, on both donor and recipient sides, had become markedly more cynical. Then came the dramatic events of 1989 and the end of the Cold War which quickly produced many signs (assisted by the worst general recession since World War II) that aid from North to South, though accepted by foreign ministries as part of an ongoing power relationship, would in fact be much harder to obtain and could no longer be taken for granted since the compulsions of the Cold War had disappeared.

In the heady atmosphere of the early 1960s Barbara Ward could say: 'Let us be clear first of all over the general aim. During the next twenty to thirty years we hope to see a majority of the developing nations pass through the sound-barrier of sustainable growth.'[3] Her hope was not realised. At about the same time, writing in *US News and World Report*, Rostow called foreign aid 'a means of buying time to protect crucial pieces of real estate'. The Barbara Ward thesis is the more appealing; the Rostow line more accurately represents what aid was about in the Cold War. More generally, it has to be asked whether aid was ever intended to assist development, as opposed to providing donors with an entry into countries where they had interests to defend or where they wished to extend their influence. Rarely has aid solved development problems; rather, it has created ongoing dependence and even its more acceptable faces – such as the Pearson Report or the Brandt Report – were in reality no more than justifications for a continuing licence for the North to interfere in the affairs of the South. The basic North–South relationship has always been one of exploitation, and aid represents a gesture towards the 'have-nots' by the 'haves' in order to keep the former in a continuing state of Micawberism – waiting for something more to turn up. Aid in fact has always been a system of largesse and spoils rather than a serious attempt to redress existing balances, for aid that worked in the sense of bringing about a genuine take-off for the whole South would undermine the dominance that the North currently enjoys. After some 40 years of aid flows the UN 1992 *Human Development Report* could still pose such questions as the following: what is the object of aid? To accelerate growth? But that is not enough. To act as a safety net? Perhaps! Withdrawing aid for political reasons, the report points out, penalises the poor who otherwise would benefit from it. It is a total indictment of the non-achievements of aid that such soul-searching can be indulged by the United Nations at the beginning of the 1990s.[4]

More than anything, aid creates dependence. Once a Third World country turns to the international aid agencies, it surrenders control over part of its development. The donors decide what is needed, how much they will provide, on what terms, and when they will come and go; this has been the pattern for more than a generation. Moreover, the donors are now headed by two of the most powerful institutions in the world – the World Bank and the International Monetary Fund (IMF). The World Bank was created to borrow from the rich to lend to the poor so as to finance sound development, but in real terms it has done little wealth recycling and in 1990–1, for example, it withdrew $500mn from poor countries. For years, now, the World Bank has worked on two broad assumptions: that it should raise and lend more money each year and that from its investments some prosperity will trickle down to the poorest. Most of its investments have been in projects – usually of major size and chosen in collaboration with Third World governments – that have often resulted in both environmental damage and adverse social consequences. Third World countries, however, will accept World Bank loans, even for projects that are obviously unsuitable, since this means regular injections of new money that can be used to service existing debts. It is a vicious circle.

In its 1992 *World Development Report* the World Bank called for a $75bn a year programme by the year 2000 to raise the living standards of the world's poor by improving their environment, and admitted that some of its own programmes had harmed the environment. Cautiously it said: 'Numerous public investments – often supported by development agencies, including the World Bank – have caused damage.'[5] The report was dismissed as complacent by Friends of the Earth, which suggested it was a bid for yet more money in the bank's coffers. The World Bank, sensing a new concern, has moved over to support 'green' policies. Thus, it argues: 'Industrialists, farmers, loggers and fishermen fiercely defend their rights to pollute or to exploit resources. Those who are hurt when the environment is degraded, and who stand to gain most from sound policies, are often the poor and the weak. They may be less potent politically than the polluters whom governments must challenge.' Such pontificating from the World Bank may read well, but nothing in the Bank's history suggests that it has ever seriously contemplated challenging governments, let alone initiating policies which do not meet with the approval of its main shareholders – and they, of course, are the rich countries of the North.

According to the UN *Human Development Report* of 1992 the IMF no longer performs the function for which it was created, which was to maintain monetary stability with the burden of adjustments shared between surplus and deficit countries; moreover, it has ceased to perform this original function because it is unable to control or exert authority over the rich industrial nations. Indeed, by the beginning of the 1980s it was absolutely clear that the rich nations (the Group of 7 or G-7) who between them can control the voting of the IMF had come to see it as their instrument and not as their mentor, and though the IMF should have become the guardian of the poor in fact it turned into the policeman for the rich. In a former age people fell into the hands of money lenders; today nations fall into the hands of the IMF. A high proportion of all Third World countries now operate IMF-inspired structural adjustment programmes (SAPs) which in essence means that the IMF instructs a government how to run its economy in return for a measure of debt relief in the form of rescheduling. Typical of this process and reflecting the state of indebtedness of so many Third World countries, in March 1992 the Nigerian central bank floated the once-proud naira and set a new starting exchange rate which reflected a 70% devaluation. This action was taken in a bid to secure a new agreement with the IMF that would lead to more favourable terms for rescheduling repayments of the country's debts, which by then had reached the $35 bn mark. Adding insult to injury, a western economic analyst was quoted as saying: 'The decision shows the government has the political will to get its structural adjustment programme back on track.'[6] Such strictures come ill from representatives of the North, and most especially Europe whose vast system of agricultural subsidies makes a mockery of IMF insistence, though only in the Third World, that subsidies should be reduced or eliminated so that market forces can work properly.

The pervasive influence of the IMF, however, now reaches farther afield than merely the Third World. In the Fund's *World Economic Outlook* for 1991, for example, the IMF chief economist suggested that after six quarters of negative growth the UK economy was probably flat in the first quarter of 1992 and 'recent indications suggest an upturn is now beginning'.[7] He was wrong and if IMF officials can get it wrong in relation to a country such as Britain where statistical and other information is abundantly available, how much more likely are they to get it wrong about Third World countries? The point is that the IMF has come to be accepted as a source of monetary wisdom whose *ex cathedra* pronouncements – let alone its prescriptions – are the final source of conventional economic wisdom. They are nothing of the kind, and its prescriptions for Third World countries (apart from any bias arising from the Fund's natural affinities with the viewpoint of the Group of 7) should not be seen in those countries as the answer to their economic problems but only as the necessary instructions to be obeyed if they want help, and that is a somewhat different matter. The IMF is likely to become even more influential now since, as a result of the events of 1989, it has the whole former Soviet Empire to deal with and instruct, and it may well turn out to be one of the great ironies accompanying the end of the Cold War that Russia and the other members of the Commonwealth of Independent States (CIS) as well as the countries of eastern Europe will now be added to the list of Third World countries operating SAPs and Economic Recovery Programmes (ERPs) in order to qualify for an IMF 'seal of approval'.

Africa, as the world's poorest and politically weakest region, is consistently bullied by the IMF, which between 1983 and

1989 drained an average of $700mn a year from Sub-Saharan Africa (SSA). Broadly, IMF conditionality is monetarist and deflationary, forcing governments to reduce imports by curtailing demand and thus stifling economic growth. And because SSA is so weak and in G-7 terms unimportant it has received minimal rather than required assistance. At the May 1992 conference of the IMF and World Bank in Washington the G-7 countries agreed to offer Moscow financial aid to the tune of $24bn; the readiness of the major donors to supply aid on such a scale (though severe conditions would be attached to it) unsurprisingly led Third World countries to voice their sense of grievance and neglect, for if the rich western donors could offer so much money so swiftly to Russia which for more than 40 years had been their principal Cold War enemy why could they not do a little better in relation to the Third World? The extent of the offer, given the history of the preceding years, underlined just how much Cold War considerations had always controlled the provision of aid for the Third World and its fears that aid would be switched or radically reduced had a secure basis in western attitudes and perceived priorities. Despite the huge problems Russia faced, following the break-up of the Soviet Union, the plight of most Third World countries was far worse and, as the UN *Human Development Report* (published just prior to the Washington conference) pointed out, the gap between rich and poor had become far greater over the preceding 30 years despite development aid, and the income of the richest fifth of the world's population in 1992 was 60 times greater than that of the poorest fifth, whereas in 1960 it had only been 30 times greater. So much for any claims that aid acted as a form of wealth redistribution. The best IMF reform (according to the *Human Development Report*) would be to tax surplus countries 1% per month on their surpluses to force them to adjust and buy more from deficit countries and increase world trade, with the IMF acting as the world's central bank to provide liquidity in hard times. Such suggestions, however, make sense only if the rich can be persuaded to submit to the same disciplines that the IMF consistently applies to Third

World countries, and in the climate of the early 1990s this was clearly a pipe-dream.

The end of the Cold War was welcomed in Africa although it left high and dry several regimes which had long depended upon Soviet support; subsequent appraisals of the new politics persuaded a majority of African countries that the most likely outcome for them was a diminution of aid flows as it became clear that the western powers were far more interested in diverting resources to eastern Europe and Russia than in maintaining what in any case had been a low level of aid to Africa (in relation to its needs). There was also a quite different fear that the West would begin to adopt a 'policeman' role in relation to the continent, attaching ever more conditions to what aid it was prepared to provide. In the case of Zambia, for example, the IMF tried to insist in 1987 that subsidies on maize should be removed as part of the restructuring programme, but following riots at the increased price of meal the government panicked and dismissed the IMF and its programme. By the end of the decade Zambia was one of the most indebted countries in Africa, was avoided as a bad risk by aid donors and owed the IMF alone some £580mn. Then came the elections of 1991 in which Kaunda was swept from power to be replaced by Frederick Chiluba as president. On a visit to London in June 1992 President Chiluba said: 'If we had known how to manage our own affairs, we would not have reached this stage. So Zambia should blame itself and everywhere else in Africa where they preached distribution of wealth before generation of wealth, we must blame ourselves. If we had known that there is no such thing as a free lunch people would have worked for their lunch.' However, after expressing such Thatcherite sentiments, the Zambian President went on to say: 'I feel ashamed that a President must go year in and year out to ask for aid. This aid is British taxpayers' money and they want to know how it is being used for the improvement of lives. We can't be a permanent parasite on the British taxpayer and on the Swedes, the French and the Americans.'[8] Such sentiments were well received in London and, indeed, might almost have been a blueprint for an IMF statement. The President then asked for more aid.

By the early 1990s sub-Saharan Africa appeared as a 'basket case', a bottomless sink ever seeking aid to solve its problems. Thus, when the civil war in Mozambique was brought to an end (1 October 1992) the immediate assumption was that the rebuilding the country required could be achieved only with massive foreign aid. The extraordinarily rapid spread of Aids in Africa has come to be seen as one more indication of the continent's apparent inability to deal with its own problems. The failure of most African countries to attract investment since independence is seen as another. New pressures, meanwhile, have challenged 30 years of one-party rule and dictatorships so that in country after country in Africa the people are demanding a return to democracy and multi-partyism. Yet even as they turn to the democracy which the West has for so long insisted is the best way of running a country their problems – economic collapse, war, famine, Aids – make it less likely than ever before that they will receive adequate help at the time when, arguably, they need it most. If the switch to democracy brings to power a new leader who is obliged at once to raise the price of food and fuel the chances are he will not last very long and that a disillusioned electorate or a power-hungry army will oust him so that the cycle begins all over again. Yet over the five years to 1992 when many African countries were both privatising and returning to multi-partyism (as well as implementing IMF-dictated economic recovery programmes) – that is, doing what the West insisted was the best way to earn its support – western aid was falling while little or no private investment was forthcoming. At the same time the British Overseas Development Institute predicted that Africa would benefit least from the new General Agreement on Tariffs and Trade (GATT).[9] A crucial question yet to be answered is whether an artifically-induced return to multi-partyism – where it is forced upon African states by the external pressures of donors and economic necessity – will solve any of the continent's problems. Part of the helplessness of Africa as well

as the contempt for its plight that surfaces too easily in the West
was illustrated early in 1992 by the extraordinary revelation
that the World Bank's chief economist had proposed increased
pollution for Africa. In an internal Bank memorandum
Lawrence Summers asked: 'I've always thought under-popu-
lated countries in Africa are vastly under-polluted. Shouldn't
the World Bank be encouraging *more* migration of the dirty
industries [to such countries]? I think the economic logic
behind dumping toxic waste in the lowest-wage countries is
impeccable.'[10] Subsequent apologies by the Bank and the claim
by Summers himself that he was merely indulging in an
intellectual exercise to sharpen debate could not erase the
effect of this appalling indiscretion. As the *Economist* pointed
out, Summers was equating the value of human life with
incomes per head, on which basis he could conclude that 'one
Englishman is worth the lives of 100 Indians'. When such
attitudes surface in the World Bank it is hardly surprising that
such institutions are so distrusted in the Third World.

In August 1991 the British Foreign Secretary, Douglas Hurd,
wrote to the European Commission to urge it to cut its aid to
governments which violated human rights, ignoring the fact
that such a policy in real terms would mean the abandonment
of aid altogether. The Foreign Office case was then spelled out
by Britain's Minister for Overseas Development, Lynda
Chalker, who wrote in the *Sunday Times*, among other things,
to say that governments receiving aid should not spend more
on arms than is required for legitimate self-defence. The criteria
which Mr Hurd was pressing his European colleagues to adopt
included respect for human rights and the rule of law, a
movement towards democracy, accountable government and
the rooting out of corruption, and the pursuit of sound social
and economic policies.[11] Built into such a list of criteria, though
unstated, was the assumption that the donors would be the
judges as to whether or not such high standards had been met.
Subsequently, in October 1991, Britain's Prime Minister, John
Major, urged these criteria upon his Commonwealth colleagues
at the Harare summit. Such conditionalities advanced by

Britain represented pious humbug on two counts. In the first place, throughout the 1960s and 1970s aid had been provided to regimes that met few if any of these conditions, always provided that they stated their anti-communist credentials; subsequently the donors enjoyed rich pickings from the large contracts on offer, most of which were tied to donor country exports, while paying little attention to either the well-being of the poor or respect for human rights. Secondly, it was totally unrealistic to suppose that Britain, or any other major donor, would keep to such guidelines when its interests demanded the provision of support to a particular country or regime. Indeed, Lynda Chalker implied this quite clearly when she wrote in the *Sunday Times* that she disagreed with those who argued against further aid for Kenya (bluster was the word she used): 'Not only is Kenya's human rights record better than that of many other developing countries but so is the openness of its society.' Britain thus started to make exceptions before the new policy was in place and though by then she was no longer providing aid (except emergency aid) to Sudan, Somalia and Burma the suspicion was bound to arise that their especially bad records were a convenient excuse for ending aid that the government wished in any case to cut back, more especially as such countries had little international influence and were currently of no commercial or investment value to Britain.

The humanitarian element in aid programmes which is strongly endorsed by the non-government agencies (NGOs) has vastly complicated attitudes to what in any case is a highly complex relationship. Many NGOs, for example, are suspicious of aid that is provided to assist the money-making process which they see as apart from and sometimes antithetical to assistance for the poorest. Few activities have lent themselves so well to hypocrisy as the aid business. If governments at least concerned themselves only with two aspects of aid the results might be both more honest and more efficient. These two aspects are providing aid to assist economic growth; and providing aid as part of foreign policy – that is, in support of those the donor wishes to influence. Then humanitarian and moral considerations could be left to the private (NGO) sector. At present it is only desperation that persuades the poorest recipients of aid to tolerate the degree of interference in their internal affairs that comes with the package.

A good deal of attention was paid to the subject of aid in Britain both during and after the UNCED conference at Rio in June 1992. Mr Major, it was said, unlike his predecessor believed in aid and in the early 1980s had been among the few Tory MPs to endorse the UN target of 0.7% of GNP for Third World aid. Lady Chalker expressed her anger at Rio that the British aid programme had slumped to a record low of 0.27% of GNP which was half the level when the Tories took office in 1979.[12] There is something very British and very hypocritical in the spectacle of the minister responsible for aid expressing her anger at the government of which she is a part at an international gathering as though, somehow, she stood outside the British record. Two African offenders against the criteria that the Foreign Secretary had proposed to the European Commission were Kenya's Daniel arap Moi and Malawi's Hastings Banda both of whom, among other things, were able to resist moves towards democracy because they received official British backing. The sudden and very public conversion of Britain to the idea that aid should only be given to 'good' or accountable or democratic governments was more than a little absurd, especially as no one could believe that such criteria would be seriously insisted upon when British interests were at stake. It was all a prelude to a new bout of meanness, and by September 1992 British Treasury ministers and officials were pressing for deep cuts in aid from both Britain and the EC when the needs in Africa, for example, had never been greater. Thus the Treasury wanted to slash about £250mn from the British aid budget – despite Mr Major's pledge at Rio to increase British aid – while the Chancellor, Norman Lamont, chairing a meeting of EC Finance Ministers, wanted to slash the Community's 1993 budget by £150mn.[13] During the period 1979–92 the British aid budget had been cut by 17% in real terms and by nearly half as a proportion of the country's national wealth, and was at a near record low at less than half the UN target of 0.7% GNP, while the other major European donors were contributing twice the British amount in relation to their national incomes. In the circumstances Britain's interest in 'good governance' as a criterion for aid became far more obviously an excuse because the government wanted to preside over a general retrenchment of its aid programme.

In recent years Germany has promoted an image of new concern with the problems of the Third World. In northeastern Brazil it is involved in a major irrigation development covering an area the size of France and Portugal combined along the Rio São Francisco. The land will be irrigated to produce fruit and vegetables for export; four giant dams are under construction and more than 120,000 people have had to leave their homes to make way for the projects. Siemens is taking part in this huge project, even though Brazil already has the highest debts of any country in the Third World, but a spokesman for Siemens said: 'The whole contract will be covered by *Hermes-Kreditversicherung* (the government-backed export credit insurance institution).' Holger Andersen, a spokesman for Hermes which is one of the largest insurance companies in the world, said: 'You can take it as read that all major projects in the Third World are covered by us.' Hermes thus provides German exporters to the Third World with a form of general cover. Recently Bonn has announced that insurance charges are to be graded and increased depending upon the perceived risks in particular countries; it is part of the export guarantees which exist to open up markets in the Third World for German industry. However, the indebtedness of the Third World countries increases with Hermes export credit guarantees, for if countries – in this case Brazil – cannot eventually pay for projects then the demands of the Hermes guarantees are added to remaining indebtedness with interest.[14] Thus extending German trade and exports in Brazil comes at high cost for that country: in the first place it incurs yet more huge debts for such projects; in the second, because so much is committed – in this case to produce fruit and vegetables for the European market – there is no money over for social and health benefits, schools or other programmes to get children off the streets. Moreover, when debts from Hermes guarantees are called in the Bonn government cuts back on payments of development aid even when this has been approved. Thus, when the Bonn government made DM250mn available for the preservation of the forest in the Amazon basin most of the money was at once blocked because, it was said: 'the Federal government is not prepared to approve payments in the form of new credits before the settlement of arrears because the Brazilian government is at present in considerable arrears for credits and trade promotions already guaranteed by the Bonn government'. Such German involvement in Brazil may be good for German exporters and may eventually lead to the production of goods that Europe requires; meanwhile, however, Brazil gets more heavily into debt, aid which has been promised and makes Germany look generous is then blocked and at the end one is bound to ask what will happen to the 120,000 poor Brazilians who were displaced so that the project could go forward. Such commercial ventures have nothing to do with real aid and everything to do with German economic penetration of a Third World market.

At the beginning of the 1990s the industrial countries were giving 0.35% of their combined GNP as ODA; the total flow was $54bn of which $52bn came from the OECD countries. (See also Table 3.1 opposite.)

Table 3.1 Public development aid as a percentage of national output, 1990

Country	% national output
Norway	1.17
Holland	0.94
Denmark	0.93
Sweden	0.90
France	0.79
UN target	**0.70**
Finland	0.64
Belgium	0.45
Canada	0.44
Germany (old Länder)	0.42
Italy	0.32
Japan	0.31
Switzerland	0.31
Britain	0.27
Austria	0.25
United States	0.21
Ireland	0.16

Note: The United States never recognised the UN 0.7% target in the first place.

Source: OECD.

4 The Poor of the World

Although the reality of a one-world society becomes more practicable all the time as communications and business techniques increasingly leap across national boundaries while the movement of men, money and ideas makes it harder for countries to maintain any form of genuine isolation, none of this appears to make any difference to the world's poorest people. They remain poor; and under the threatening economic circumstances of the early 1990s seem destined to be ignored even more than has been their lot in the past. Even allowing for rapid economic growth in Asia, especially in the Newly Industrialising Countries or NICs such as Taiwan, South Korea or Hong Kong, or in parts of India and China, three-quarters of the world's poor are found in Asia and development strategies hardly touch their plight. The 1991 report of the UN Economic and Social Commission for Asia and the Pacific pointed out that 'More than 800 million poor people, 72% of the world's total, reside in the Asia–Pacific region; of these 633 million are extremely poor.' Of the rural poor only a minority owned land and the majority subsisted as day labourers while in the cities few efforts had succeeded (or been made) to narrow the gap between rich and poor.[1] Of the world's 41 poorest countries (according to World Bank criteria) with a total population of 2,948.4 mn, 27 were in Africa with a combined population of 418.4 mn (1989); 13 (including China and India) were in Asia with a combined population of 2,491.5 mn; and one in Latin America (Haiti) with a population of 6.4 mn. (No reliable figures were available for either Afghanistan or Kampuchea.)[2] Now all these 41 countries had per capita incomes below $700 and should not have been obliged to borrow at commercial rates; yet India, with an average per capita income of only $340, was obliged to borrow at commercial rates through the 1980s with the result that during the decade her debts rose from \$5bn in 1980 to \$70bn in 1991. If this kind of relentless increase in debt is to be reversed new strategies are required as a matter of urgency. Essentially, as the UN *Human Development Report* suggests, this means making poor people both the means to development – by removing their poverty – as well as its end. At present donors and aid agencies only speak of the poor in a Victorian sense as those whose poverty has to be relieved. Relief is no substitute for equipping them with the means to develop and that, too, often, is not considered. Relief of the poor is easy; turning the poor into productive elements in a world community is not only demanding as an exercise but threatening as a political concept, and so far it has largely been avoided.

Of possibly even greater – and growing – importance is the question posed by the UNDP: 'In a period of rapid economic globalisation, who will protect the interests of the poor?'[3] Moreover, are we now entering an era in which the poor will be helped only if they are seen to be useful to the North? Such questions are not often asked, yet they underly the growing indifference to the plight of the world's poor which is becoming apparent in the attitudes of the rich North. It may well be that in a world which threatens to become more inward-looking as recession bites deeper only major institutions such as the World Bank, the IMF and the United Nations will have both the capacity and the authority to assist the poor and even then, probably, only according to guidelines set down by the North. The riots in Los Angeles during 1992 (the worst in the United States for 30 years) demonstrated how much the American poor – blacks and Hispanics and ghetto dwellers of the big cities – had been marginalised and forgotten in the richest country on earth. Only an explosion such as a riot brings their plight to the attention of the government and the redress they then receive is largely cosmetic in the hope that they will resume their relative quiescence and allow 'contented' America to continue in peace. Now, the 1992 riots in America had profound implications for the poor of the South: if the richest, most powerful country on earth is not prepared to implement any significant programme to assist its own poor, of whom there are now many millions, it is simply unrealistic to suppose it will show greater concern about the poor of the South. And if the United States will do little or nothing neither will the other major economies of the North be prepared to do more in relation to the poor of the South.

Poverty is the single most important factor dividing North and South. That is why almost all North–South dialogue concerns aid, terms of trade and the transfer of technology. Between 1960 and 1989 the top 20% (world-wide) increased the differential from 30 times more than the bottom 20% to 60 times more, while real disparities between people as opposed to country averages became even greater. The absolute difference in per capita income between the top 20% and the bottom 20% of world population expressed in 1989 US dollars increased between 1960 and 1989 from $1,864 to $15,149. In 1989 the top 20% enjoyed 82.7% of world GNP, 81.2% of world trade, 94.6% of commercial lending, 80.6% of domestic savings and 80.5% of domestic investment. The bottom 20% accounted for only 1.4% of world GNP, 1% of world trade, 0.2% of commercial lending, 1% of domestic savings and 1.3% of domestic investment. There was a 65 to 1 difference between the richest 20% of countries in per capita income and the poorest 20%. And there was a differential of 140 to 1 between the richest 20% of people in per capita income and the poorest 20%. The global gap in GNP between the richest 20% with 82.7% of it and the poorest 20% with only 1.4% of it was in the order of 59 to 1. At the same time (between 1960 and 1989) Sub-Saharan Africa and South Asia increased their share of world population from 27% to 32% although their share of global GNP declined by 20% and their share of global trade was more than halved, with the result that some 1.7bn people have been marginalised in world economic terms. When particular factors essential to development are compared the South, once more, is retarded by the general lack of educational opportunities; at the crucial level of tertiary education, for example, enrolment in this sector in the South is only 8%

while in the North it is 37% and in the least developed countries it is no more than 2%. The ratio of scientific and technical personnel (per 1,000 of the population) is only 9 in the South to 81 in the North. The South has only one-eighteenth the telephone connections of the North, one-eighth the newspapers and one-sixth the radios, while only 5% of the world's computers are in the South. Developing countries are responsible for only 4% of global research and development, although they account for 80% of the world's population.[4] The list can be extended more or less indefinitely.

One of the most important suggestions of the 1992 *Human Development Report* is its call for a radical change of the UN structure including a 22-member 'Development Security Council' which would have 11 permanent members – the current five (Britain, China, France, Russia and the United States) with, in addition, Japan and Germany, and then four of the most populous developing countries – Brazil, Egypt, India and Nigeria – with a further 11 seats rotating. This new council would co-ordinate development policies and humanitarian aid and formulate global policies on food security, protecting the environment, dealing with the debt problem and so forth. However, such reforms can only be implemented and made to work if the political will to make them succeed exists, and that must come from the rich nations of the North for they alone have the capacity to force such reforms through. On the other side of the equation, many countries of the South spend far more on their military than upon education. Thus, of seven selected countries the ratio of soldiers to teachers was as follows: Iraq 6.2 to 1; Somalia 6 to 1; Ethiopia 4.2 to 1; Nicaragua 3.5 to 1; Syria 3 to 1; Mauritania 3 to 1; Vietnam 2.9 to 1. In the United States the ratio is 1 to 1 and in Britain 0.6 to 1.

The fundamental problem is one of attitudes: the rich believe that on the one hand their wealth also makes them the natural arbiters of world problems and on the other that problems should only and naturally be viewed from the standpoint of the North. As long as this attitude prevails in the main institutions responsible for North–South relations then the South has little chance of altering world trends that work against its interests. Thus, for example, the OECD analysis of the world economy to 2015 takes its models from the 20% free market industrial countries, and by so doing assumes that the remaining 80% of the world is either of only marginal importance or that it should automatically (no matter what its actual capacities) get into line with the 20%. The arrogant assumptions of the North have now become such an ingrained part of any calculations about development and how it should be pursued, about trade and investment and market forces, that it becomes increasingly apparent that the primary concern of the North is to establish and maintain criteria to bind the South absolutely to the needs and objectives of the rich. The longer this process continues the less real the possibility that countries of the South will ever be able to break free of the shackles which the rich impose upon them.

Existing disparities in economic power between the major economies and the rest are enormous, and growing bigger. Many of the major countries of the South hardly made any gains at all during the 1980s: of 18 of the most important developing countries only three saw any income growth during the 1980s while the rest (measured in dollar terms) grew poorer. During the 1970s, at least, all but two of the 18 achieved some per capita growth, the two exceptions being Argentina and Pakistan. Korea, Taiwan and Thailand grew through both decades with Korea and Taiwan overtaking the poorest developed countries like Greece and Portugal to join the ranks of the industrial world. Nigeria had an appalling record during the 1980s and saw GDP per head decline by 15% a year. Argentina and Venezuela also performed exceptionally badly: in 1970 their GDP per capita was equivalent to 35–40% of the OECD average; by 1990 it had fallen to 12–14%.[5] There were, of course, some special factors at work. One fault was that certain countries (including the USSR) used their natural resources to fuel growth rather than encouraging greater productivity by offering higher incentives to labour while the countries achieving the greatest advances did so largely because productivity increased. The second factor concerned investment: the higher the investment levels, the greater the success levels. But investment presupposes the prevalence of a number of conditions which will attract external finances. These include political stability, resources that the investor seeks, a disciplined work force and a reasonable-sized market. Export-oriented businesses are essential to developing countries, for it is exports that produce the foreign exchange required to service debts and necessary imports, and if a developing country relies only upon the export of raw materials – minerals or commodities – its development is liable to suffer from devastating setbacks when world prices fall as they did through the 1980s. One of the greatest problems of all concerns the extent to which the western economies will open their markets to goods from the south; in 1992 every sign pointed to more rather than less protection.

The North, with about 25% of the total world population, consumes 70% of the world's energy, 75% of its metals, 85% of its wood and 60% of its food. And though variations constantly occur, over the 15-year period 1965–80, while the average rate of world growth was 2.4% that for the OECD countries was 2.9%. In area after area there is persistent evidence of the growing gap between North and South; between 1980 and 1990 the share of world trade of developing countries dropped from 24.8% to 19.3%. During 1991 and 1992 great attention was paid to the needs of the former Soviet Bloc states with Russia's problems assuming paramount importance. In May 1992 at the Washington conference of the IMF and World Bank the G-7 countries agreed to offer Moscow $24bn; unsurprisingly the Third World felt both neglected (that the attention of the rich had been switched to Russia) and fearful that the level of aid could be provided only at the expense of aid to the South. Despite Russia's problems, which are formidable, most Third World countries faced even greater difficulties, yet at Washington little attention was paid to them. But while aid is important, trade is far more so and the greatest harm has been caused to the South because the industrialised countries have shut off their markets to the products of the developing countries. As a result exports from the Third World are reduced by the equivalent of $100bn a year, which is twice the figure for aid.

In the first 10 months of 1991 the nine most important markets for the South were as shown in Table 4.1.

Table 4.1 Nine most important markets for the South (1st ten months of 1990)

Country	Imports (bn dollars)
United States	135.1
Japan	64.6
Germany	42.2
France	22.0
Britain	21.6
Italy	19.0
Canada	10.7
Holland	10.1
Spain	9.5

Note: These imports exclude those from OPEC countries.
Source: OECD.

For at least 10 years up to 1992 there was a decline in prices paid for crucial Third World export commodities. Raw material prices fell by 20% during the 1980s and the tendency increased at the beginning of the 1990s so that in 1991 Third World countries received, on average, only two-thirds what they had received for raw materials in 1980, and the effects have been devastating. In Malaysia, which is at the upper end of lower-middle income countries, wages for workers on palm oil plantations were halved over the two-year period 1990–2. Generally, the poorer a country the more it depends upon exporting raw materials and, for example, Uganda (admittedly after years of civil war which drastically reduced the promise of the economy at independence) was 99% dependent upon raw material/commodity exports at the beginning of the 1990s: in Uganda's case principally coffee, whose price on world markets had been halved since 1989.

Protection in the North, already severe and now growing, penalises the South in two principal ways. Since the North regards most developing countries as poor risks for investment it charges them exorbitantly for its loans. Thus, while on average during the 1980s the industrialised countries operated on interest rates of 4%, developing countries were obliged to pay an average of 17% for monies borrowed. Secondly, wherever developing country exports were seen as potentially dangerous competitors the North created a high protective wall of customs and excise duties and other non-tariff barriers such as health regulations, industrial standards or agreements involving self-restraint. The UNDP estimates that unequal access to world markets costs the South $500bn.

The formation of a North American Free Trade Agreement (NAFTA) comprising the United States, Canada and Mexico which was announced in August 1992 was hailed as a political triumph for Mexico's President Carlos Salinas. Over 15 years the three countries intend to eliminate all barriers to trade and investment; the agreement is due to come into force on 1 January 1994 provided the draft treaty is ratified by the three countries, and there is much opposition to it in both Canada and the United States. If it does succeed it will create a single market of 360mn consumers worth an annual $6,000bn. The Japanese complained at once that the NAFTA agreement 'discriminates against foreign investors and runs the risk of violating the intent and spirit of the General Agreement on Tariffs and Trade'.[6] The agreement was seen as a form of rehabilitation for Mexico following the debt crisis of 1982 and as a confirmation of just how seriously the United States now takes its southern neighbour. The statistics of the agreement (from Mexico's viewpoint) are impressive: the United States is Mexico's principal trading partner and takes 69% of its exports

(worth $18.1bn) and supplies 68% of its imports (worth
$19.3bn) (1990 figures). Mexico is now ranked as the world's
13th largest economy and has achieved impressive growth since
the mid-1980s. Just how this deal will work in the long run is
impossible to predict but from Mexico's point of view the
immediate object was to accelerate growth and the actual
agreement might be seen as the bridging operation which
moves Mexico from the Third World of under-development
into the industrialised North. However, that is far from certain.
The tough bargaining between Mexico and the United States
concerned ways of cushioning the impact of the change for
Mexico's most vulnerable sectors such as oil, financial services
and agriculture (in relation to the United States) and at the
same time securing favourable deals for its competitive
industries (cars and spare parts). On the other hand, US fears
concentrated upon the possibility that unskilled jobs will now
move southwards to Mexico although free trade with Mexico
should also create jobs in the United States while increasing US
exports to Mexico by an estimated 20–30%. At one level the
agreement can be seen as an example of a Third World country
'moving up' to become integrated in the industrialised
economy of the North. On the other hand it might find that
it becomes the poor and dirty industrial sector for North
America as a whole, attracting the unskilled dirty industries
southwards and seeing its own most advanced industries or
financial management being swamped by more sophisticated
US industries. Whatever eventually results it is at least an
example of a possible developing trend: the gradual integration
of poorer markets into richer ones. However, the model is at
present unique and subject to particular geographical circumstances that do not apply to North–South relations generally.

The civil war which forced Siyad Barre from power in
Somalia escalated steadily during the first years of the 1990s
to become one of Africa's greatest man-made disasters but
apart from NGOs providing humanitarian aid it was largely
ignored by the world community until the UN Secretary-
General, Boutros Boutros-Ghali compared the readiness of the

North to intervene in Yugoslavia with its indifference to
Somalia, thus raising many of the issues which divide North
and South. However, leaving aside the attitude of the North
what was the attitude of the South to this war? Somalia belongs
to the Organisation of African Unity (OAU), the Arab League
and the Islamic Conference (IC) and none of them took any
initiatives to tackle the problem. As Rakiya Omaar, the
Executive Director of Africa Watch, pointed out in a letter to
the *Independent*: 'Some of the richest countries in the world
belong to the Arab League and the IC. The Emir of Kuwait
recently gave £1m to London Zoo; he has given nothing for the
starving millions in Somalia. Nor have Arab countries given
anything to Yemen to help it absorb 60,000 Somali refugees.
The IC talks of military intervention to save the Muslims of
Sarajevo. Muslims as victims seem to interest the Muslim world
only when they can be used as a political football with the
West.' Ms Omaar's letter goes to the nub of several problems
which characterise both the relationship of North and South
and the approach of the South to what are fundamentally the
South's problems. Just because the South does not have the
means to do much about a disaster like that in Somalia is no
excuse for ignoring it. And if the oil-rich countries can deploy
wealth to make an impression in the North how much better if
they used that wealth to do something about disasters in the
South. The temptation for the South – in this case its Islamic
wing – to concentrate upon the perceived or real injustices
perpetrated by the North has proved stronger than the more
urgent need to do something about a problem on its own
doorstep. Such attitudes at once illustrate just how deep the
divisions and suspicions between North and South have
become. And as Rakiya Omaar also asked: 'Why should
Europeans care about Somalia when Africans and their
regional organisations appear not to care? . . . Somalia has
been ignored partly because it is an impoverished country with
no strategic importance in a continent whose concerns appear
irrelevant to the world at large. But Africa has also been an
accomplice in its marginalisation.'[7] The habit of Africa leaving

its problems for the North to resolve must also be seen as part of the Somali question and such acquiescence (in this case in doing nothing) by African diplomats at the United Nations, for example, is a sad indictment of African indifference on the one hand, and its learned subservience to endless pressures from the North on the other.

The Somali question, indeed, illustrates just how impotent Africa has become. At a time when the OAU should be in the forefront of African affairs, making maximum efforts at solving some of the continent's problems, it is doing nothing of the sort while Africa's leaders seem to have lost the will even to try to do things on their own. It is as though a brutal decade of mounting debts, declining trade and devastating wars and famines has finally reduced Africa's leadership to a state of permanent neo-colonial dependence upon the Paris Club and the World Bank and the IMF and big power intervention, so that they have finally been deprived of the capacity any longer to face up to their problems, let alone produce solutions. At present Africa has become so used to its role as underdog – at the mercy of market forces it can never hope to control, mired in debt and aid-dependent – that it has fallen into the dangerous habit (a form of neo-colonialism in reverse) of expecting all its problems to be solved for it by outside agencies. If it continues with this line it can hardly complain if such agencies – the United Nations, the World Bank, the IMF, the big powers – also take control again (as Britain's Foreign Secretary, Douglas Hurd, has already indirectly hinted). Africa cannot have things both ways, and never since independence has it been in greater danger of losing even the little genuine freedom of choice it enjoys than at the present time.

It is against such a background of both impotence to solve problems and the failure of the new independent leadership to improve the lot of their people in many parts of the south that the rise of militant Islam has to be viewed. Anwar Haddam, a leading member of Algeria's banned Islamic Salvation Front (FIS) warned in May 1992 of 'an explosion' in Algeria and of 'a new Iron Curtain, a wall between the West and the Islamic world'.[8] When in December 1991 the FIS had won the first round of voting in the Algerian elections and was clearly set to win power in the second round the electoral process was called off by the military in a take-over that was designed to prevent the Islamic upsurge. The rise of militant Islam in North Africa reflects both anger and despair on the part of a new generation of young people who see little or no gain from 30 years of independence. If the models adopted by the post-independence leadership have so blatantly failed to improve the lot of the people as a whole, so the argument runs, why not try something else, something that is not modelled upon western practices? That, at least in part, is the explanation for the rise of militant Islam. The failure of the West to protest at the hijacking of the electoral process in Algeria, despite a general readiness to preach democracy at Africa, merely reinforced the suspicions of many Africans (and in this case angry Moslems) that western principles are paraded only when it is politically expedient and hastily withdrawn if their operation works against western interests. Since the overthrow of the December 1991 election results in Algeria it became clear that the West fears Militant Islam far more than it believes in democracy. Moreover, this growing conflict between Islam and the established political regimes is not confined to Algeria. Tunisia, like Algeria, is trying to control a rising tide of Islamic disaffection; so is Egypt and though the most militant countries such as Iran and Sudan are accused of financing and arming dissident groups, this is to miss the point. Most of these Islamic movements have grown up spontaneously as a protest against what is seen as a failed system: it is the social and economic discontent of a generation of young people that by the 1990s was fuelling militant Islamic opposition to governments which were either corrupt and unable to solve problems or regarded as too subservient to western capital and western interests.

One of the major effects of economic decline in the South is to increase migration to the North, as has long been occurring between Mexico and the United States, often illegally. And it is one of the ironies of the developing gap between rich and poor that migration from South to North is rapidly developing into a political 'bogey' in the North, and especially in Europe. Germany, which faces many problems as it integrates the former East Germany into the greater whole has reluctantly come to recognise that it is now a multicultural society, a land of immigrants. Increasingly, western Europe sees itself as a magnet for migration from eastern Europe and Africa; in the end, fear of being swamped by a tide of migrants from the South who seek the prosperity they are unable to generate at home could be the spur which forces the North to consider genuine policies of world wealth redistribution, although the pressures will have to grow far more menacing before action on any significant scale is forthcoming.

5 Pressures on the Third World

When the United Nations Development Programme (UNDP) published its 1991 *Human Development Report* it called for aid to poor countries to be made conditional on curbs to military spending and progress towards human rights. The first reaction to such demands must be that they are entirely reasonable; problems arise, however, once such demands are analysed for, as usual, it is the Third World that is told how to behave if it is to qualify for assistance while the First World which will supply or withhold the finances is once more cast in the role of judge and arbiter over developments in the South. This does not excuse the military and human rights excesses to be found in many Third World countries though it does make their resentment at the rising list of conditionalities more understandable. The UNDP calculated that up to $50bn a year of misused money could be released for human development if Third World governments were to change their spending priorities; at the same time it blamed donor countries for only earmarking one-twelfth of aid for essential human development needs such as basic education or primary health care. The UNDP argued that much of the extra spending required for basic human development needs could be met by cuts in military expenditure. It calculated that a cut of 3% a year in military spending in the industrial countries would release $25bn for such objectives while a freeze on military spending in Third World countries would release another $10bn for the same purpose. The UNDP argued that developing countries which spend more on their military establishments than on the education and health of their people should have their aid cut off. Since one of the largest industries in the North is the arms business and a large part of its sales goes to Third World clients this UNDP suggestion comes close to providing a licence for the arms trade to expand in direct competition with aid: the more arms they can sell in the Third World the easier for their governments to cut back on aid.

The 1991 *Human Development Report* also provided a Human Development Index, listing countries under three categories: high level of human development, medium level and low level. Unsurprisingly most Third World countries fell into the third category, not through choice but largely the result of necessity – they had no money – for, as the same report demonstrated, with 77% of the world's population they only had 15% of the world's income and it is money that ensures high educational or health standards.[1] But in 1992 the UNDP dropped its Human Development Index which had ranked countries according to the freedoms enjoyed by their citizens; it did so in response to objections from Third World countries that had done badly in the index but who also saw such rankings as yet another device whereby the North links possible development aid to definitions of 'freedom', which in any case are both controversial and subjective, depending upon the ethical considerations prevailing in particular countries or regions.

A principal problem for Third World countries is combating fashion! In 1992 the fashion was the environment so that, for example, even the Scandinavian countries which usually are the most generous in relation to the Third World took the line that they were so committed to funding for greenhouse controls that there was no surplus over for immediate but low-profile issues that also required funding. If the rich are (temporarily) to be concerned with the greenhouse effect they can use this as an argument for not providing aid for other more mundane ongoing problems such as ordinary health or education. No doubt, once the various environmental concerns voiced at the Rio Earth Summit have been forgotten, a new set of concerns will again divert the attention of the world community from ongoing problems in the South. It sometimes appears as though the North wants such diversions, since these provide a plausible excuse for cutting back on development aid which in any case has lost its political and electoral appeal.

Arguably, Mrs Thatcher's greatest contribution to Third World problems during the 1980s was to make market forces the principal world economic catchphrase; insistence upon the application of market forces – privatisation of state run corporations, the abolition of subsidies, devaluation – in effect all those measures which made the economies of the South more easily subject to penetration from the North were constantly advocated by the IMF as the surest way to earn its 'seal of approval', without which developing countries had increasing difficulty in obtaining aid from such donor groups as the Paris Club or having their debts rescheduled.

As political changes appeared distinctly possible at the beginning of the 1990s in South Africa, Angola and Mozambique so the bankers of the North reassessed the development possibilities for the region. One senior banker with responsibility for Africa put the problem as follows: 'It's a question of saying, if you want your lollipop, you'll have to mow the grass. It sounds condescending, but it's the only way we can protect ourselves.' Accepting that bankers now employ such extraordinary language which presumably means that borrowers must first trim their economies according to the dictates of the banks, what in fact does this mean for southern Africa, the region under discussion? It is a region rich in resources: South Africa, Angola, Zimbabwe, Namibia, Botswana and Zambia between them possess a large share of some of Africa's most valuable minerals including gold, diamonds, oil, platinum, chrome, copper, lead, zinc and a range of others as well as rich agricultural potential. The region is also large in area – more than 7mn square kilometres – and in South Africa and Zimbabwe possesses two of the most advanced infrastructures on the continent. These countries were looking hopefully for an end to their regional conflicts and, therefore, to a new surge of development. But this required financing, hence the interest of the bankers from the North who, however, expressed doubts as to whether money would be forthcoming: 'We want to see evidence of where the money is coming from. Loans and deals are done on the basis we'll get paid back. This is not aid.' And as another African specialist said: 'Many businessmen will base decisions on whether the party in power proposes a market-driven economy.'[2] In a variety of ways the bankers were all saying the same thing: if you want finances from the North you must adopt a market-forces approach. The big prize was South Africa, which western investors had reluctantly left or at least stopped investing in during the latter half of the 1980s; they wanted to return but waited for political stability first. After years of civil war in Angola and Mozambique and the progressive breakdown of apartheid-based white dominance in South Africa during the 1980s the region was desperate for new investment in the 1990s. In part its politicians put out clear signs that they would work according to free market rules; in part, whatever the local problems, they had little option if they sought finances from the North.

An entirely different kind of Third World problem surfaced in Mexico when an industrial explosion in Guadalajara, whose underground blasts killed more than 200 people, occurred in April 1992. The disaster was deeply embarrassing for the Salinas government which was then negotiating the free-trade agreement with the United States and Canada. The disaster was the result of lax environmental controls as Mexico continues its headlong rush to industrialise; it was caused by a gas leak in the city's sewer system and was a direct consequence of unregulated and unrestrained economic growth, for in many parts of Mexico growth has far outstripped the development of an adequate infrastructure as the country moves over as fast as it is able from an agricultural to an industrial base. Mexico is close to joining the North as an industrialised, self-sustaining economy and, as this becomes more obvious, it is likely to face a different kind of restraint from the North than those applied to far less developed countries in Africa. Mexico poses a potential threat to the North with its abundant cheap labour; as a result such disasters as that in Guadalajara could be used as a reason for preventing its entry to the rich club. The event also drove home some of the arguments that were later to be debated, more or less fruitlessly, at the Rio Earth Summit two months later. As a Mexican government official explained, more such accidents are bound to occur because so many of Mexico's industries use outdated equipment: 'If you want to enforce environmental laws you need resources and these will only come with a North American free trade agreement.'[3]

It is, however, over the question of population growth that the greatest pressures are mounted by the North upon the Third World, and in this connexion it is worth noting that in the 1960s both President Johnson of the United States and President de Gaulle of France presided over congratulatory ceremonies in their own countries to mark the arrival of the 200 millionth and 50 millionth American and French babies respectively. In the North, size of population is a matter of pride; in the South, it is to be deplored. The statistics of population growth, nonetheless, make startling enough reading. As of the last decade of the twentieth century 90% of the world's population growth will take place in the developing countries and by the year 2000 it is estimated that 80% of the world population will belong to the Third World. On 1 July 1989 world population stood at 5,324,000,000 and was growing by 93mn a year (an annual increase of 1.78%). China with a population of 1,103,900,000 and India with 835,000,000 between them accounted for 37% of the total. Predictions of doom about population are likely to become one of the main North–South themes over the next few years. Already old estimates have had to be revised upwards and the UN Population Fund now assumes that the world population will pass the 6bn mark in 1998 rather than 2000, when it will be 6.4bn. The fastest rates of growth generally are now in Africa, the world's overall poorest region, while the lowest rates of growth are in the industrialised countries of the North, with Germany and Hungary actually experiencing a fall in populations. The logic of these findings must be to concentrate upon development first; then the problem of rapid population growth will begin to right itself.

Even with the implementation of maximum family planning demographers expect the population to at least double by the middle of the next century; this, however, is the most optimistic assessment and assumes that couples using contraceptives will increase from a present 50% to about 75% in the year 2000. Such a development is unlikely to occur unless industrialised countries increase their contraceptive aid to the Third World. According to Timothy Black, chief executive of the Marie Stopes International Foundation, 'overpopulation is a major threat to mankind'.[4] The subject of family planning is fraught with controversy, with two main strands of opposition: the first is religious and most notably emanating from the Roman Catholic Church; the second is political–emotional opposition on the grounds that population control is yet another weapon of the North in its attempts to control the South.

Britain's Minister for Overseas Development, Lynda Chalker, told a meeting organised by the charity Population Concern in July 1991 that family planning should be more integrated into the development programmes of the Third World. The budget of her department spent on supporting population programmes had increased in the previous year by 28% and by 120% since 1981: 'I am keen that we should do even more', she said. But despite calls for population control from the North such control in real terms is likely to take place only when development has produced higher living standards all round, including low infant mortality, so that people in poor countries for the first time have a reasonable guarantee that their children will survive. The argument thus becomes a circular one: over-population leads to the destruction of the environment, for example desertification as scarce trees are used for firewood, and only massive long-term development aid which provides an alternative to such destructive cycles will halt the process. At present over-population leads to accelerated agricultural production which ultimately damages the soil; over-grazing of pastoral land; deforestation for fuel; over-urbanization, with the drift to the towns in search of employment and the consequent growth of disease-prone shanty-

towns; and an accelerated depletion of non-renewable resources. The experience of the rich countries of the North –
more than a century ago – was the reverse of what they now
attempt to force upon the South. In countries like Britain the
huge rate of growth that characterised much of the Victorian
era began to fall only when better economic standards were
extended to the population at large, yet despite this experience
policy makers from the North insist that the South must control
its birth rate first, as though huge rates of population increase
are the cause of poverty in the South: they are one of its
principal effects. But concentration upon the population
explosion is politically attractive, since it allows the North to
blame the South for its fecklessness while also pandering to the
prejudices of the North that it will be swamped by southern
hordes; instead, the North should direct its efforts at the
development of the South, for only when poverty has been
overcome will there be a real chance of persuading people to
exercise population control, for then it will make sense to have
small families. It does not do so at present. It is, however, to be
expected that the rich North would concentrate its attention
upon the one area where progress is unlikely until fundamental
poverty has been eliminated because to do so provides an
excuse for not taking the steps necessary to eliminate the
principal cause of over-population which is poverty. That
would be too costly.

Drought and famine have become almost endemic in some
regions of Africa; in part they are beyond human control,
though not always, and those affecting countries such as
Ethiopia or Sudan in the Horn or Angola and Mozambique
in southern Africa can be traced to the effects of long-lasting
civil wars as much as natural causes. A drought may be the
work of nature; a famine is usually man-made. And here, too,
the North has played a role. Thus, in Angola through 15 years
of civil war the United States, for its own Cold War reasons,
supported Jonas Savimbi of UNITA against the government,
and in the aftermath of the Cold War has a responsibility to
help bring about a peace while no longer having any excuse for

assisting one side in a murderous conflict by supplying money and arms. These famines highlight the problems and development failings of the Third World for such countries, even when provided with food aid to meet the emergency, are often unable to distribute it to those in need for they lack adequate infrastructure, vehicles or foreign exchange to pay for petrol, since taking the food to the hungry in remote rural areas is an expensive business. Starving children excite pity in the West and famine relief in its many forms has become a major aspect of western aid, especially in Africa. One of its lessons needs to be related closely to the arguments about birth control that come too readily from those who would make policy for the Third World. A phenomenon that aid workers have become all too familiar with is that of children consciously excluded from a group of the starving to die so that there is more food for the remainder. Further, in a real famine situation the adults eat first because their survival is essential if the group is to survive; the children, or some of them, are expendable. These harsh facts of behaviour which emerge out of famine situations should be remembered when birth control is advanced as an obvious solution to some of the South's problems. In an environment where famine and starvation are regular occurrences people cannot be expected to think about birth control. Moreover, if children are expendable, as they are in such circumstances, they are also replaceable.

By mid-1992 Zimbabwe was suffering from severe drought, part of the wider catastrophe affecting the whole of southern Africa. Normally Zimbabwe is a food exporting country and has a surplus that provides it with a measure of food security. In 1991, however, the year before the drought, the Zimbabwe government had given way to pressure from the United States and the World Bank and sold a million tons of surplus grain so as to meet its debt obligations to the North. When famine came, it had no reserves.

Famine exacerbated by wars has done possibly irreparable damage to the image of Africa in western eyes, turning the continent into a disaster zone always in need of aid, peopled either by the starving or by warlords and tribalists who put little value upon human life and yet constantly expect the North to bail them out with relief aid. Moreover, relief has often been hampered by sometimes inexcusable inefficiency, by internecine squabbles as to who should receive the aid, and by denials (as in Sudan for many months) that a famine situation existed at all. In such circumstances it is not surprising if the reaction of aid donors turns from horror and pity at the plight of the starving to indifference and the assumption which surfaces all too quickly in the North that life is cheap in such countries in the South. Famine disasters do not make the relationship between North and South any easier; rather, they assist in the development of myths: either that half the problems could be avoided with political stability (that is, multi-party democracy); or, that the South really needs the permanent presence of donors or other agencies to deal with its problems (what appears likely to be a new fashion during the 1990s, the call for some form of re-colonisation). And by early 1992 a food crisis of unprecedented proportions through much of Africa simply served to emphasise such appraisals. In the Horn (Ethiopia and Sudan) crop failures and war had placed more than 15 mn people at risk. In Somalia disintegration and anarchy appeared to be the order of the day. In Liberia continuing civil war put the entire population of one of Africa's smallest countries at risk. In Angola and Mozambique years of civil war had reduced some people more or less permanently to the margin. And across the continent as a whole perhaps 30 mn people faced severe food shortages.

By the spring of 1992 an estimated 700,000 people faced starvation in Mogadishu, Somalia, while the Security Council debated whether or not to send 500 troops to guard food convoys and the Somali capital had been reduced to one of the most dangerous places in the world where most people go armed while much of the city had also been reduced to rubble. According to the UN World Food Programme it was the general insecurity which had resulted in an almost total lack of food in the country. At the same time Kenya was dealing with a refugee population in the north of 180,000 which was being increased at the rate of 1,500 a day from either Somalia or the fighting in southern Ethiopia. In southern Sudan the Islamic government of Khartoum had launched a fierce onslaught upon the non-Moslem Sudan People's Liberation Army (SPLA) of the south, had seized up to 12 towns in SPLA territory and was accusing aid relief agencies of assisting the rebels with arms. Some 80,000 refugees from southern Sudan had crossed into Uganda since the turn of the year.

In southern Africa the effects of drought in Malawi were only slightly less damaging than in neighbouring Mozambique. And in this instance one of the increasingly bizarre results of the politics of aid became apparent, for while donors had suspended all non-humanitarian aid in May 1992 until they saw 'tangible and irreversible evidence' of human rights improvements, they nonetheless pledged $170mn in drought relief. In the circumstances, the relief aid was provided reluctantly. In Mozambique the Renamo guerrilla leader, Afonso Dhlakama, said he would allow international aid groups to take food into rebel-controlled areas where thousands faced starvation. Previously he had refused to allow relief convoys access to such areas. Ironically, it was the increasing famine in Mozambique that brought the two sides to agree a ceasefire which came into effect in October because drought and famine made a continuation of the war close to impossible.

In Zimbabwe, which in normal times is a food exporter, the drought had reduced hundreds of thousands of rural people to eating wild plants with malnutrition across the country estimated at 45% and in remote areas as high as 70%. Up to 17 mn people in southern Africa faced famine with little hope of obtaining the food they needed. It was expected that the harvest for southern Africa as a whole for 1992 would be only two-fifths the normal for the region, with eight countries reaping less than half as much grain as in 1991; with South Africa and Namibia harvesting less than a third; and Botswana and Zimbabwe no more than a quarter their normal crops. The drought came at an especially difficult time for southern Africa with South Africa itself attempting at last to move from apartheid to some form of a multiracial state, with Zambia just having returned to multi-partyism and Namibia nursing a newly gained but fragile independence and Angola and Mozambique – hopefully at least – bringing their long civil wars to an end. As the African director of the British aid agency Save the Children said in April 1992 'It is awful to have to sound the alarm for Africa every year.'[5] Constant alarms from Africa do not help its cause in the North and in 1992 the rich nations had made known that they did not intend to increase their world-wide food aid over 1991 levels.

In April 1992 what was left of the harvest in nine southern African countries was estimated as shown in Table 5.1.

Table 5.1   Percentage left of the harvest in nine southern African countries, estimated April 1992

Botswana	24
Lesotho	47
Malawi	46
Mozambique	41
Namibia	30
South Africa	30
Swaziland	38
Zambia	36
Zimbabwe	26

In any emergency it is to be hoped that the world community will respond, and a famine in Africa requires and should receive food aid and other forms of relief from the rich nations of the North. This happens. But if Africa is asking for such aid year after year the willingness of the donors is liable to be blunted. And if in addition natural disasters are made worse by civil strife then it becomes increasingly likely that donors will be tempted to ascribe the disasters to men and governments first and make this an excuse for ever tighter conditions for their assistance. It may seem a terrible thing to claim but perhaps the civil war in the former Yugoslavia with its brutalities, ethnic cleansing and ruthless killing at least provides a bonus for the Third World by demonstrating what the North had almost forgotten: that a civil war in the rich North can be every bit as devastating and destructive as one in the poor South. The North should be careful about making hasty or facile judgements over civil wars in the South.

As southern Africa faced its worst drought in 50 years various members of SADCC were implementing (or trying to implement) World Bank prescribed structural adjustment programmes (SAPs) which forbid food subsidies. An abandonment of such SAPs, whether temporary or permanent, would permit these countries to subsidise agricultural inputs so as to enable farmers to plant sufficient crops to meet the needs for 1993, and by cutting food prices enable the poorest to afford what food was available. Perhaps few situations better illustrate the extent to which countries of the Third World have ceased to be their own masters than the fact that in a great emergency they remain tied to policies dictated from outside. In Europe the EC agreed its largest food aid programme ever (£160mn) but failed to find any consensus on two aid-related issues: how to use aid against oppressive regimes; and whether to abolish 'tied' aid which forces recipients to spend it only in the donor country. Ministers of individual EC countries were reluctant to cede to the European Commission the right to suspend aid; they clearly wished to retain this right to safeguard their own interests. Similarly the proposal that tied aid (EC countries disburse $10bn of tied aid every year) should be freed so that recipients could spend it anywhere in the EC, a move that would add an estimated 20–30% value to such aid, was resisted, especially by France, on the grounds that such a move would discriminate against the more generous donors and that the less generous donors should first increase the level of their aid. As with so many other arguments about North–South relations the greater concern appeared to relate to the comparative advantage of the donors rather than to the well-being of the recipients.

6   Special Cases

During the 1990s attitudes of indifference or hostility, accompanied by a determination to manage or punish, increasingly marred the relations of North and South, with foreign ministers and ministers responsible for aid in the North lecturing and hectoring the South for its shortcomings. This is not a healthy relationship but most indications in 1992 suggested that it would become worse. Certain countries in the South, though for very different reasons, help to highlight this deteriorating North–South dialogue. Three – Libya, Somalia and South Africa – are worth looking at in some detail.

Few international figures have ever been treated as though they are such threats to western interests as Colonel Gaddafi of Libya; only Castro has been treated worse by the United States and only Nasser by Britain. Why? What is it about Gaddafi that so infuriates the western powers? And why do his brother Arabs also see him as a threat? He is a 'maverick', it is true, and has been responsible for actions that, from time to time, have both angered as well as threatened other interests, yet in this he is no different from a good many other Third World leaders and his activities have certainly been no more threatening (and a good deal less destructive) than those of figures such as Saddam Hussein of Iraq or the Ayatollah Khomeini of Iran. Yet despite their 'crimes' (in western eyes) being on a greater scale than anything Gaddafi has achieved, only he has been the subject of such obloquy in the West. The reason for this is as much psychological as anything else, for Gaddafi's greatest crime has been his refusal to be 'bought in' by the West, a crime compounded by the fact that his country is not remotely as powerful or as strategically important as either Iraq or Iran.

On 1 September 1969 a group of young soldiers, the Free Officers, mounted a coup against the ageing King Idriss and declared a republic, and on 13 September Gaddafi became

71

chairman of the Revolutionary Command Council. In the five years following this coup Gaddafi played the role of the classic nationalist: he moved against western interests, which in Libya's case meant those of the United States and Britain, forcing the Americans to relinquish their huge Wheelus base, the British their smaller facilities and nationalising British controlled banks. Then he tackled oil. Indeed, it was Gaddafi's determination to take on the major oil companies in the early 1970s, forcing them into a series of deals that both increased the price paid for Libya's oil and gave Libya a controlling stake in its own oil for the first time that provided OPEC (which had existed almost unheard of for 10 years) with the teeth which turned it into the most formidable cartel ever to threaten western economic hegemony. Therein, perhaps, lies the secret of western antagonism, for none of the other Arab oil states at that time dared take on western oil interests. Having successfully tackled the oil giants, and in the process provided himself with enormously increased 'oil power' in the form of huge revenues, Gaddafi felt able to turn his attention to other fields.

An uncomfortable person to deal with, Gaddafi's vision (or visions) have always been greater than his immediate Libyan background, and outsiders – whether westerners or leaders of the Arab world – have not known how to deal with him, especially because what he has demanded, when stripped of its flowery rhetoric, has had great appeal, whether it is for an end to western interference in the Arab world, greater Arab unity or hostility to Israel. Always controversial, Gaddafi has used Libya's oil wealth to support a variety of nationalist and more dubious causes around the world. At the same time the small population of Libya and its relatively large oil resources enabled him to provide his people with major improvements in housing, education, employment and social services and still have a large surplus of money to pay for his external policies, certainly during the oil boom years. But though Gaddafi's support for anti-western causes around the world produced its denunciations from Washington or London as well as distrust from conservative Arab leaders, oil wealth always provided him with a 'pull' that made outright breaches more awkward than his detractors cared to enforce, for while the West detested Gaddafi it nonetheless wanted both his oil and the lucrative contracts for developments in Libya. The West thus developed its own brand of hypocrisy when dealing with Gaddafi: denunciation of his support for terrorism has been coupled with advice to its citizens to remain working in Libya 'for the time being' as governments have stood back one remove from the greedy business world. The result has been to make the West paranoid about Gaddafi and his doings.

Following the explosion early in 1986 of a terrorist bomb in a Berlin disco which killed an American serviceman President Reagan decided upon retaliatory action against Gaddafi and contacted Britain's prime minister, Margaret Thatcher, to ask to use the F-111 bombers which were based in Britain, supposedly for NATO purposes only, for the raid. Three months earlier Mrs Thatcher had said 'I do not believe in retaliatory strikes that are against international law' but, nonetheless, she agreed.[1] So in April 1986 the US Air Force mounted what in theory was a high technology precision air raid upon Libya with the object of killing Gaddafi but not hurting civilians. The raid failed in its purpose. Civilians were killed, including Gaddafi's adopted daughter, but he himself had been in his tent that night, a fact that was worth a great deal of propaganda in the aftermath of the raid, and was unhurt though substantial damage was done to property in Tripoli. President Reagan had wanted a soft target to demonstrate American toughness on terrorism and Syria and Iran (both at least as much if not more involved in anti-western terrorism, at the time) were seen as likely to be too costly as targets and able to damage too many western interests in return, so they were left alone. As a result, the West conferred upon Gaddafi the unique distinction of being the only Arab leader openly to confront the United States. Subsequently, when it became clear that Syrian rather than Libyan terrorists had almost certainly been responsible for the Berlin outrage, neither the United States nor Britain made any form of apology. Later that year (1–3 September) Gaddafi attended the Non-Aligned Summit in Harare, Zimbabwe, to tell a bemused and outraged conference that it was irrelevant (he was undiplomatic, but correct).

It is possible to draw parallels between the bombing of Libya in 1986 and the invasion of Egypt (Suez) by Britain and France 30 years earlier. In both cases powerful western nations attempted to overthrow 'awkward' Arab leaders; in both cases they called upon the Arab people to rise against their leaders; in both cases they attempted to bring about their objective by using force; and in both cases they failed, while their armed interference worked to increase the popularity (or at least the heroic stature) of the targets – Nasser and Gaddafi – though Gaddafi was never in the same league as Nasser. No uprising followed the raid on Libya for, whatever Libyans thought of Gaddafi, they distrusted outsiders more and the United States most of all. The sordid fact is that the United States chose Libya as a target because it could not retaliate, whereas both Syria and Iran could.

The destruction of the Pan American flight 103 over Lockerbie, Scotland, by a terrorist bomb on 21 December 1988, in which 270 people were killed, caused justifiable outrage in the West, yet the subsequent determination to pin the responsibility upon Gaddafi outran the evidence and if he has responsibility so too do Syria and Iran, yet western fury was concentrated upon Gaddafi. As reprehensible, dangerous and threatening as Gaddafi might appear in western eyes reactions have been disproportionate to his offences if judged by western responses in other cases – towards Saddam Hussein gassing the Kurds or Iranian behaviour over Salman Rushdie. By November 1991 western governments were putting the finishing touches to a package of demands to be made upon Libya which, if not met, would be followed by western recourse to 'all necessary means', which clearly implied the threat of force. The warning came from the United States, Britain and France who were demanding the handover of the two Libyan intelligence agents indicted in the West for the Lockerbie crash. In addition, they demanded of Libya compensation for the crash victims and renunciation of terrorism. Sanctions were to follow non-compliance by Libya with the United Nations being asked to make the already existing EC embargo against Libya world-wide. At this point western diplomats said the next stage would be a UN resolution demanding that Libya comply with the tripartite demands (of the United States, Britain and France), to be followed if necessary by a resolution similar to Resolution 678 which had authorised member states 'to use all necessary means' to evict Iraq from Kuwait. As a British diplomat said (in language uncomfortably akin to that used by Hitler in the late 1930s): 'At stake now is a new Arab order, which is part of the new world order. Still, we want to avoid a naked threat at this stage.'[2] The western demand that the two Libyan suspects be handed over for trial in Britain or the United States would not for a moment be tolerated by other more powerful countries while both western countries would have responded to such a request (had the position been reversed) with scorn, asserting that their nationals could not hope for a fair trial in Libya. As the British newspaper, the *Independent* asked in a leader: 'Ought great powers to threaten diplomatic and ultimately military sanctions to enforce what are only indict-ments, not convictions, in their domestic courts? If this is sauce for the pariah goose, to how many ganders should it apply? Should we threaten military force to persuade Iraq to hand over Saddam Hussein to Western justice? What about other dictators? What is needed is a sense of proportion in the enforcement of national law abroad and a new respect for international law.'[3] By the middle of 1992 Libya had not complied and western sanctions were being applied to it, while the Libyan parliament said it would allow the Lockerbie bombing suspects to be heard by a 'fair and just' court chosen by the United Nations or the Arab League in agreement with Tripoli.

By this time Libya was clearly being harried by the western powers in what had all the appearance of a crusade against a particular Arab leader: demands for the handover of the two men accused of the Lockerbie bombing for trial in Scotland or America would be unlikely to result in a fair trial given the way they had already been publicly adjudged guilty in those countries; and pressures upon the United Nations to act as a justifying cloak for these western pressures placed the world body at serious risk of losing any appearance of impartiality. This is not to exonerate Libya of any justly deserved blame, but if Libya is to be taken to task for aiding and abetting terrorism why do the same powers (the United States, Britain and France) not mount comparable campaigns against other Middle East countries as or more guilty of terrorist tactics, including Syria and Iran, and Israel which has conducted endless terrorist raids into Lebanon with impunity for a decade or more? The fear must be – and especially for the South – that the western powers who now control the Security Council without any threat of a Soviet veto are prepared to use it to justify any policing activities which suit them.

Writing in the *Observer* in June 1992 the British business tycoon R. W. 'Tiny' Rowland called in question the legality of the western demands that Libya should hand over the two suspects and demonstrated that it was contrary to both the Charter of the United Nations and international law as accepted by the United States, Britain and Libya. He claimed: '1. Libya has acted in accordance with its treaty obligations; 2. The US and UK have not acted in accordance with their treaty obligations; 3. In order to get their own way, despite the Montreal Convention [this convention of 1971 deals specifically with bombs in aircraft and the duties of states in relation to such terrorist tactics], the US and UK have not only threatened the possible use of unlawful force against Libya, but also appear to have manipulated the Security Council by rushing through resolutions to block Libya's case before the International Court.' As Mr Rowland concluded: 'The credibility of the UN cannot be maintained without an acceptance by the US and the UK that, however inconvenient, they must abide by their treaty obligations, even towards a country as small and as unacceptable – to them – as Libya.'[4] Unfortunately for the South and, in this particular case, for Libya, all the signs point to a growing determination on the part of the big powers to flout international laws, especially in relation to weak powers, when it suits them to do so; and since they control the Security Council the probability is they will get their way more often than not.

The UN Security Council imposed sanctions upon Libya on 15 April 1992 for failing to hand over the two Libyans wanted by the West over the Lockerbie disaster. The following September, not having surrendered to the demands of the West, Gaddafi called for direct talks with the United States and urged a committee set up by the Libyan legislature 'to negotiate directly with America' without going through the United Nations. Perhaps the saddest aspect of this dispute has been the unwillingness of the United Nations to stand up to the big powers. On 20 August a senior UN official had told Gaddafi to expect tougher sanctions if he did not comply, but he made plain he did not intend to do so. If there is to be an international rule of law, and if the major powers are to be its guarantors, it must be applied equally to all states and all cases at all times. Nothing is more likely to destroy the rule of law – and even the concept of it – than if the big powers take it upon themselves to twist and bend it for their own convenience and, in relation to Gaddafi and Libya as it would seem, for revenge as well. The tactics used by the United States, Britain and France in relation to Libya are reminiscent of the tactics employed by big powers prior to World War I before the League of Nations had been set up at a time when the world accepted – because there was then no alternative – that might is right. For 45 years since 1945, even if at times only negatively, the world has paid lip-service to the rule of law and the role of the United Nations. If the end of the Cold War and the withdrawal of the Soviet readiness to veto mean a return to the big power arrogance of pre-1914 days that indeed represents a black outlook for the Third World.

The awful and apparently unstoppable tragedy that un-folded in Somalia following the overthrow of Siyad Barre has made headlines mainly in terms of what has not been done about it. An Amnesty International report of August 1992 which examined the human rights abuses in Somalia said: 'It is Somali political organisations and their leaders who have prime responsibility to end this cycle of abuse,' a statement with which no one should quarrel, but Amnesty added that the problems of Somalia had met with 'a mixture of despair and neglect by the outside world'.[5] The comparison made by the UN Secretary-General, Boutros Boutros-Ghali, between western attitudes to Yugoslavia and western attitudes to Somalia has been referred to already. What events in Somalia have brought out clearly is the extent to which such a disaster is considered actionworthy as opposed to merely newsworthy. The terrible famine in Somalia during 1992 was the result of two years of drought and four years of civil war, yet only slowly and creakingly did relief go into action and this only after the growing scandal of UN ineptitude and red tape and western indifference had been sufficiently highlighted that it became impossible any longer to ignore the problem. The failure of Africa to do anything at all about Somalia was an additional scandal, and though the general weakness and poverty of the continent might justify its inability to do much on the ground the total quietude of its politicians in the face of western indifference was inexcusable. Boutros-Ghali illustrated what will be the problem of the Third World for the rest of the century when he described the conflict in Yugoslavia as the 'war of the rich' while that in Somalia was 'the war of the poor'.

One problem is what has come to be called 'compassion fatigue'. With so many conflicts, famines and refugees it is possible to overwhelm those who normally respond, but though that might affect the media – making for indifference – or the public who give to charities (though on the whole they show a remarkable continuing generosity), it ought not to be a reason for major governments or the United Nations to be slow in their responses. By August 1992 it was estimated that 1 mn Somalis had fled the country since President Siyad Barre was ousted in

January 1991: 300,000 to Kenya, 500,000 to Ethiopia, 15,000 to Djibouti, 65,000 by boat to Yemen and perhaps 100,000 of the wealthier Somalis to Europe. At the same time the UN Special Envoy to Somalia, Mohammed Sahnoun, called for the United Nations to send a far larger force of guards to Somalia than the 500 proposed by the Security Council. He suggested that 6,000 peace-keeping troops were required. A UN mission arrived in Somalia in the first week of August 1992 and managed to arrange a fragile ceasefire between the self-styled president, Ali Mahdi Mohamed, and his principal rival for power, General Mohamed Farah Aideed, whose rivalry had by then led to the maiming or deaths of many thousands of Somalis, but as Sahnoun said: 'If only we had intervened before November [1991]. Because of that delay we now pay the price.'[6] The question he could not answer was why the United Nations had not intervened earlier. How long should a conflict be allowed to escalate before external action to halt it or bring relief is mounted? And how much does the delay in taking action depend upon the importance attached to the conflict by the major powers? That, really, goes to the heart of the matter.

An agreement to permit a 500-strong UN force to operate in Mogadishu to guard relief supplies was finally accepted by General Aideed in mid-August, once it was made clear that such troops were not peace-keepers. Subsequently, a visiting UN delegation met with representatives of the NGOs who up to that point had been responsible for most of the humanitarian relief activities, but while refusing to tell them what it would recommend to the UN Secretary-General, it did say they would be asked to distribute much of the relief food to come. The NGOs reacted with anger at being taken for granted and David Shearer of Britain's *Save the Children* said of the UN mission: 'They still don't realise that what they intend to do impinges not only on our work but our safety. They assume we are going to be working at the sharp end. But after 10 days flitting about in aeroplanes they don't want to share their ideas with the people who've been here for some time.'[7] The principal problem raised at this point was what the UN force of 500 would do if shot at or attacked. Would the United Nations then pull out? It was somehow entirely in keeping with the Somali tragedy that the NGOs and United Nations failed abysmally to understand each other or discover a common aim or policy. Nonetheless, by late August the report to the United Nations called for 3,500 troops to guard relief supplies and said that they should be armed. At the very end of the month, as if to emphasise the mission's point, two UN observers in Mogadishu were shot. Mike Aaronson, the overseas director of the British charity *Save the Children Fund*, then claimed that the UN record in Somalia had been pathetic. The collapse of any form of law except that of the gun in the hands of armed bands was testimony to the long period of inaction when nothing was done. During the whole year to September 1992 the UNDP had $68mn budgeted for Somalia lying unspent for want of a signature. By mid-September the first of the 500 UN troops arrived in Mogadishu where the primary need was to restore order at the port where 10,000 tons of American sorghum had been sitting in a dockside warehouse for two weeks because a clan dispute prevented aid workers from distributing it.

By this stage in the convoluted Somali story sufficient publicity had made a reluctant West begin to take more formal notice, but the fact that France, Britain, the EC and the United States each became involved separately was not calculated to solve the problem. Visiting Mogadishu the French Minister for Health and Humanitarian Action, Bernard Kouchner, said 'international aid to Somalia will stop if insecurity persists', although how the insecurity was to be stopped he did not explain. A French ship arrived at the port while M. Kouchner was in Mogadishu bringing 2,000 tonnes of food aid and 100,000 litres of fuel. 'France is here', said M. Kouchner grandly 'in response to an appeal by the UN Secretary-General.'[8] Meanwhile both the French humanitarian group *Médecins Sans Frontières* and the British *Save the Children Fund* reported widespread malnutrion and called for the United Nations to spearhead a seaborne operation to inundate the country with food aid so that at least some of it would reach the starving population rather than be waylaid by armed gangs. In mid-August 1992 France began an airlift of food to Somalia.

The north of the country (the former British Somaliland protectorate) had already proclaimed itself the Republic of Somaliland in May 1991 and here the prospects of relief were complicated by international red tape. As Alun Michael MP, the Chairman of the (British) All-Party Parliamentary Group on Somalia claimed, writing to the *Independent*, the international community had left 'Somaliland in a Catch-22 situation: development aid is refused until there is effective government and until there is development aid there is no way effective administration can be created out of the ruins.' A second correspondent, Robert Forsythe, suggested a return to some form of UN mandate: 'In the interests of the starving children, should not the UN look to appoint – on a term of, say, 10 years – a single country with sufficient military presence and international standing to rule Somalia and try to instil a rudimentary system of central government strong enough to disarm the warlords, feed its people and rebuild its base infrastructure?'[9] This suggestion is doubly interesting: first, because it does not come from Africa; and second, because it raises a comparable thought in relation to Yugoslavia. If intervention on the scale suggested is to take place then surely the initiative for it ought first to have come from Africa. The fact that it did not and that nothing came from Africa is a measure of the continent's weakness and unwillingness to give any hostages to fortune, almost as though Africa were saying collectively: 'we are a basket case for aid and Somalia must take her chances with the rest of us'. Second, if it is right to consider imposing a UN mandate on Somalia (and maybe it is) then surely it is equally right to do the same thing in Yugoslavia (with sufficient military presence to disarm the warlords). And if it is, where does the United Nations stop? In fact the newly proclaimed Republic of Somaliland had been largely ignored by the United Nations or the international community.

By September 1992 the EC had decided to send a battalion of Belgian paratroopers to Somalia, using Third World aid funds to pay for this logistical and military support for relief convoys. The move was opposed by Britain which has consistently resisted EC moves to forge a common foreign policy at the United Nations, since London fears this could ultimately result in both Britain and France losing their seats on the Security Council in favour of an EC seat. Meanwhile, in Mombasa, the Americans were preparing to airlift 145,000 tons of food into Somalia over 60 days although their operation ran into initial difficulties because they had failed to clear it properly with the Kenyan authorities so that subsequent wrangling delayed the relief flights; an unnamed Kenyan source complained that the Americans appeared to have taken over Kenyan airspace 'from Mombasa to the North Eastern Province'.[10] The misunderstanding was soon smoothed over but that it had occurred at all was symptomatic of the African sensitivities at stake: rescue comes from the West; and the West treats Africa as though it is colonial territory again.

During August and September 1992 international efforts at relief finally gathered momentum, by which time an estimated 4.5 million Somalis were in danger of starvation; American and French planes brought in relief supplies, Britain announced further aid of £18mn in addition to an earlier commitment of £23mn worth, and Germany announced it would provide $13.7mn worth of aid and sent two planes to Mombasa to help transport food. Britain's Foreign Secretary, on a flying visit to Mogadishu early in September, said the world had been too slow in reacting to the famine in Somalia: 'We were all collectively too slow', he said. He was leading a European Community delegation which also included the Danish Foreign Minister, Uffe Ellemann-Jensen, and the Portuguese state secretary, Dura Barroso. After lightning visits to three feeding centres and a hospital Mr Hurd told a news conference: 'Now at least we have a short but vivid impression.'[11] By this time, it seemed, everyone had become involved in the Somali tragedy, though sometimes they gave the impression that they were more concerned with political constituencies back in their own countries than the tragedy on the ground. As the more successful of the NGOs which had been operating on the ground for some time pointed out: the first rule for functioning successfully was to work with and through the local people. That, however, is a rule that governments and the United Nations do not seem to have understood while western journalists talk only to expatriates and only credit foreign organisations with efforts to solve the conflict and relieve the famine. As T. E. Lawrence wrote in an earlier age: 'Better to let them do imperfectly what you can do perfectly yourself, for it is their country, their war and your time is short.'

The high hopes raised by President de Klerk's speech of 2 February 1990 were not being met in 1992. Despite the white referendum of March 1992 which gave de Klerk a decisive vote for constitutional change subsequent events threatened break-down. The massacre of ANC supporters at Boipatong by members of the Inkatha Freedom Party, consistent and growing evidence of police and military intransigence (the police reportedly brought into Boipatong killers from a local hostel for migrant Zulu workers) and a parallel suspicion that de Klerk either could not or would not control them pointed to the growing possibility of a collapse into disintegration rather than a new South Africa. Against this depressing background there were calls for greater international involvement in South Africa and in particular for a UN special representative to facilitate negotiations, monitor violence and report responsi-bility for it. The country has been living in a fool's paradise for decades. Apartheid made it possible for the white minority to persuade itself that its high standards of living, based largely on the export of raw materials such as gold and diamonds, could be extended indefinitely. Then, following Nelson Mandela's release, whites continued to fool themselves into believing that provided the ANC could be weaned from its left wing which advocated nationalisation there could be a return both to better economic times and to international respectability. On the other side, black expectations that an end to apartheid also means that the population as a whole can share in such prosperity is another myth. Essentially, South Africa is a Third World country with huge problems to solve, and this fact is not altered by the presence at the top of a large white elite which has long controlled the politics and economics of the country to its own advantage. Any genuine change in South Africa that extends the vote to everyone must bring such delusions to an end.

Ironically, if privatisation and greater competition are to be applied to the new South Africa, it is the whites who will suffer most; a bloated state bureaucracy and semi-guaranteed permanency of job tenure have long been used to assist the poorer whites and today South Africa has a bureaucracy whose size and inefficiency is matched only by those in eastern Europe. In 1992 the country had high inflation at 15% and high interest rates, with an economic growth rate that had declined by 2% a decade since the early 1970s and fell into negative figures in 1991. Fixed investment has fallen since the mid-1980s and existing capital would be insufficient to fund economic expansion. South Africa remains primarily an exporter of raw materials, and as such is both dependent upon the world market and effectively a Third World economy. Assuming that a political settlement can be achieved (and it remains a major assumption to make) this will work only if there is also a massive economic improvement in the lives of the black majority who will at once expect political advance to yield them jobs, better homes, proper education and cheaper staples (mainly food). It is at this point that the relationship of South Africa with the North becomes all important. Are countries such as Britain which argued against pressures to end apartheid, on the grounds that it was an internal matter, going to extend that argument so as to avoid any responsibility for the economic settlement that must follow a political one? For decades, as world agitation against apartheid mounted, powerful western interests in Britain, the United States and the EC worked to protect white South Africa from pressures for change while also safeguarding their lucrative investments in the country. And sanctions were opposed on the grounds that they would hurt the blacks rather than make the whites change their politics. Now, like the USSR under Gorbachev, South Africa under de Klerk has changed anyway and cannot revert to apartheid. But it has not begun to solve its problems and may fall apart. At one stage there was talk of a Marshall Plan for the new South Africa since the Republic would be unable to produce the wealth needed for economic and social reforms from its own internal resources. By 1992, however, the message from the West – principally Britain and the United States which are the most heavily committed to South Africa – was that development funds would have to come mainly from the World Bank and the IMF and that these would come only at a price. Much of South Africa's attraction for the West during the years of the Cold War was derived from her possession of scarce minerals and her strategic situation; these advantages have now become mainly redundant as the West becomes increasingly inward-looking. The West is more interested in developing eastern Europe than in salvaging a South Africa which could prove an endless drain on resources without yielding any quick returns.

Suspicion marked ANC relations with de Klerk's government throughout 1992 as one crisis succeeded another: continuing violence, splits in the ranks on both sides as the hardliners moved closer to outright confrontation, the breakdown of the talks in the multi-party Convention for a Democratic South Africa (CODESA) on 16 May, and the Boipatong massacre each contributed to a growing sense of foreboding, although fear of isolation if talks do collapse constantly persuaded the two sides to keep trying. De Klerk's principal problem is white fear at being ruled by blacks and given South Africa's history this is understandable; his solution lies in a constitution providing for 'checks and balances' which in simplistic terms means a white veto on majority (black) decisions. As this deadlock continued the ANC mounted a 'mass action' campaign to demonstrate the strength of its following in the country, and out of this came the Boipatong massacre.

By September 1992 with deadlock between the government and the ANC the EC was able to play a role when a foreign ministers' delegation led by Douglas Hurd visited South Africa; its aim was to prod the two sides into resuming talks once more. The visitors' itinerary inside South Africa emphasised their concern with rising violence and came at a time when new revelations of deaths in police custody showed that little had changed and certainly not in relation to the behaviour of the police or security forces. At least at this point there was an EC initiative to bring the two sides back to the negotiating table; it was in no one's interest to see a total breakdown in South Africa, though this then seemed appreciably closer.

Nelson Mandela scored a major international success in July 1992 by securing an invitation to address the UN Security Council on the violence in South Africa and the deadlocked talks. At the same time a scandal broke in the British press about South African spies and hit squads operating in Britain which was calculated to cause de Klerk maximum embarrassment when Mandela addressed the Security Council. British officials leant over backwards to emphasise that de Klerk was 'Mr Clean', but their efforts backfired since, as Abdul Minty of the UN Special Committee against Apartheid was able to point out: 'There is now enormous evidence of state complicity [in violence] . . . If De Klerk doesn't know what is going on then how can he negotiate South Africa's future, because he is clearly not in control.'[12] Then Nelson Mandela appeared before the Security Council to say he would resume talks for a non-racial government in South Africa only when the violence in the black townships had subsided and accused de Klerk's government of organising and orchestrating the violence against democratic movements like the ANC. He called on the Security Council to intervene to end the stalemate in South Africa and on the Secretary-General to appoint a special representative to South Africa. Britain, as usual, lobbied busily to prevent any attacks on Pretoria appearing in the draft resolution. South Africa's Foreign Minister, Pik Botha, subsequently accepted the idea of UN observers in South Africa but ruled out any UN peace-keeping troops. Subsequently Cyrus Vance visited South Africa as a UN special envoy on a 10-day mission and following his report the Secretary-General, Boutros-Ghali, recommended an inquiry into the South African Defence Force, the police, the KwaZulu police and the armed wings of the African National Congress and the Pan-Africanist Congress as well as a 30-strong monitoring force to be stationed at 'flashpoints'. Some two weeks after the submission of the report the Security Council unanimously authorised the stationing of observers in South Africa. The South African government accepted the United Nations report and welcomed the stationing of observers in the country so here at least the United Nations had achieved a substantial breakthrough in a country and with a government whose past intransigence had been notorious.

At the end of August 1992, following its agreement to a UN monitoring force, the South African government admitted the collapse of confidence in the police (and by implication their guilt in relation to the many accusations of collaboration in violence) when it purged a number of senior officers who had failed to adapt to post-apartheid politics, announced a 'positive discrimination' policy to promote blacks to senior positions and established an independent unit to investigate accusations of police crimes or police obstruction of justice. Then came the Ciskei massacre early in September when troops of the 'independent' Ciskei Homeland fired on a mass demonstration march of the ANC. The result of that massacre was to shock both sides into renewed talks. Even Britain on this occasion insisted that Pretoria must take full responsibility for keeping the troops of Ciskei and other 'homelands' under control; indeed, it was one of the most forceful statements to be made by Britain since de Klerk had begun his 'reform' process.

The real problem for South Africa remained and could be described under several headings: (1) Whatever the political solution, how could generations of racial oppression and bitterness be eliminated? (2) Would the extremists on both sides reduce any solution to violence and sectarian confrontations, and if so would either the United Nations or the big powers intervene? (3) How could the new South Africa finance the huge programmes of economic and social improvements for the black majority without which no political solution could work? (4) And what attitude would the major powers of the North take towards the new South Africa: one of 'wait and see' or one of providing active assistance to ensure that the political solution could be made to work? Most of the indications at the end of 1992 suggested that the leading powers who had for long interested themselves in South Africa – Britain, the United States and then the EC – would adopt 'wait and see' tactics at a time when South Africa required help from outside more than at any other time in its history. Just as the West did a minimum to bring an end to apartheid during the 40 years from 1948 to 1990, so it seems equally likely it will do a minimum to assist South Africa make the transition from an apartheid state dominated by whites to a Third World country requiring massive economic assistance if it is not to collapse into chaos. Should South Africa collapse into chaos, the blame will rest squarely upon western shoulders.

7　The Question of Debt

No other problem threatens the South with such continuing and forbidding menace as does that of debt, for nothing else remains so clearly beyond its control. The South can be blamed for its huge debts since in absolute terms it did not have to borrow in the first place, but although that is strictly speaking true such a judgement represents only a part of the story. At the end of the 1970s, before the OPEC-induced oil boom collapsed, western bankers, only too anxious to lend their money to an oil-rich country, were happy to tell Nigeria that it was 'under-borrowed' while in 1980, following its independence, Zimbabwe found plenty of would-be creditors ready enough to offer aid and credits – at a price. The North, indeed, has been only too anxious to lend to the South in good times and to do so without paying too much attention to orthodox banking criteria when the prospects for a high return looked reasonable. There have been at least as many willing lenders as there have been willing borrowers to create the massive problem which faced both North and South by the beginning of the 1990s.

Current international debts owed by the developing countries of the South to the developed countries of the North now amount to US$1,700bn and annual debt servicing comes to $100bn, while there is a net resource outflow from developing countries of $80bn a year, of which $70bn is from the highly indebted countries. The problems of debt have been aired many times – with increasing desperation on the part of the debtors – since 1982 when Mexico suspended interest payments and sparked off the debt crisis. Much less aired but certainly acknowledged has been the belief of bankers that for all practical purposes they will never recover a large part of their lending.

Between 1983 and 1989 the rich creditor nations received $242 bn in net transfers from the developing countries on their long-term lending, and the bigger the overall debts the faster the problem grows. The debts of the developing countries mount steadily and apparently inexorably no matter what temporary forms of relief are proposed and tried out. In 1970 such debts stood at a mere $100bn, a figure which increased sixfold to $650bn by 1980 and then doubled to $1,350bn by 1990. Though more than half the debt is concentrated in only 20 countries, led by Brazil, Mexico, Argentina, India and Egypt, in a sense this is irrelevant, for the amount of debt has to be related to the size of the economy of the borrowing country and its ability to repay. The debts of Sub-Saharan Africa at $150bn, although just over a tenth of the total, are nonetheless equivalent to that region's entire GNP. On the other hand, debts in Latin America which are of a far greater magnitude, are equivalent to only half the region's GNP.

The overall position is coming close to the absurd, with too many debtor countries finding that most of their export efforts go principally into servicing debts. Africa, which is the world's poorest region, saw its debts grow by an average of 10% a year throughout the 1980s and an increasing number of developing countries are now caught in the debt trap in which new borrowing – whatever its ostensible purpose – is made to meet repayment commitments, with the result that any new borrowing simply increases both the debts and the annual level of servicing which has to be met. World recession, moreover, has exacerbated the problem because it has decreased export earnings, mainly of commodities, even as debts to be serviced have increased.

Debt relief – either in the form of rescheduling or amortising (forgiveness) – has generally been politically haphazard, with little effort at helping the poorest in a systematic way, so that these countries have not necessarily received more in lower interest rates or debt forgiveness than richer countries. A general awareness of the debt burden and periodic relief gestures have proved a poor response to what, arguably, is the most dangerous and compelling of all the problems which divide North and South. The search for a solution to the question of the South's debts should take priority over other North–South problems because (as various Third World leaders made plain at the Rio Earth Summit) there is little point in expecting a country whose every initiative is constrained by debts and the need to meet repayments to embark meanwhile upon other policies which, however worthy, might hamper its freedom to earn hard currencies from the North and so deal with its debts. What, then, makes sense as a solution?

The huge existing debts and the sense of almost hopeless indebtedness that shackles development for a growing number of countries in the South is close to turning into a cause of deep resentment between South and North, for as long as debt hangs like a pall over so many poor countries it is unrealistic to suppose that other North–South agreements, for example over pollution control, can be entered into with any chance of success. The search for a solution, therefore, is as much in the interests of the creditors as it is of the debtors.

One suggstion advanced has been for the banks to write off about $300bn and then finance this by a tax on GNP in the bankers' countries and by increased subscriptions to the World Bank and IMF. Yet $300bn is still only to tackle the problem at the margin. Debt relief so far has never had an impact on the problem in the sense of moving it towards a solution. At most, such measures have brought temporary relief to some of the most hard-pressed debtor countries. The usual approach to debt relief is to postpone interest payments or capital repayments and add the arrears to the overall capital sum owing. The net result of this approach is to make the total long-term debt position worse, extending the debtor's horizon of indebtedness indefinitely. Borrowing more to provide immediate relief has the same effect. So far, indeed, even apparently generous debt forgiveness has only reduced indebtedness in Africa (the poorest region) by 10% and this is not on a sufficient scale to alter the nature of the problem.

Any solution to the debt problem must first take account of political attitudes in the North where, through the 1980s, it became increasingly obvious that new 'guidelines' were beginning to affect the way the rich countries viewed the problems of the South. Even before the end of the Cold War and the collapse of the USSR countries such as Britain were putting increased emphasis upon different political values in the South as the price for aid, tying assistance to 'good governance', by which was meant an abandonment of one-party rule and a return to multy-partyism, or insisting upon an end of human rights abuses. Following his election victory in November 1991, the new President of Zambia, Frederick Chiluba, when visiting Britain in February 1992, asked the British government to support a write-off for Zambia's $8bn debts. What he said on this occasion was instructive, for though he insisted that the North did not *owe* anything to the South, nonetheless he suggested: 'Countries in the developed world – indeed they owe us nothing – but they have a duty to move along with us to ensure new democracies do not crumble.'[1] It would be hypocritical as well as dangerous for the North to insist upon new criteria for its aid and then, when such criteria are put in place, do nothing new in response. But the danger of this happening exists and should a complaisant North first encourage political change on the grounds that this is a prerequisite for continuing support, but subsequently not provide the support which it has implied will be forthcoming, the end result will be to widen still further what is already a dangerous divide.

The debt crisis crept up on the world by degrees. Originally money was loaned by governments to assist development projects and by banks to make commercial profits. And then, gradually, the huge debt problem emerged with both sides liable for blame: the lenders for not calling a halt sooner and failing to apply proper banking criteria to many of their loans until they had become greatly over-extended; and the borrowers for assuming they could continue indefinitely meeting one economic or political crisis after an another by the expedient of borrowing. The two sides continued along this path until the debt problem had grown to unmanageable and potentially destructive proportions, nearly exploding in 1982 when it threatened to destroy the entire international financial system. And yet, in all examinations of this problem, a crucial question is never asked. It is simply this: do the creditors really want to solve the debt problem and allow the debtors to get free of their control? Or is the bulk of the debt forgiveness which has taken place so far no more than a series of political gestures designed to look good but never enough or intended to alter the basic relationship between North and South which, of course, is one of economic dependence? Is the real explanation of the debt problem the desire of politicians in the North to keep the South so dependent that it also remains manipulable? For example, in the 1992 *Human Development Report* the UNDP points out that the World Bank has not forgiven Africa debts (where insistence upon repayment means net negative transfers) but instead has accelerated disbursements – and only in some cases – so that the immediate situation appears better though in reality the debts become greater.[2]

The fact is that at the present time there exists deep two-way suspicion and mistrust between North and South. The North sees the South as a burden. And the South sees the North, exemplified through its mammoth debts, as an economic oppressor.

The only way the debt burden can be alleviated so that debtors become permanently better off and feel free – at last – to develop along their own lines would be by total forgiveness of all debts, a wiping clean of the slate. So far, all efforts at providing relief have been too little to make an impact that is meaningful. Thus, the 1989 Brady Plan to reduce debts absolutely rather than just rescheduling them was a step in the right direction but still dealt in sums that were insufficient to alter the overall dependence – and debt desperation – of the South. A discussion of means – whether a particular initiative such as the Brady Plan or income growth, an efficient fiscal system, a trade surplus or better levels of domestic investment – always brings us back to the elementary fact that none of these has been sufficient to resolve the problem. Quite simply, this is because the debt burden has now grown to almost unmanageable proportions and each and every expedient so far tried, either on its own or jointly, has been unable to achieve more than provide temporary breathing space in what remains a deteriorating situation. The debt problem is not a temporary crisis; it is a permanent state and if it is to be resolved in a way that is beneficial to the world economic community as a whole then its resolution also requires a permanent reordering of the present creditor–debtor relationship. Thus, as always, the real question is one of political will.

We *know* the debt problem, which has been exhaustively analysed, just as we are acquainted with the various part-solutions which have been advanced, but in the end it boils down to how willing the North is to think and act in terms of a global approach rather than one that is primarily concerned only to safeguard the interests of the rich. This is not a question of charity; it is about a decision to break a deadlock that threatens the entire global economic structure.

Unlike so many of the relationships between North and South which as much as anything resolve themselves into a question of attitudes, the problem of debt is capable of a solution if only because it is a precise, concrete problem to which there are equally precise answers. It can be solved. But for a solution to work it must benefit – and be seen to benefit – both sides in the debt equation. It is worth examining the debt problem as if both sides were equally concerned to find a solution, for if this particular irritant in North–South relations could be removed much else of benefit to both sides would then be likely to follow. If, for a moment, we suppose that a way could be found to eliminate the entire debt burden of the South, what results would flow from such an achievement? Would total debt forgiveness, whatever the apparent cost to the North, open up such new opportunities for world trade, stability and development as to compensate for the original sacrifice? The most likely answer to this supposition is a resounding 'yes', for there is no other area of international relations where a single imaginative initiative could lead to so many beneficial spin-offs of equal value to both rich and poor, both North and South.

Before considering either the results of total relief for the world community or the modalities necessary for its implementation, another set of questions has to be addressed. The first is: what do we actually want as a solution, not to the debt problem as such but to the wider problem of North–South relations? Given the growing gap between North and South and the further possibility that the end of the Cold War may precipitate a return to an older and more dangerous style of big power politics a resolute attack upon the debt problem could have a profound impact in the other direction. An imaginative initiative from the North that demonstrated a true willingness to eliminate the vast debt burden of the South would dispel many of the current fears in the South that it is about to be marginalised as a direct result of the end of the Cold War and the consequent disappearance of the compulsions that drove both sides to seek allies in the South. On the other hand, if the debt burden is allowed to increase it will fuel all the other antagonisms which are wrapped up in questions relating to the population explosion, emigration, the control of pollution, or freer trade and access to the markets of the North. Would a major onslaught on the debt problem produce a knock-on effect capable of changing the climate as well as the economics of North–South relations? A fundamental change of political and economic attitudes is possible, but only if these questions are approached in this light from both sides.

If all debts, that is the total of \$1,350bn owed by the South to the North (as of 1990), were to be forgiven, what would be the effect on the world economy generally, for both the indebted and the creditors? There is the question of mechanisms to be resolved. And there are the results to consider – what would actually happen?

The end of the debt burden for the nations of the South would be like a blast of fresh air, rejuvenating the politics as well as the economies of countries which at present have little or no freedom of movement. The first result would be to release the \$100bn a year now employed to service their debts; this would at once become available to purchase goods and services from the world market. Were such a sum to be injected into the world economy, as an addition to current flows, it would act as the tonic needed to bring the recession to an end. Moreover, almost the entire sum would be spent in the markets of the North to purchase goods which at present are not produced in the South. The release of funds on such a scale would automatically create a new surge of business with the North that the current level of debts has made impossible and this in turn would have a knock-on effect that must work to the advantage of both sides. This huge injection of funds into the market place would be the *return* which the North would earn for its own act of statesmanship.

Of course, there will be objections: that, as a matter of principle, banks cannot permit a write-off on such a scale; that such mammoth forgiveness once practised must only encourage the developing nations to run up similar debts again in the hope that the operation could be repeated in the future; that to do so in a time of recession must add impossible extra burdens to already hard-pressed economies in the North. These are the views of caution although in fact the debt problem was created, at least in part, because bankers did not originally act with caution at all.

The object of any forgiveness exercise should be twofold: to end the current state of permanent indebtedness and dependence in which the poor nations find themselves; and, by ameliorating the prevailing economic conditions of the South, help the world emerge from a major and dangerous recession. Political rhetoric and hyperbole are often expended upon the concept of a 'one-world' society, though rarely does action follow to suit the words. Here is an area where action could begin to benefit both sides as soon as a programme was put in place. Exercises of amelioration have been carried out from time to time but none has made any real or lasting impact upon the problem – and perhaps none was meant to do so. If the real aim, the starting point, is genuine debt forgiveness and if, for a moment, we assume that the huge current debts no longer exist, what difference will this make to development in the South?

How much foreign exchange will it release for other purposes? And to what extent will some of the more advanced economies of the South, such as India or Brazil, then be able to play a formative, focal role in the market place for the first time? For the North, how much would such a move create a new climate for its relations with the South and enable it to become involved in the South's development not, as at present, as though part of a permanent rescue operation but rather in a South that is seen for the first time to be part of the whole global market?

The aim makes sense; what of the means?

The massive debts of the South divide between government-to-government debts (the result of aid loans), those owing to the multilateral institutions (the World Bank and IMF) and those owing to the private sector (mainly the commercial banks) so that any write-off exercise will require a number of different approaches. An operation on this scale can only make sense if it originates with the G-7 and if they are prepared to give the lead by writing off both government-to-government loans and publicly guaranteed loans (the private sector contribution). The second step would be the provision of funds to enable the World Bank and the IMF to do the same, and again the initiative has to come from the G-7 who in any case command the necessary voting power in the global banking institutions. Essentially the G-7 has to create a fund equivalent to the total of debts to be written off and, as forbidding as this may seem, such a fund could in fact be created on a yearly basis.

A number of suggestions for funding partial forgiveness exercises already exist and though the global sum in question – $1,350bn – is forbidding it need not be daunting. The idea of a new Marshall Plan has been mooted from time to time to cover one-off aid packages to assist particular countries or regions. Could the North, therefore, launch the equivalent of a Marshall Plan to eliminate the debt problem as the United States launched its plan in the post-war period to rehabilitate Europe and get it back on its feet again? The objective is remarkably similar.

First it is necessary to examine the statistics. One possibility, for example, would be a tax of 1% on the GNPs of the rich nations. In 1988 the combined GNPs of the G-7 – the United States, Japan, Germany, Britain, France, Italy and Canada – came to US$11,402,904,000,000 so that 1% of that would be equivalent to US$114,029,040,000, or slightly more than the annual debt service costs which the South now faces. In the same year the combined GNPs of all the OECD countries came to US$13,053,179,000,000 to yield a slightly larger 1% figure of US$130,531,790,000. As it stands, that is not enough.

The debtors can be divided into those with per capita GNPs below $700 – the poorest – and the rest. In 1989 the total debts of the 41 low-income-countries including China and India came to US$310,641,000,000. The total debts of the next group of lower-middle-income countries (also 41 in number) came to US$674,041,000,000. And the total debts of the 17 so-called upper-middle-income countries stood at US$248,002,000,000.[3] How then can they be tackled?

In the case of the 41 poorest countries virtually all their debts are either public or publicly guaranteed or IMF credits. Given the huge total of the combined debts of the South total forgiveness would cost approximately 10% of current OECD GNPs, which is too much for even the richest nations to contemplate in one operation. It must be taken in stages. There are several possible approaches. One which might make the greatest economic sense would, however, not be politically acceptable. That would be to select a handful of important countries (as to size) with real potential for growth and eliminate their debts entirely so as to enable them to become 'motors' for growth in their regions. In order to achieve a semblance of equity a major country in each region could be selected for such treatment: Mexico in Latin America with debts of $95bn, Nigeria in Africa with debts of $32bn, India in Asia with debts of $62bn. But though such an approach might appeal to detached economists it would be bound to raise fierce political objections from all those who are excluded as well as the rich nations who prefer other candidates. So it would make more sense to approach the problem by tackling the indebted according to group or class, and the easiest way to do this would be according to the World Bank criteria of least-developed and less-developed. But a third way makes the most sense of all: that is to make all the indebted tackle the problem together. This could be done by the creation of an amortisation bank.

An amortisation bank or fund could be created with a single purpose: to work towards the eventual elimination of the South's debts. The bank would be funded by the annual debts repayments from the South. Each year, all official aid repayments to OECD countries would be paid by the OECD recipients direct into the bank. This annual handover of repayments by the rich countries of the North would be their contribution to solving the problem. It is, moreover, always easier to forgo repayments which have already been made than to find new funds – and this is what the rich would be expected to do. The money paid into the bank each year (beginning at approximately $100bn of repayments) would be used to buy out private banks or amortise debts (capital only). On an annual basis, in addition to the actual total of repayments made (which at present are insufficient to alter the overall state of the South's indebtedness), an equivalent sum would then be written off the total of capital outstanding with the added bonus of reducing the interest due for the following year. Such a revolving amortisation fund would have the great merit that debtors – year by year – could see their repayments having a double effect: meeting the current year's burden and then reducing by that amount again their total of capital debts. Moreover, the real reduction in debt (represented by the second part of this annual transaction) would come increasingly in line with what the debtor nations could actually afford. The rich, for their part, could claim that they had doubled their aid contribution (in the least painful way) and the charge that the North is now taking out of the South more than it puts in would fall away. Debts would actually begin to be reduced, as opposed to growing ever more unmanageable as at present.

The operation of such an amortisation fund need not be complicated. First, the bank would register each country's debts and a debtor country would repay its annual capital and interest to its account at the bank where the repayment would be offset against the various national (credit) accounts of that particular debtor country's donors. The example of Mozambique, currently listed as the world's poorest country, can be used as an illustration of how the process would work. In 1989 Mozambique's total of public and publicly guaranteed debt stood at $3,885,000,000 and that year Mozambique repaid $13mn in capital and $31mn in interest to make a total of $44mn. Under the amortisation scheme this sum would be paid to the bank, where it would be offset against the appropriate creditor accounts. Then, at the end of the year (in this case it would have been at the beginning of 1990) Mozambique would have had its share of total debt further reduced by the amount she had repaid, in this case by $44mn, all of this sum being offset solely against capital.

However, though the total repaid in any year by the 41 poorest countries would be used to amortise part of their debts it need not necessarily be applied to these, country by country, on a pro rata basis. Instead, other criteria could also be used to weight amortisation in favour of the poorest each year. Weighting which favours the poorest might include such criteria as per capita GNP, total indebtedness and ability to repay (foreign exchange earnings). If such a procedure were to be followed then Mozambique (as outlined above) might have qualified for a greater amortisation than the $44mn which she would have repaid that year (possibly $50/55mn) while the better off among the 41 least developed countries might receive somewhat less in amortisation than the sum they had repaid during the year. Probably, however, the politics of equity would dictate that annual amortisation equals annual repayments. Over 10 or 15 years such an approach could eliminate the greater part of the South's debts without putting too great a strain upon the economies of the North, while the scheme's great merit would be twofold: that debt repayments would now have the effect of more than doubling the rate of debt reduction and that all money originally provided by donors as aid would continue to be used as aid.

This annual exercise applied to the 41 poorest countries (in the same way as to Mozambique above) would work out as follows. In 1989 total repayments from the poorest 41 countries of principal on their long-term public and publicly guaranteed loans came to US$11,252,000,000 while total repayments of interest for the year came to US$10,742,000,000 to give a combined repayment figure of US$21,994,000,000. This latter figure would have been paid into the amortisation bank to be subsequently written off against the total capital debts outstanding of the 41 at the end of that year. In 1989 the total public and publicly guaranteed debts of the 41 poorest countries came to US$310,641,000,000 (and assuming this to have been the figure at the end of the year when the repayments worth US$21,994,000,000 had already been set against these debts) then the overall figure would have been reduced to US$288,647,000,000 which would then have become the starting figure for 1990.

A comparable exercise for the 41 lower-middle-income countries would have worked out as follows: total debts (1989) came to US$674,041,000,000 while principal repayments amounted to US$25,734,000,000 and interest repayments to US$24,602,000,000, combining to give a repayment figure of US$50,336,000,000 for the year. At the end of that year this repayment sum of US$50,336,000,000 would then have been written off against the total debts of US$674,041,000,000 to reduce the capital owing to US$623,705,000,000 which would have been the new starting debt for 1990.

Such an exercise, repeated each year, would soon make itself felt throughout the economies of the indebted countries as it would in the North by progressively releasing more purchasing power in the South each year. Now solutions to world problems are never as simple as this and, for example, in 1992 Russia which faced every sort of economic problem as it tried to alter

course after more than 70 years of communism wanted to call
in the $8bn of debts owed to it by Ethiopia. The possibility of
obtaining agreement among the rich to such an approach to
debt would in any case be highly problematical. Yet the fact
that formidable problems exist is no reason for not trying to
tackle them. It is not enough to overcome the debt crisis; more
important, the indebted countries must also be restored to a
satisfactory medium-term rate of growth. Something of this
nature is required if the debt problem is not to overwhelm the
world economic system. The real problem – as always – is one
of political will. We know the debt problem and its scale, as
well as the possible ways to tackle it, but in the end the question
resolves itself into one of the willingness of the rich to act: it is a
question of political will. Whether the political will exists or
whether the rich and powerful would prefer to keep the South
permanently indebted is another matter.

8 Resources

An analysis of relations between North and South shows the former to hold all, or almost all, the advantages, which leads us to the crucial question: whether the North needs the South at all? Many appraisals of North–South relations tend to emphasise the power of the North, in the sense of its control of the global economy, and the weakness of the South, its debts and poverty, while at the same time it is assumed, and has sometimes become part of the conventional wisdom, that at least the South possesses massive resources which the North needs and that this fact acts as some kind of counterweight which gives to the South a degree of leverage upon the more advanced technologies of the North. However, an examination of resources must throw doubt even on this assumption. The activities of the 'greens' world-wide, the representations of the various aid lobbies or the immense amount of publicity that preceded the Rio Earth Summit, often in the form of comparing and contrasting the wealth of the North with the poverty of the South, have between them brought awareness of the huge problems that divide North and South. But underlying these arguments and presentations has always been the assumption that the North needed the South if only for the wealth that lies underground and, therefore, that there was a long-term possibility of redressing the balance between North and South; this assumption was greatly strengthened by the oil experience of the mid-1970s when OPEC, if only briefly, did hold out the prospect of change and the implementation of a New International Economic Order (NIEO) based upon the South's control of the marketable surplus in one major commodity. Subsequently that experience affected the way the North saw the South: as a storehouse of raw materials. And though they do not say so openly there are undoubtedly many politicians and businessmen in the North who would like to keep the South in just such a state – a permanent storehouse of raw materials to be supplied on demand to the industrialised North.

Although cynics will claim that the Rio summit achieved little or nothing, this would be wrong. It did achieve one astonishing breakthrough – foreshadowed by the UN Conference on the Human Environment at Stockholm in 1972 – and that was to bring together 160 governments and ask them to begin acting as though all resources belong to all mankind. It is a demand that goes contrary to every historical experience up to this time, and if it is only a quarter successful will nonetheless represent an advance of unprecedented proportions. Rio did at least focus our attention upon the fact that the world faces a problem and as such the Earth Summit also represented a tentative advance in world government. Both the League of Nations after World War I and the United Nations after World War II were created to keep the peace but not to manage the resources of the planet, which were assumed to be the business of the particular nations which controlled them. What might be described as the new science of environmentalism sees the world as a single interconnected system that must be regulated in such a way that it benefits everyone or, if damage has to be inflicted upon the globe, that this should be as minimal as possible compatible with the need to exploit resources. A world which claims that carbon emissions in California can damage forests in Europe is a world inextricably linked; environmentalism thus becomes 'the first ever truly global crusade'.[1] Assuming that such arguments are generally accepted (which at least in theory appears to be the case) then at once two further questions arise: the first, who is going to control the environment and attacks upon its resources for the benefit of all mankind? The second, what price can be extracted by those who control large resources in exchange for agreed methods of conservation for the benefit of the world community? These questions were already beginning to take shape at the Rio summit. In a gesture prior to Rio that at least acknowledged the existence of such questions, President Bush increased US support for the conservation of forests in the developing world as a sign of American concern for the world environment. Whatever their motives for attending the Rio summit – and many in fact were not notable for any previous understanding of or concern with environmental issues – over 100 heads of state did attend it and by so doing brought the issue of resources closer to the centre of world politics. The subject will now remain at the centre of world attention, even if real control of resources on anything like a global scale for the benefit of the world as a whole is unlikely to become viable as a proposition for several generations.

Meanwhile, resources and their control (in the absence of political considerations of the kind that dominated the Cold War) will come to dominate relations between North and South. The North – and most especially the United States, Canada, Russia, Australia and the EC – has huge resources at its disposal and often imports from the South either because it is cheaper to do so or because by so doing it may preserve its own resources that much longer. This was certainly the case in the United States during the oil crisis of the 1970s. Indeed, a likely scenario for the future is one in which the North extracts as much as it possibly can from the South before the latter is sufficiently developed to need those resources in any quantity to support an improved lifestyle. At its worst such a scenario would see the South (or particular countries in the South) exporting their most valuable resources to the North to finance development, only to find when they have finally achieved developmental breakthroughs of their own that they have no resources left. Such a scenario becomes more likely when other techniques employed by the North are taken into consideration. At the present time the North concentrates its energies upon exporting its manufactures to the South while taking only raw materials or semi-processed goods in return and thus restricting the industrialisation of the South. The answer to the question what the North *wants* of the South must determine the future relationship of North and South and, in terms of present performance, the answer basically is raw materials.

And though it can be argued that the South offers the North huge markets for its trade even this appears to be doubtful, for by far the greater part of world trade is North–North, and the more advanced an economy the more it trades with others as equally advanced as itself.

Forests, and especially the tropical forests of Brazil and southeast Asia, have become symbols of this environmental concern. The 'greens' say they are to be preserved, but the markets for their wood are in the North and, for the countries which possess them, they represent ready money. They are, of course, a wasting asset and though it may make sense to emphasise the importance of reafforestation it is still more important to stop felling natural forests which cannot be replaced. Conservation arguments are often divorced from the requirements of the local populations, although Friends of the Earth argue cogently enough that: 'Planting trees in itself is not a bad idea. There are many reasons why we should do a lot more of it. But the expansion of tree cover in the tropics should be geared to local needs – for fuel, fodder, fruit – rather than global priorities.'[2] Present evidence suggests that this is not taking place and, for example, the Intergovernmental Panel on Climate Change estimated in 1990 that an area the size of Europe from the Atlantic to the Urals would have to be reforested each year to balance the annual anthropogenic emissions of carbon dioxide from all sources. If that is indeed the case we are in deep trouble. In 1990 a \$1.5bn Rainforest Pilot Project in Brazil was approved by the Group of Seven (G-7) (which promised to finance it) and then declared by the World Bank to be 'an example of cooperation between developed and developing countries on global environmental issues'. Two years later, however, only \$53.5mn had been raised and then only after President Collor of Brazil had written to the G-7 heads of government: the United States at that stage had contributed just \$5mn. As Brazil's Environment Minister, Jose Goldemberg, said: 'The first world is being very hypocritical – it annoys me tremendously. We get a lot of advice and rhetoric but very little money.'[3] Incidents such as this leave the impression that concern for the environment is largely for show and that threats to resources will have to become far more compelling than at present before effective action is taken, by which time it may well be too late. And this absence of real concern in the North was highlighted during the Rio summit when the European Commissioner for the Environment, Ripa di Meana, objected to plans by the British Ministry of Transport to destroy part of an ancient woodland in southeast London to make way for a road. The squabble, common enough in the EC, made the high-minded concern of ministers from the North appear hypocritical and tawdry. Meanwhile, according to the UN Food and Agriculture Organisation (FAO), about 17mn hectares of forest land are destroyed every year, most of this at present in South and Central America. The world has 4.9bn hectares of forests but the amount destroyed annually surpasses the amount that is replanted. At present 50% of Latin America, 33% of Asia and 27% of Africa is covered by forest.[4]

One of the South's most able champions is the Prime Minister of Malaysia, Mahathir Mohamad, who defends his country's massive exploitation of its forests and attacks the North for its hypocrisy at the same time. As he claims: 'Fear by the North of environmental degradation provides the South with the leverage that did not exist before.' Such a claim, however, can make sense only if the North is really concerned about what happens to the environment of the South, as opposed to demonstrating concern to appease its various 'green' lobbies or to distract attention from its own environmentally destructive activities. In April 1992 Prime Minister Mahathir addressed the ministerial conference on environment and development at Kuala Lumpur which was attended by 55 developing countries; he advanced an unequivocal challenge to the North: 'If the rich North expects the poor to foot the bill for a cleaner environment, Rio will become an exercise in futility . . . There will be no development if the poor countries are not allowed to extract their natural wealth. The only way for them to develop and yet avoid damage to the environment is for

them to receive substantial material help.' He made what is
going to be a standard form of criticism when he took the North
to task for destroying its own environmental heritage and then
suggested that it now wants to argue that resources which are
left in the South also belong to the North. Speaking of
Malaysia's forests he said: 'But we are also acutely conscious
that we are a developing country which needs the wealth
afforded by our forests . . . If it is in the interest of the rich that
we do not cut down our trees, then they must compensate us for
the loss of income.'[5] Arguments about preserving forests
become entangled with arguments about terms of trade. Thus
Japan, which is one of the world's largest wood importers, does
not tax imported logs but imposes a 15% import tariff on
imported plywood; ostensibly this tariff is designed to safeguard
Japan's own industry against competition but, at the same
time, it also has the effect of inhibiting the development of
wood processing industries in logging countries and so prevents
a greater proportion of the profits being retained at home.

The extent to which the world environment is under threat
can be readily illustrated by the plight of the world's
mountains. The world's uplands cover 20% of the earth's
surface and provide living space for 10% of the world's
population whilst also being a vital source of minerals, food,
timber and – most important of all – water. But mountains are
now under threat world-wide from pollution, tourism, mineral
projects and hydro-electric developments. Mountains represent
one more area where global attention and action is necessary if
huge resources are not to be eroded and their value destroyed,
or at any rate damaged beyond easy recovery. Such issues as
the forests and mountains make the headlines because they are
attractive subjects for the 'greens' to focus upon but in reality
they are part of a far wider problem: the rapid destruction or
running down of world-wide resources to meet the needs of a
voracious and growing world population. Despite periodic
outcries in the North about the destruction of resources in the
South, there is little evidence that the North is prepared to do
anything except extract what it wants from the South as

cheaply as possible. It is, therefore, unsurprising that leaders in the South, such as Malaysia's Mahathir, respond in the way they do. Even so, the forests represent only one particular area of exploitation, and a relatively minor one in terms of the global picture; they attract attention for romantic reasons and because their destruction is so highly visible. An examination of the overall position in relation to all resources shows that Mahathir's belief in a capacity for leverage by the South is at best tenuous.

An examination of international commodities – who produces, trades and controls them – reveals the extent to which they are all, or nearly all, dominated by the North. It is not simply that the North collectively provides the main market for such commodities – this is to be expected – but in a surprising number of cases it also produces far more of them quantitatively than does the South. Some 50 internationally traded commodities are considered here. In some cases, such as aeronautics, the North dominates the field completely: that is, it produces the commodity virtually in its entirety while trade in it is 90% a question of North–North activity with the South playing at most a peripheral role. In the case of other commodities such as aluminium the South produces a substantial proportion of the commodity for export, even if the end use is overwhelmingly a matter of consumption in the North. Only in a minority of cases such as tropical foodstuffs like cocoa or coffee is the South the only producer, and even then its markets are almost all in the North.

Aeronautics as a highly sophisticated industry demands an ever-greater concentration of technology, and this in turn means an ever-greater concentration of resources and investment, with the effect that the industry is found in only a few of the most advanced economies. By 1990 the leading producers were the United States, Britain, the USSR, France and West Germany; the main exporting countries were the United States, Britain and France; and the main importing countries were the United States, Britain and the rest of Europe. Moreover, by that date most aeronautics industries had either merged or been forced to collaborate; the industry was dominated by the United States with only Airbus-Industrie in Europe as a serious contender outside North America. Now aeronautics is one of the most sophisticated of all industries so this pattern of concentration is not surprising, but this or a similar pattern is repeated again and again.

The field of computers and electronics is dominated both as to imports and exports by the North although certain countries of the South (generally the Newly Industrialising Countries or NICs) are also developing this sector; they are led by Hong Kong, Taiwan, China, South Korea and Malaysia.

Financial services, principally banking and insurance (the provision of credit), is almost entirely in the hands of the North; the monumental frauds associated with the Bank of Credit and Commerce International (BCCI) may well set back similar banking ventures emanating from the Third World. There are a growing number of Third World countries which have launched small-scale stock markets of their own in recent years; these include Singapore, Nigeria and Kenya.

The production of machine tools is a primary indicator of industrial capacity and the leading producers are Japan, the United States, Germany and the USSR (though the break-up of the Soviet empire may expose many flaws here as elsewhere in its productive capacity). The main exporters are Germany, Japan, Switzerland and Italy while the main importers are the United States, Russia, Germany and France. The production of motor vehicles is mainly a North–North affair though with increasing assembly activities in the more promising markets of the South. The main producers of pharmaceuticals are all in the North – the United States, Japan, Germany, France, Britain, Italy and Switzerland – but joined by South Korea from the NICs. The main exporters of pharmaceuticals are the United States, Germany, Britain and Switzerland and the main markets are in the United States, the EC and Japan.

The production of semi-conductors (crystalline solids or chips) for the computer market is entirely in the hands of the North at the top end of industry, with production in the approximate ratios of Japan (4) to the United States (3) to Europe (2). Telecommunications is dominated by the North with Japan, the United States and the EC as the principal exporters, although here both South Korea and Taiwan are competing and while the main markets remain in the North an increasing number of developing countries such as Brazil or Nigeria do offer rapidly expanding markets.

What are known as 'white goods' – such as refrigerators and washing machines – are principally traded North–North, although there is significant potential for exports to the South, at least to supply the upper end of the market for the local elites.

All the above traded commodities are at the most sophisticated end of the market and are produced, controlled and traded overwhelmingly between the countries of the North. However, a few countries such as South Korea have made significant breakthroughs into at least some of these sectors and their success represents the starting point for greater activity by the South.

The arms trade stands in a category of its own. It is the biggest single trade in the world and though the sophisticated arms all originate in the North many countries of the South – whatever other problems they may face – find the means to purchase arms. Moreover, certain 'pariah' countries in the South such as Chile under Pinochet, South Africa, Rhodesia during the UDI years in the 1960s and 1970s, Israel, North Korea and Taiwan have made enormous efforts to develop arms industries of their own, thus breaking the general pattern of dominance by the North. During the 1980s, for example, Iraq was the biggest importer of arms world-wide while in 1990 developing countries accounted for 60% of the total arms trade.

The second category of resources are minerals, where many countries in the South are well or at least significantly endowed. The extent to which they can add value to their minerals by processing (bauxite into aluminium, for example) before exporting them is a measure of their success. In a number of cases, however, large resources do not necessarily mean significant exports. There are, for example, huge coal resources world-wide and the big users in the North such as the United States have their own sources of supply and do not need to import, though they may do so if coal from the South is available at significantly lower prices.

In the case of aluminium (with bauxite processed to aluminium in the country of origin) the main producing countries are the United States, Russia, Jamaica and Canada followed by Norway, Germany and Australia, while the main exporting countries are Jamaica, the United States, Canada, Brazil and Surinam (three out of five from the Third World). When it is a question of exporting bauxite before any processing has taken place the leading exporters – Jamaica, Guinea, Indonesia, China and Ghana – are all from the Third World while the main importing countries are the United States, USSR, Canada, Japan and Germany.

Four countries from the South – Chile, Peru, Zaire and Zambia – formed the copper cartel (CIPEC) which accounted for 55% of the non-communist world's supply but the United States and Canada rank respectively as the first and third world producers while there are substitutes for copper if the price rises too much, as CIPEC found to its cost in the 1970s.

The four leading producers of diamonds are Australia, Zaire, Botswana and the USSR (now Russia) while almost all the remaining important producers are found in Africa: South Africa, Namibia, Ghana, the Central African Republic, Sierra Leone, Liberia, Tanzania (now virtually worked out), Angola and Guinea.

When the Bretton Woods agreement linking the dollar to gold was terminated in 1971 gold became a commodity like any other, though one that is much sought after and used as a hedge in financially bad times. In 1990 South Africa accounted for 29% of world output, the United States 11% and the USSR and Eastern Europe for a further 10% (estimated). They were followed as producers by Australia, Canada, Brazil and China.

There are abundant world resources of iron ore. At present the principal producers are Russia, China, Brazil, Australia

and the United States; the main exporting countries are
Australia, Russia, India, Canada and Venezuela; and the
main importing countries are Japan, Germany, the United
States and South Korea. Lead and zinc are generally found
together. The main producers of lead are Australia, the United
States, Canada, Peru, Mexico and then Europe, and the main
importers/consumers are the United States, Japan and Europe.
The picture is nearly identical for zinc, whose main producers
are Canada, Australia, Peru, the United States, Mexico, Japan
and Europe while its main importers/consumers are the United
States, Japan and Europe.

Of the world's top seven producers of natural gas – Russia,
the United States, Canada, the Netherlands, Algeria, Britain
and Indonesia – only two come from the South, while of the
main exporters – Russia, Canada, the Netherlands, Algeria,
Norway and Indonesia – the same two appear again. The
main importers are all in the North. The main producers of
phosphorites (the basis for fertilisers) are the United States,
Russia, Morocco, Jordan and Tunisia followed, on a smaller
scale, by Togo, Syria, Senegal and Algeria. The main
exporters are Morocco, the United States, Jordan, Russia
and Syria while the main importers are Europe, Japan, the
Philippines, India, China and Iran. In this case at least the
South is a significant importer as opposed to merely producing
for export.

Four other important metals are chromium, platinum, silver
and tin. South Africa and Zimbabwe are major producers of
chromite while Gabon in Africa is also an important producer.
In Latin America it is found in Brazil, Bolivia, Chile, Cuba and
Mexico. South Africa is the world's leading producer of
platinum, accounting for about 77% of western supplies; other
significant producers are Russia and Canada. The main
producers of silver are Mexico, the United States, Peru,
Canada and Australia while the main consumers are the
United States, Japan and Europe. The world's main sources
of tin are all in the South – Brazil, Malaysia, Indonesia, China,
Thailand, Bolivia – while the main exporters are Brazil,

Malaysia, Indonesia, Thailand and China and the principal markets are the United States, Japan, the EC and Russia.

Petroleum is in a class of its own and 'oil power' during the 1970s gave the Third World a brief glimpse of how a more equitable economic realignment might be achieved in relation to the North (see Chapter 2). Countries such as the United States have large oil resources but an even greater rate of consumption, so that it has long been American policy to import a significant proportion of its total needs. Petroleum is easy to extract and market and is in world-wide demand so that it has provided a number of Third World countries with their main source of foreign exchange. The main world producers are the USSR (Russia and Ukraine), the United States, Saudi Arabia, China, Iran, Iraq and Mexico while the main exporters are Saudi Arabia, Russia, Iraq, Iran, the UAE, Nigeria and Norway. The main importers are the United States, Japan and Europe.

Tropical fruits and nuts and a range of commodity foods and beverages such as bananas or coffee found only in tropical or sub-tropical countries are the resources which at least in theory should give the greatest advantage to the South. Tropical fruits and nuts are important to many Asian, African and Latin American countries; their main importers are the United States, Japan and Europe.

Bananas are the product of tropical or sub-tropical climates and the main world producers are Brazil, the Philippines, Ecuador, Honduras and Indonesia while the main importers are the United States and the EC. However, the largest producers are not necessarily the countries most dependent upon exports; small countries such as the Caribbean islands may depend for as much as 70% of their foreign exchange earnings upon banana exports, even though their contribution to total world sales is very small.

Cocoa, which is one of the world's principal tropical food commodities, is produced on a major scale in seven countries; these are Brazil, Ecuador, Cameroon, Côte d'Ivoire, Ghana, Nigeria and Malaysia (all from the South). Of these seven countries five are major exporters – Côte d'Ivoire, Ghana, Nigeria, Brazil and Cameroon. Their main markets are the Netherlands, the United States, Germany, Russia and Britain.

Coconuts are one of the very few commodities whose production and trade is almost entirely confined to the South. The main producers are Malaysia, the Dominican Republic, Sri Lanka and Guatemala while the main importers are Singapore, Hong Kong and El Salvador, where the copra is extracted.

Coffee is produced only in countries of the South and is one of its most valuable commodities which is sought by all advanced economies. For certain small countries such as Burundi and Rwanda in Africa it accounts for as much as 75% of their exports although their output only represents a tiny proportion of world output. Such countries, in consequence, are extremely vulnerable to the impact of price fluctuations. The main producing and exporting countries are Brazil, Colombia, Indonesia, Mexico and Côte d'Ivoire; the main importers are the United States and the EC.

Cotton is both a tropical and sub-tropical plant whose main producers are China, the United States, Russia, India and Pakistan while the main exporters are the United States, Russia, Pakistan and Australia, although it is immensely important to a number of other countries such as Egypt and Sudan. Jute is the second fibre after cotton. The main producing countries are India, Bangladesh, China and Thailand and they are also the principal exporters of both fibre and raw jute. The developed world imports approximately twice the volume of jute and fibre as does the developing world.

Although the three top producers of groundnuts are India, the United States and China and the three leading exporters are China, the United States and India groundnuts are in fact far more important absolutely to a number of West African countries which have established the African Groundnut Council and this, often, is the pattern: thus the United States is one of the top exporters in volume and value of groundnuts although they are a minor factor in its overall trade while for a number of Third World countries they form a significant part of total exports.

In the North meat forms a principal component of the ordinary diet; in the South it is very often either a luxury or a sign of status. The main meat exporting countries are the Netherlands, the United States, France, Australia and Canada and the main importing countries are Japan, Germany, Italy and the United States. Both Latin America and southern Africa which produce meat for export are subject to drought. In the case of three southern African countries – Botswana, South Africa and Zimbabwe – the EC has adjudged their controls in relation to foot and mouth disease to come up to its standards, and so permits imports of their meat to Europe. Given the EC meat 'mountains' this is really the result of special pleading, a form of aid.

The main producers of rice (which is one of the world's great staples) are Thailand, the United States, Vietnam, Pakistan and Italy while the principal importers are Iran, China, the UAE, France and Iraq. Rubber, which has to compete with synthetics, is produced only in the South – Malaysia, Indonesia, Thailand and India – while the main importers are the United States, Japan, China and India. The main producers of silk are China, Bangladesh, Russia and the United States while the main importers are Japan, Italy, Hong Kong and South Korea.

Pepper and spices come from the South. The main exporting countries for pepper are Indonesia, Singapore, Malaysia, Brazil and India and the principal importing countries are the United States, Singapore, Germany and France. The main spice producers are Indonesia, Sri Lanka, Zanzibar, Madagascar and Grenada while Madagascar, Comoros and Indonesia are the main producers of vanilla. The principal importers are the United States, Germany, Japan and Saudi Arabia while Singapore and Hong Kong are significant re-exporters.

Cane sugar is tropical in origin, beet sugar comes from temperate lands and the main producers from both sources are India, Russia, Cuba, Brazil, the United States, China and

Thailand while the principal exporters are Cuba, Czecho-Slovakia, Australia, Thailand, Brazil and South Africa, although it is also very important as an export to small countries like Swaziland. The main importers are Russia, Japan, the United States, China, South Korea and Canada.

The main producers and exporters of tea are India, China, Sri Lanka and Kenya while the principal importers are Britain, Pakistan, the United States, Egypt and Iraq. In the case of tobacco the main exporters are the United States, Brazil, Italy, Turkey and Zimbabwe and the principal importers are the United States, Germany, Britain, Japan and the Netherlands.

On the whole the pattern is the same: the principal markets for all these commodities lie in the North and though the South enjoys a monopoly in the production of a number of products – principally tropical fruits – these do not provide it with the leverage to alter what is essentially a fixed trading pattern, with the South producing the raw materials and the North providing and controlling the markets. In many cases, particularly in relation to minerals, although the South may possess abundant resources it does not enjoy a monopoly and certain countries of the North – most notably the United States, Canada and Australia – also have abundant resources of the same minerals.

A few other commodities are worth brief consideration. Textiles have become one of the principal exports of the South for they are one of the easiest, most cost effective and labour intensive of all commodities to produce. Fisheries are in a special category, for many countries in the South have rich offshore fisheries but lack the means to farm them properly. As a result they have leased out their fishing rights to the fishing fleets of the North. Countries like Namibia and Mozambique in southern Africa, which possess exceptionally rich offshore fisheries, have licensed the fishing fleets and factory ships of the North to take much of the catch and have benefited only marginally from the catches when these are considered according to their full market value. Non-tropical fruit and vegetables are mainly produced in the North where they are

also marketed, although there are certain important exceptions. Mexico, for example, is a huge producer while a number
of arid countries in the Gulf have now become significant
producers as a result of irrigation. The main exporters of olive
oil are Greece, Italy, Spain, Tunisia and the UAE.

The huge international trade in wheat is dominated by the
United States, France, Canada and Australia while several
countries of the South – China, Algeria and Iran – are major
wheat importers. Wine is mainly produced, exported and
consumed in the North though certain countries of the South
have real potential for capturing a significant share of the world
wine market and in the case of South Africa have already done
so. The trade in wood and paper, wool and timber (apart from
tropical hardwoods) is dominated by the North.[6]

Tourism, which cannot be classified as a commodity, is
nonetheless of great importance to both North and South. It is
basically an activity of the North though countries such as
Morocco or Thailand earn substantial incomes by acting as
hosts to tourists. Finally, there is the trade in narcotics which
falls into a very special category of its own. It is now the second
largest trade in the world after the arms business with an
estimated annual value of $500,000mn (covering cocaine,
heroin and marijuana). The main opium producers are
Afghanistan, Iran, Pakistan, Myanma, Laos, Thailand, Mexico, Lebanon and Guatemala while the main coca producers
are Peru, Bolivia, Colombia and Ecuador. The huge trade in
narcotics in the United States and Europe in particular might
almost be seen as the South's revenge for other injustices. In
this trade, at any rate, the market forces so beloved of the West
appear to be winning the battle against the anti-narcotics
police of the North.

An overall analysis of the world trade in commodities reveals
that a high proportion of both trade and production is confined
to the North; that in most cases the South or developing
countries cannot afford to bargain but must sell their commodities for what they can get since these are often their only means
of earning hard currency; and that the mechanisms which

control the markets are all located in the North. In a number of cases, as the copper cartel, CIPEC, discovered, there are substitutes for products if the producers try to force the price up too high while the alternative to this is stockpiling, which the North can afford to do as the cocoa producers discovered when they attempted to withold supplies. In most cases the balance of advantage lies overwhelmingly with the North. The South has people, oil, a surplus in certain minerals, exclusive control of tropical fruits and vegetables and tropical forests. The South also possesses a range of minerals which, however, are not exclusive to it but parallel and supplement similar minerals in the North while a handful of Middle East countries possess the world's greatest reserves of petroleum.

One commodity of great significance that the South has in abundance consists of its populations and this, arguably, is the most significant long-term factor of all because it engenders fear in the North. The huge and growing numbers of the South offer large potential markets for the future and, as an alternative, threaten mass migrations northwards as the current concern of the North with numbers and the promotion of family planning in the South so obviously demonstrates. Instinctively, the South is right to resent the North's concern with its population growth for the North's concern is not for the South but for its own peace of mind.

What comes across from this analysis is the fact that, with certain exceptions, the North could get by tolerably well without the South and that much North–South trade is a convenience as much as it is a necessity. In 1989 all the developing countries accounted for only 19.3% of world trade while the least developed countries accounted for only 0.4% of that figure. The industrial countries of the North accounted for the remaining 80.7%.

9 The Turn to the East

The many turmoils resulting from the end of the Cold War will continue throughout the 1990s and to try to predict the eventual outcome would be pointless. But three obvious general developments are already making themselves apparent. The first of these has been the turn eastwards by the West whose interest is to salvage as much as possible from the break-up of the Soviet empire and to support the countries of Eastern Europe in their search for a new market-oriented economic model. This interest will extend – though how much is far from clear – to providing assistance to the successor states of the USSR including Russia itself. The second development, which in any case depends upon the first, is a loss of interest in what used to be seen as the Third World, and a growing indifference to its problems unless these impinge directly upon western interests. The third development, whose consequences may well be devastating, is the collapse of certainty. This collapse of the certainties which the Cold War provided can be seen in the sudden heightening of inter-European rivalries centring round the Maastricht Treaty, with the EC becoming increasingly uncertain of its future even as it advances ever greater claims about its long-term potential; in the disintegration of Yugoslavia, with the attendant indecisiveness as to just what should be done about it; and in the growing readiness to wait for the United States as the only power now seen to be capable of effective interventions.

The challenge to the Soviet system posed by Gorbachev in order to revitalise it soon turned into open questioning of everything it stood for, and developments in the USSR led most of Eastern Europe to abandon communism during the latter part of 1989. That year, indeed, was a world turning point and in retrospect it appears that the West did not know what to do or how to grasp the opportunities it offered. There were many factors making for change in Eastern Europe: an ageing leadership under challenge from a new generation of younger, more progressive politicians; intellectual challenges to an increasingly sterile communist monopoly of power; popular mass demands for change which had already – and significantly – brought about changes in both Poland and Hungary; and the general realisation (in a time of world recession) that the planned economies were not succeeding. On top of these factors came the admission by the Soviet leadership that communism in Eastern Europe was no longer viable, with the corollary that the former satellites would be allowed to go their own ways. And from the top Gorbachev encouraged the various reform movements in Eastern Europe. Moscow, in fact, was gambling that post-reform regimes would be more stable than increasingly unsupported communist ones. As a result of these pressures the autumn of 1989 witnessed mass demonstrations and demands for change throughout Eastern Europe leading to the collapse of the communist governments of Czecho-Slovakia, East Germany, Romania and Bulgaria either totally or to the extent that they were forced to carry out far-reaching reforms. Thus in Romania, after a fight against the powerful secret police, the Ceauçescus were executed; in Czecho-Slovakia the dissident Vaclav Havel became president; although in East Germany and Bulgaria – if only for the time being – the communists just held onto power.

The most significant developments took place in East Germany (the German Democratic Republic or GDR) following its 40th anniversary celebrations. These were attended by Gorbachev who on 7 October warned Honecker to reform; subsequently there was a rapid collapse of the government and huge anti-government demonstrations occurred all over the country so that by 18 October Honecker was forced to resign to be replaced by Egon Krenz, though the change did not stop the demonstrations nor the exodus to the West. On 7 November the entire government resigned and on 9 November the border with the West was opened. The opening of the German border and the subsequent destruction of the Berlin Wall marked –

symbolically – the end of the Cold War and the collapse of the communist system in Eastern Europe. At the same time the rapid eruption of nationalist–separatist movements which had been repressed for decades in central Asia, the Caucasus and the Baltic threatened to destroy the cohesion of the USSR itself. In China, on the other hand, the pro-democracy movement was ruthlessly crushed by the intervention of the army in Tiananmen Square on 4 June when more than 1,000 students were killed, altering China's international standing and image in the process. But although China made plain it was not prepared to make concessions to the anti-communists as in the Soviet empire, the hostile world reaction to China's use of force against the students had the effect of inhibiting leaders in Eastern Europe from using similar force when they faced challenges to their own rule later in the year.

By the end of 1989 and as 1990 opened it seemed as if the prospects for world peace were the best since 1945; for a brief period a widespread sense of euphoria blinded people to the true significance of events or the likely developments that would follow. But the euphoria was not to last long. 1990 witnessed growing tensions in the USSR and Eastern Europe, the Iraqi invasion of Kuwait, the reunification of Germany in October and growing civil disturbances and civil strife in the southern tier of Soviet republics where demands for autonomy set the pace and indicated something of the shape which the new world order was likely to assume. Nonetheless, in Eastern Europe the first half of 1990 was a time of hope, a celebration of the end of communism; the second half of the year saw greater realism, the coming to terms with new and often unpalatable political and economic facts. The old system may have been grim, but at least it guaranteed everyone a job; one of the first effects of the new freedom and the acceptance of market forces appeared to be the possibility and likelihood of widespread unemployment. The realisation that adjustments to the new freedoms would be both economically hazardous and politically dangerous soon took the gilt off the euphoria. However, on 3 October 1990 the GDR formally ceased to exist and a single Germany re-emerged after 45 years of division; whatever the subsequent problems, a formidable new power had been created. During the year the problem of nationalities in the USSR became increasingly threatening. Lenin had argued that nationalism would disappear under communism; he had been profoundly wrong. The repression of nationalisms for 70 years merely ensured that the subsequent release from control was all the more dangerous. Gorbachev reached the height of his international popularity abroad during the year – he was awarded the Nobel Peace Prize for his contribution to ending the Cold War – but at home his standing steadily declined for he was not solving the problems that his policies of *glasnost* and *perestroika* had unleashed.

1991 saw the formal end of the Cold War and the dissolution of the USSR, with the various soviet republics declaring their independence. The attempted hardline coup against Gorbachev in August signalled the beginning of the counter-revolutionary process that will be a major factor throughout the former USSR for the balance of the century. Gorbachev survived the abortive coup, though his position was much weakened; then, on 25 December 1991, he resigned, conceding that the USSR no longer existed. The collapse of the USSR – one of the world's two superpowers – meant the end of the structures that had dominated world politics since 1945; now Russia and the Commonwealth of Independent States (CIS) were obliged to turn, humiliatingly, to the West for economic assistance. Indeed, the sudden replacement of the USSR by 15 independent states, the majority of them poor, landlocked, seeking aid and beset by violent upheavals, transformed the world political landscape.

Three of the newly 'released' independent states were in a category of their own: the Baltic states of Estonia, Latvia and Lithuania had been incorporated into the USSR during World War II and had never seen themselves as a permanent part of the USSR despite their substantial Russian minorities. With a combined population of just under 8mn they are small enough to be absorbed into the general European system without too much difficulty although both Estonia and Latvia have Russian minorities of 30% or more to absorb or otherwise come to terms with, and given past history that will not be easy. Russia, with a population of 150mn, remains a great world power though what happens there through the 1990s will have enormous repercussions in the other ex-Soviet states and in Eastern Europe. Ukraine with a population of 51.7mn and major resources is potentially on a par with countries like France in Europe. The remaining 10 successor states to the USSR present far greater problems: they are generally poor and under-developed, almost all landlocked, beset by ethnic divisions, small in population and geographically sandwiched between Russia and Ukraine to the north and the major Islamic countries of the southern Asian rim – Turkey, Afghanistan, Iran and Pakistan – to the south, with India and China at their eastern extremity. Thus 10 weak 'Third World'-type countries have suddenly emerged in the centre of a highly volatile region where, inevitably, they will be subject to immense geopolitical pressures from several different centres. Azerbaijan has a population of 7 million, Kazakstan 17mn, Kyrgyzstan 4.3mn, Tajikistan 5.36mn, Turkmenistan 3.6mn, Uzbekistan 19.91mn. These six are predominantly Moslem with strong historic ties southwards ethnically to Turkey and in religious terms to the Islamic world. The other four successor states – Armenia with 3.3 million population, Georgia with 5.45mn, Belarus with 10.26mn and Moldova with 4.34mn – will look in different directions; Belarus and Moldova may turn first to Europe while Armenia and Georgia must settle for uneasy independence sandwiched between far more powerful neighbours.

The six Moslem republics face a difficult future; in 1979 out of a combined population of 46.2mn 9.8mn were Russians. Now some of these are leaving while those who remain face many uncertainties, for their status has changed from that of being representatives of the imperial power to that of ethnic minorities often viewed with suspicion if nothing worse. There is resentment for what some Central Asians see as 130 years of exploitation, there are threats to personal security, the rise of Islam and decrees to make local (non-Russian) languages official. But if there are ethnic problems in these successor states there are far greater economic problems throughout the CIS (including Russia itself) and the combination of ethnic divisions and economic collapse could make the entire region dangerously volatile for years to come. It is that possibility which has engaged the attention and fears of the West, for disintegration and collapse in the former USSR will destabilise the entire world. In the circumstances it is unsurprising that the South faces increasing marginalisation in terms of the priorities that govern western decisions.

Early in 1992 the Group of Seven (G-7) agreed that the CIS should hold a 4.2% stake in the IMF which (in principle) would allow them to borrow between $15bn and $16bn; at the same time the G-7 pressed the IMF to work out full IMF membership for Russia and some of the other new republics.[1] The involvement of the IMF marked a major step towards integrating members of the CIS into the western-dominated economic system. Full membership of the IMF entitles a country to apply for loans, but the size of the loans will depend upon the kind of economic reforms which are initiated and the mere fact of applying will, at least to some extent, relegate such states to the ranks of the Third World or South: that is, into the position of those who seek western economic aid but must first obtain an IMF 'seal of approval' by inaugurating economic reforms that will move their economies closer to the western market system which was always anathema to the communist world.

Western doubts about the size of any aid package to Russia were in part a reaction to confusion in Russia and uncertainty as to just how far any economic reform programme would be pushed and in part, during a recession, about who would actually produce the money. The fact that Mikhail Gorbachev had been invited to the 1991 London economic summit of the G-7 only to return home empty-handed and face a coup attempt reinforced the need for caution in 1992. In the end a

$24bn financial assistance package for Russia was announced. Later in the year the President of the World Bank, Lewis Preston, talked of possible World Bank lending to the CIS of $5bn a year, provided the IMF approved Moscow's programme of free market economic reforms.[2] Thus, within two years of the end of the Cold War, the exigencies of Russia's economic crisis on the one hand and the western response on the other seemed set between them to force the CIS countries into IMF-controlled debt crises similar to those which are now all too familiar throughout the South.

When in March 1992 Britain's Foreign Secretary, Douglas Hurd, told EC foreign ministers in Brussels that the community should not launch its own aid programme for Russia and the other republics but see aid handled through the IMF he was implicitly arguing that still greater power should be given to the West's single most important instrument of economic control. Apart from whether the IMF is intellectually equipped to oversee so profound a change from the communist system to a western system – its rigid application of financial orthodoxies in Third World countries makes this seem unlikely – the broader question arises as to whether more power should be given to either the IMF or the World Bank. There is much hostility world-wide to the IMF, especially in Latin America and Africa but also, for example, in Poland where it is criticised for trying to force through too rapid an economic transformation with consequent harsh burdens imposed on the Polish people. In pursuit of its economic orthodoxies the IMF has rarely demonstrated much sensitivity about the social and political problems of the developing countries in which it operates and it seems unlikely that it will prove any more sensitive in Russia or other CIS republics. Indeed, it is far more likely that by insisting upon too many market reforms too quickly the IMF will serve western economic interests badly rather than well and come up against hardline Russian opposition while also upsetting Russian pride, so that in the end Russia will fail – perhaps deliberately – to qualify for the IMF's 'seal of approval', opting instead for its own much slower path to economic reform or transformation. However, the IMF enjoys a major advantage in that it is the only body whose judgement is trusted by the world banking system (which means the western banking system) and international investors.

The western banking system took a battering during the 1980s from its over-extension in the South – much of this being its own fault – with the result that in 1992 it was extremely cautious about new commitments in Russia or other CIS republics. Whatever the faults of the IMF – as seen from the South or indeed from the new republics of CIS – it is the key to any major flow of funds from the private sector in the West whose resources are vastly greater than those of the international agencies. By the end of 1992 such caution seemed justified as counter-revolutionary forces grew steadily stronger in Russia while civil–ethnic tensions threatened to overshadow economic questions in at least some of the other republics. Poland may well provide a test case for the effectiveness or otherwise of IMF-imposed reforms. By April of 1992 the IMF was warning the Polish government that its economic reforms were in danger of going off the rails, a warning that Warsaw was obliged to heed since its international credibility and, therefore, its chances of obtaining further reductions in its foreign debts and attracting more investment depend upon continuing IMF support. It was an all-too-familiar scenario, and in Poland's case was made more difficult precisely because the country had returned to western-style democracy and the electorate was becoming increasingly dissatisfied with the harshness of the economic reforms that for them did not appear to bring any compensating benefits. The Polish Prime Minister, Jan Olszewski, urged the IMF to be more flexible towards Poland and argued sensibly that normal IMF criteria do not fit post-communist countries where the market economy has been destroyed and has to be rebuilt from scratch.[3] It seems unlikely that, with or without IMF support, Poland will be able to effect a total transformation from a state-directed communist economic system to a western-style free enterprise one, for the pain could well prove too great for a people at last free to express their disagreement with the government. If Poland is unable to make the transition effecively or quickly its failure will have a profound influence upon the approach to change in the rest of Eastern Europe and the CIS.

By the end of April 1992 the World Bank and the IMF had agreed full membership for Russia; Boris Yeltsin promptly declared that he would never allow western financiers to dictate to Russia and though his comments were mainly directed at his own conservatives rather than the outside world this was only partly the case. Asked by reporters whether Russia risked the kind of social upheavals that some Third World countries have experienced after complying with IMF prescriptions he said: 'We do not intend to work to the direct dictation of the IMF. We do not share the views of this organisation on everything and we will stick to our point of view.'[4] As a result of its full membership of the two financial bodies Russia became eligible for up to $24bn in aid but as Mr Yeltsin also said: 'We do not want to throw ourselves head first into the abyss and grab all the $24bn at once.' At least he was aware of the abyss. As Yeltsin was to discover during the remainder of the year Russia is deeply divided about the extent and speed of economic change, and though the younger generation generally favours integration into the world economic system the older generation and the conservatives are profoundly sceptical and fearful of major economic changes and would resent too much outside (western) interference as a humiliation. In January 1992 the radical First Deputy Prime Minister, Yegor Gaidar, began freeing prices that had long been subsidised but without any parallel increase in salaries. By mid-December Yeltsin had apparently lost his confrontation with the Congress of People's Deputies which had convened on 1 December and was obliged to ditch Gaidar, who had been in charge of economic reforms, and replace him with a former communist apparatchik, the conservative Viktor Chernomyrdin. By then it was clear that Russia was not going to be stampeded by the West into adopting free market reforms.

When the Russian minister for foreign economic relations, Piotr Aven, visited Washington in September 1992 for the annual meeting of the IMF he revealed that Russia was owed $142bn in foreign debts by Third World countries. It is unlikely that Russia will get much of this back, it was a poignant reference to a superpower past. Mr Aven claimed that Cuba owed $28bn but had turned down requests for discussions; Iraq owed $10bn, presumably for arms, and also seemed unlikely to repay it. On the other hand India also owed Russia $10bn and was regarded as more likely to repay it. Thus, almost overnight, Russia had changed from a superpower source of aid to client states round the world to a supplicant for aid itself, for Mr Aven was trying to reschedule some $70bn of debts owed by the former USSR.[5] At least Russia was moving to take over responsibility for all the CIS debts. It was only able to repay $2.5bn in 1992, which was far below western demands. Germany, which had shown itself the most responsive to Russia's requests for aid and is owed about half the total of Soviet debt, was nonetheless unwilling to allow repayment delays of more than two years, urging more financial assistance from the West instead of debt relief. But whether Russia obtains debt relief or more aid, by the end of 1992 she was already firmly enmeshed in the aid–debt webs of the West and the IMF. In 1992 Russia was scheduled to receive $18bn in grants, food aid and loans from the IMF and World Bank with the possibility of similar amounts for 1993 though these were thrown in doubt by Boris Yeltsin's surrender to the hardliners at the Congress of People's deputies in December 1992. Later he was to recover the initiative.

When in November 1992 Boris Yeltsin visited Hungary the relationship between Eastern Europe and his country had been transformed. Yeltsin apologised to the Hungarian parliament: 'The 1956 national uprising was not in vain. It showed that not only individuals, but an entire people understood that they have no future without ridding themselves of Communist dictators.'[6] Yeltsin was seeking a new relationship with Eastern Europe while the East Europeans try to decide just how the new Russia is going to behave, for Russia is more important to them than even the newly unified Germany. By the time of his visit the last Russian combat troops had left Poland (they had already left Hungary and Czecho-Slovakia in June 1991) although the promised withdrawal from the three Baltic states had just been suspended on the grounds that there was nowhere for the troops to go, itself a humiliating admission for Russia to have to make. The Hungarian President, Arpad Goencz, told Yeltsin: 'We believe the integration of Russia into Europe is vitally important. We cannot imagine the European security system without the participation of Moscow.' This, almost nostalgic, admission from Hungary's president was a reflection of the dilemma into which the countries of Eastern Europe have been thrust.[7] After years in which they have seen the USSR as an unwelcome imperial overlord and have yearned for the democratic freedoms of the West they were beginning to discover the hazards that western freedoms represented and, not least, were finding how reluctant the EC was to open its doors to their membership. And this reluctance may well come to be seen as symbolic of the West's lack of certainty: it was so much easier during the Cold War to represent the European Community as a bastion of freedom than to expand it after the Cold War by embracing the countries of Eastern Europe with all the political and economic costs that their inclusion in the Community would entail. Already by the end of 1992 Eastern Europe was coming to understand this reluctance and to wonder just where it was left as a result; the leaders of Czecho-Slovakia, Hungary and Poland had returned home empty-handed from their meeting with EC leaders in London the previous October and by then western economists were suggesting that it might take as long as 20 years before they would be able to join the EC. Thus, by the end of 1992 with a renascent unified Germany and an increasingly reluctant EC to the west, a disintegrating Yugoslavia to the south and the old Russia possibly reverting to hardline big power politics to the east the newly 'freed' countries of Eastern Europe were feeling far from secure.

Although the likelihood that Yugoslavia would break up had long been apparent the actual process of disintegration got underway in mid-1991 when in June Croatia and Slovenia declared their independence, to be followed by hostilities between Croatia and Serbia. By August 1992 when brutal hostilities for over a year had reduced Yugoslavia to a state of misery and destruction the *Washington Post* posed the awkward question of 'how to enforce international law and human rights without occupying the country with infantry on the ground, as no government is prepared to do'. There was, of course, no answer and the fact that there was no answer was in itself an indictment of western policies over the preceding two years. By September Britain's Foreign Secretary, Douglas Hurd, was cautioning that any military intervention to stop the civil war in Bosnia would bring a halt to humanitarian aid, as though such aid to the victims of civil war was more important than bringing an end to the creation of victims in the first place. By December Britain's Defence secretary, Malcolm Rifkind, was pontificating that it would need 100,000 troops to stop the civil war and that it could go on for years. That it would be 'inappropriate' for the United Nations to impose peace in Bosnia was then the British line, though what was appropriate the minister failed to say.[8] The real fear in the West was any commitment of troops on the ground who would have to fight, because the West is deeply fearful of the impact upon its electorates of high casualty figures; ultimately, however, such an attitude is an abnegation of responsibility. The West, it appeared, wanted to be the arbiter of the new world order but not at too high a cost. Learning slowly, but learning, the United Nations decided in December that it should deploy a battalion-strength force of military observers in Macedonia in the hope of heading off conflict before the gathering dispute over its international recognition led to a new war front. Here at least was an initiative that introduced a new principle of deploying a preventive force before hostilities break out. But even as the United Nations embarked on this new policy Greece warned its EC partners that it would oppose any EC move to recognise Macedonia. Meanwhile NATO, the EC and the United Nations became embroiled in discussions as to whether or how to impose an air embargo over Bosnia, air strikes against Serbia or the deployment on the ground of peace-keepers. Then the United States raised the possibility of using force to protect the delivery of humanitarian aid and preventing further atrocities against civilians. The underlying problem which all these discussions carefully skirted was the simple fact that nothing short of full-scale military intervention would actually prevent what was happening in Yugoslavia.

By early November 1992 there were 850,000 displaced persons in Bosnia and Herzegovina; these ethnically cleansed Bosnians were mainly within a short distance from their homes. By this time the Croatian government in Zagreb was refusing to allow any more refugees to cross its frontiers; it had already received 800,000. What had become clear was the fact that western or UN expressions of concern had not stopped the Serbian onslaught and without effective action on the ground the situation would deteriorate further.

The Balkan tragedy represented a monumental failure of policy by the EC which, while wishing to demonstrate that it can act effectively with a single foreign policy, had succeeded only in demonstrating that it was as divided over the issue of Yugoslavia as the people of that unhappy country were themselves. Even after the break-up of Yugoslavia had clearly become inevitable the West continued to insist that its republics should remain united on the general though untenable grounds that disintegration in Yugoslavia would encourage disintegration elsewhere (it was most concerned with what might happen in the USSR). The West behaved as though nationalism – and nationalism of the most virulent kind as it appeared in Yugoslavia – could somehow be ignored. It was neater and easier to have a united Yugoslavia and so the West acted as though that must continue to be the case despite the evidence. This western approach in the early days of the crisis encouraged Serbia, the most powerful of the republics, to use force to hold the country together. But Croatia and Slovenia were not prepared to accept this solution and fought for their independence and Germany then broke ranks with its EC partners and forced the pace of disintegration by recognising Croatia. Thus the two northern republics demonstrated the value of fighting and the lesson was not lost on the rest of the contenders for individual statehood; the result was a general descent into bloodshed with the weakest – Bosnia and Herzegovina – most at risk.

In the event, the European Community showed itself quite unable to come up with a single, consistent policy towards Yugoslavia but lurched from one expedient to another, its performance being an unhappy augury for those who believe in the possibility of a united Europe with a single foreign policy. It would not use NATO because that, inevitably, was bound to mean American domination of whatever plan was adopted. The Council of Europe was bypassed and the Conference on Security and Cooperation in Europe (CSCE) was also persuaded to stand aside for the Brussels policy makers. And while various solutions were examined and then discarded the Serbians ignored international appeals and continued their ethnic cleansing operations: from being the champions of a single state which the West began by wanting, the Serbs became the villains of the civil war because they sought what all the other groups sought – a state for Serbs alone. By Christmas 1992, as the United Nations debated the use of force against the Serbs, Bosnia had been mutilated and at best might be able to survive in truncated form. The Europeans of the Community, meanwhile, had bickered for two years about what might or might not be done while the Serbs fought ruthlessly to gain as much as they could. The lessons, stark and depressing, were there for all to see: if the EC could be so incompetent, so divided and so uncertain about how to handle a problem on its doorstep the chances of it giving any better lead elsewhere in the world appeared drastically reduced. When the civil war in Yugoslavia is finally concluded, more or less to the satisfaction of the stronger ethnic groups, then the question will arise: where will these successor states to Yugoslavia belong? Inside Europe? Or as fringe countries of the old Third World, for by then they will have been so devastated that it will require many years for their economies to be properly revived. In any case they form one of the poorest, least developed corners of Europe.

The reluctance of the West (through the UN) to discipline Saddam Hussein of Iraq as he suppressed the Shias in the south of his country was bound to invite comparison with the approach to Bosnia. By mid-August 1992 it had been agreed to commit a battalion of British troops to guard relief convoys in Bosnia as well as possible air cover; at the same time, as President Bush of the United States faced the Republican Convention, he suddenly became more concerned with the plight of the Shias. Talk of air exclusion zones thus came to cover both Bosnia and southern Iraq, yet both problems highlighted western uncertainties about the role the West should play in either conflict. As the British *Independent* asked: 'If the Shia Muslims and Marsh Arabs of southern Iraq deserve protection, what about the Slav Muslims of Bosnia?'[9]

By the end of 1992 the EC was moving slowly yet logically towards military intervention in Bosnia, Germany (whose unification had raised many quesions about its roles inside the EC and also in Eastern Europe) had admitted officially that it was in recession, while Czecho-Slovakia was in the process of dividing (as everyone hoped peacefully) into the two successor states of Czechland and Slovakia to complicate still further the ethnic jigsaw of Eastern Europe. These developments in Eastern Europe and the CIS had occurred so swiftly in the three years 1989–92 that their long-term impact upon the Third World or South had still to be properly assessed. Yet as early as the last quarter of 1989 the West had adopted a French proposal to create a new international development bank, the European Bank for Reconstruction and Development (EBRD), with overtly political objectives of fostering multi-party democracy and market economies in the former communist countries. By May 1990, in an astonishingly short period for such an international body of only five months, the articles of agreement had been initialled by the member states. Here at least was a clear demonstration of Europe's determination to provide finances for the successor states to communism. The decision to give the EBRD a mandate to foster open market economies reflected the determination of the West to sustain the break with communism.[10] The first question the Bank will have to face is the extent to which it will provide aid to those countries that have only partially broken with their communist pasts. A 40% upper limit on lending to the public sector was written into the Bank's mandate so as to safeguard the management against what might otherwise prove to be endless ongoing requests for support for public sector infrastructure projects. The second question concerned the old or former Third World: how much aid will the Bank divert from the South to the new needy of Eastern Europe, and was this just one more sign of the declining interest in the North for the problems of the South? What, ironically, may work in favour of the South could be the tenacious nature of the old systems of Eastern Europe; embracing the market economy in theory is very different from making it work in practice and by late 1992, in both Russia and other East European countries, moves to block swift transitions to a purely market system were becoming increasingly evident. Clearly the speed with which Eastern Europe does transform its economies will be crucial to the flow of funds either eastwards or southwards. The end of the Cold War and collapse of the communist economic systems altered the entire environment for aid; what the South feared, and was right to fear, was a change in the political attitudes of the principal aid donors. Not only will the West provide less aid but aid from Eastern Europe is also likely to diminish, if it does not disappear entirely. Only if there is general economic expansion of the joint West–Eastern European economy as a result of the events of 1989–92 could the South truly benefit from what has happened, but that possibility lies a long way in the future. Immediately, therefore, the South must view the changes in the communist world with concern for their most likely effect is to turn the West eastwards at the South's expense – and that plainly has already occurred.

Perhaps even more threatening for the future of the South is the way in which the West assumed, incorrectly, that the end of the Cold War affected only the East and that western structures would remain in place as strong as ever while the new East adjusted to them. In fact the structures which the West had come to take for granted – such as the EC and NATO – were themselves the creation of the Cold War and with its passing much of their *raison d'être* has passed as well. A reunited Germany which was unthinkable as late as 1988 can now dominate the EC which was formed, in major part, to contain it. The rivalries of the great western powers that 45 years of the Cold War subordinated to the common purpose of uniting against the Soviet threat are once more surfacing. The ordered control of Eastern Europe in the Warsaw Pact has given way to a chaotic power vacuum and the democracy which the West extolled so readily during the fixed confrontation of the Cold War seems unlikely readily or quickly to provide many answers to the economic and ethnic challenges that now beset Eastern Europe, where by late 1992 the rise of a new form of fascism seemed more probable than anything else. The deep problems that beset the EC during 1992 were less about the implementation – or not – of the Maastricht Treaty than about Europe's long-term view of its own future: will it embrace the countries of Eastern Europe, and if so, how soon? Will they want to be embraced? And if the EC expands as far as Ukraine and Turkey would it any longer represent, even remotely, the EC of the Twelve? The end of the Cold War put everything, all the accepted structures, back into the melting pot of what President Bush was pleased to describe as a 'New World Order'. Once the Cold War parameters had been removed bickering and distrust among the powers escalated, since there is no longer the compelling need for unity against a perceived enemy, while the creation of a number of new fringe countries in Eastern Europe and the southern tier of the former USSR has enlarged the number of countries qualifying to belong to the South even as the justification for non-alignment on the one hand or the need to secure allies (or at least clients) on the other has disappeared.

10 Western Racism

As the problems developed, following the end of the Cold War and the evaporation of the initial euphoria, so the signs multiplied that western energies were more likely to be used to keep the rest of the world at bay than for any other purpose. The high standard of living which the West alone enjoyed needed to be safeguarded and, ironically, it appeared more at risk from the flood of new world developments which an end of superpower confrontation had set free than ever it had during the Cold War. The possibility of using the huge energies released from Cold War confrontations to tackle problems of poverty in the South did not appear to have any serious place on the agenda of the New World Order which President Bush had so grandly announced. Instead, a number of new orthodoxies surfaced while old forces, and most notably racism, became strident. It became orthodox to say publicly that the West was threatened with an influx of immigrants which could swamp its way of life. It became orthodox to speak once more of the poor 'always being with us' as a prelude to arguing that little could be done to alter that state of being. And it became orthodox to advance arguments about 'good governance' as a reason for cutting back on aid to countries whose governance, good or bad, had not been a bar to western assistance during the Cold War with its very different priorities. The doyen of American economists and elder statesman Kenneth Galbraith pinpointed two underlying necessities of the western world (although he was concerned primarily with the United States): the contentment of the 'haves' which precluded action to change conditions among the less fortunate; and the need (in a contented society) for an underclass.[1]

Like poverty, racism has always been with us; what changes is the manner in which a society works to control it or the extent to which it is allowed a free rein. By late 1992 the signs

were not good, and the latent racism in all western societies was
strengthened by the mere fact of governments tightening or
looking at ways of tightening immigration controls so as to
prevent influxes, imagined or real, from the South. The politics
of contentment which dominate political decisions in the
United States and Europe were nonetheless threatened: in
the United States by an underclass that saw no point in voting;
in the newly united Germany by the quarter of the population
from the old DDR who discovered that unemployment and
insecurity were part of the new dream while the racism and
nationalism which communism had suppressed could surface
once more, sometimes in virulent form; and in the EC as a
whole by the collapse into civil war of the former Yugoslavia
which presented the West with choices about intervention that
it was desperate not to take. At the same time western smugness
was reflected in the new morality which had so suddenly and so
conveniently been discovered in the wake of the Cold War's
end. This new morality, which has its roots in nineteenth
century imperial proselytising, not only bodes ill for the Third
World – that was to be expected – but will also cost the West
dear for it has no firm basis in any principles of enlightened self-
interest, despite appearances to the contrary but, rather, is a
feeble weapon that will be waived whenever it conflicts with
real western interests.

The rise of virulent forms of right-wing racism – neo-Nazis
in the United States, the skinhead sub-culture in Britain, the
National Front of Jean-Marie Le Pen in France and the neo-
Nazi violence against incomers in east Germany – became
sufficiently important in the early 1990s to be the subject of
wide debate, giving rise to two broad arguments: that these
manifestations were insignificant in real political terms and
not to be compared with the rise of fascism in the 1920s; or,
despite the small minorities involved, that they were potentially dangerous and had to be nipped in the bud and not
ignored. As Irwin Suall, the fact-finding director of the Anti-
Defamation League of the B'nai B'rith in New York suggested:
'Today's racists like to see themselves as a true international

movement, just like the Nazis did in the Thirties before the war.'[2] Neo-Nazis are now reported to look to British skinheads for inspiration with the Union Flag a popular symbol used by various nationalities of racists, while US neo-Nazis and Ku Klux Klan members have been making recruiting trips to Germany since 1991. Such extremist groups have long had international links though for many years these have had little importance or impact. What became worrying in the early 1990s was the extent to which they came into the open. The depressed economic conditions and unstable political climate in eastern Europe encouraged such groups to seek greater publicity and offer each other solidarity. A growing generation of young jobless in Europe are prepared to turn to right-wing politics as an outlet for their frustrations and, as Dr David Cesarani of the Wiener Library in London has noted: 'Right-wing violence has got out of control because of the failure of political leadership . . . In Britain, France and Germany, central politicians are so afraid of losing votes that they are afraid to confront the right.'[3] A great deal of attention has been devoted, rightly, to the rise of right-wing violence in Germany where fire-bombings, beatings and killings have been carried out by young people, frustrated or otherwise. But making Germany the scapegoat for a general rise of European racism is too easy and does not address the problem which is widespread and by no means confined to that country. Such extremist groups are not going to achieve political power; but their activities certainly assist the mainstream right-wing politicians such as Le Pen in France, Jörg Haider in Austria or Franz Schönhuber in Germany when they demand clampdowns on immigration or tightening of the asylum laws. Right-wing racist thuggery on the streets may still be only a small part of the political problems which the West generally has to face, but it is a highly visible manifestation of discontent, and the disturbing element about it is the degree to which its perpetrators now feel free to come into the open as though, quite suddenly, they are a step closer to political respectability.

The fundamental political problem concerns who does and who does not belong in Europe; that is what the rise in racism is about. In western Europe overt racism has become most apparent in Germany and France although countries with more tolerant traditions have also seen its increase. And though economic distress is often the natural ally of racism this is not always the case. Thus, in Baden-Württemberg which is one of the most prosperous areas in Europe the Republican Party of Franz Schönhuber has won 11% of the vote. As a German academic, Erwin Faul, has argued about minority groups: 'If the right to participate in politics is granted, ethnic groups (just as in the United States) will attempt to gain decisive influence on immigration policy and open the floodgates, thus withdrawing sovereignty from the traditional leading national group.'[4] Such an argument attracts as many followers in Britain, for example, as it does in Germany and is likely to prove decisive in considerations relating to immigration control and asylum. European fear of immigrant impact is likely to be compounded by fears of Islamic fundamentalism for many of the areas from which immigrants have come or are likely to come – Turkey for Germany, North Africa for France – are overwhelmingly Islamic. As Britain discovered in relation to the Salman Rushdie affair and subsequently over the argument about state-funded religious schools (they already exist for Jews and Roman Catholics) the Moslem minority is developing into an important political force, at least in certain cities where large numbers of Moslem immigrants have settled.

Although the EC has been successful at coping with old ethnic rivalries it has paid all too little attention to the claims of new immigrant groups. European citizenship which came into being on 1 January 1993 was for the old Europeans while the millions of new migrants who have settled in Europe during the 1970s and 1980s remain essentially migrants in European eyes. The reluctance to admit Turkey to the EC despite many years of acceptance as a NATO anchor has more to do with its Islamic heritage than its relative poverty or anything else. The idea that has gained credence in Brussels is of a Europe of

Christian or formerly Christian states. During November 1992 there were attacks upon minority groups in Italy where the Interior Ministry reckons there are about 1,000 'Naziskins' in the country, mainly concentrated in the big cities; the desecration of a Moslem cemetery in France; the murder of a man in Germany by German skinheads who mistook him for a Jew and then took his body across the border to dump it in Holland. In Austria the right-wing Austrian Freedom Party, led by Jörg Haider, began a campaign to halt immigration and segregate non-German-speaking children in the schools. There were other signs of growing xenophobia, with increasing references to hordes from the south – just across the Mediterranean in the Maghreb countries for example – waiting to come into Europe.

The possibility that the far right was once more on the move in Europe became an important political speculation during 1992; the catalyst for both the rise of racism and such speculation was the growing alarm, shared by electors of most political hues, that Europe faced mass immigration, legal and illegal, which it would find increasingly difficult either to absorb or prevent. The fact that in France Le Pen's National Front could obtain 13.9% of the national vote was eloquent testimony to these fears but was also put down to the efforts of the Socialist Party to demonise Le Pen and raised a question of a different kind: to what extent should centre parties target racism and to what extent should they ignore it or treat it as only a passing phenomenon? The danger of doing nothing brought renewed fears about the way fascism had risen in the 1920s; the alternative was to attack and denounce racism even if to do so gives the extremists the publicity they seek. Avoiding either of these extremes tended to produce a third approach of sweet reason: the argument that many of the fears of ordinary people were justified and had to be taken into account by sensible politicians, an approach whose end result would be to keep immigrants out which was just what the extremists were demanding. The size of the problem could be related to the 4mn recent immigrants from North Africa that France is currently attempting to absorb. The difficulty about this middle-of-the road approach is that it assumes the majority are inherently reasonable and reject racial hygiene theories of the kind adopted by Hitler. Then, in the middle of 1992, the whole question of racism in its most virulent form was thrust to the forefront of European considerations by the 'ethnic cleansing' which the Serbs began to practise against their former partners in disintegrating Yugoslavia.

There is considerable irony in the immigrant problem for though Europe has come increasingly to fear Third World immigrants it began by inviting them in (as did Britain from the Caribbean Commonwealth in the 1950s) in order that they might provide the cheap labour of the underclass necessary to the maintenance of the contented society. During the days of its economic miracle West Germany opened its doors to millions of Turkish *gastarbeiter* while also wishing to demonstrate its liberal intentions in a conscious rejection of its Nazi past. Yet by July 1992 a draft of EC ministers' immigration proposals suggested that harsh measures were being planned to keep Third World refugees out of the Community with an EC definition of 'manifestly unfounded applications for asylum' to be used by all member countries. The draft reaffirmed the policy which insists that refugees stay in the first safe country they reach. This 'safe country rule' means that the great majority of Third World refugees will be confined to camps on the borders of their own countries with only a minority able to claim asylum in Europe if they can manage to fly or sail directly to a European port. But even this minority may be excluded in the future if, as the draft report suggests, such refugees must first seek redress for human rights abuses in their own courts before an asylum claim can be entertained by the EC.[5] This represents a Catch-22 situation without remedy. These deliberations were secret rather than open, with mounting evidence that EC restrictions upon immigration would be drastically increased. The issue of immigration into Europe was the subject of a Global Partnership '92 conference held in London during November 1992, at which it was claimed that the idea of a 'fortress' Europe to keep out immigrants would not work unless the West tackled the problems of poverty in the Third World which produced the migrations in the first place. As Nicholas Hopkinson, associate director of Wilton Park (a British foreign policy think-tank), argued: 'What the West does not give in aid and trade concessions, it will have to pay in increased costs to police borders, protect the innocent in the streets, screen asylum seekers and house and feed immigrants.'[6] The fact that western thinking has reached such a point demonstrates the extent of the fears about immigration even if these are deliberately highlighted; and, moreover, the thesis advanced by Nicholas Hopkinson came at a time when the evidence suggested that Britain was determined to cut back its aid in real terms.

Prosperity in western Europe (despite current economic depression) which the collapse of communism in eastern Europe has emphasised is offset by poverty and conflicts in the Third World. The result has been a huge increase in the number of asylum seekers, with East–West migration growing from 200,000 in 1987 to 1.4mn in 1990 while in 16 developed nations of the West the number of asylum seekers rose from 71,000 in 1983 to 500,000 in 1990. The great majority of applications for asylum in Britain, for example, come from sub-Saharan Africa and the Indian sub-continent which are the two poorest regions in the world. During 1991 some 12 wars or civil conflicts led to the displacement of 30mn people. As long as catastrophe on this scale persists in the Third World immigrant pressures upon the West – whether of refugees or economic migrants – will continue.

A new and brutal phrase, 'ethnic cleansing', entered the international vocabulary during 1992 as minorities in the various race enclaves of the former Yugoslavia were 'cleansed'. The displacement of these refugees in the worst violence Europe has witnessed since 1945 served to highlight growing racist attitudes throughout Europe. Although governments condemned 'ethnic cleansing' and called upon the Serbs or Croats or Bosnians to stop the practice they were also quick enough to put up barriers when faced with a massive influx of refugees for fear of racial explosions in their own countries. Confronted with the first major test of its tolerance – putting into practice the principles it is so ready to preach – Europe showed many signs of panic and little readiness to control its own racists. Tara Mukherjee, President of the Migrants' Forum of the European Community, suggests that the EC has done little to tackle racism within its own borders, let alone confront it; he would like to see a Commissioner for Racial Affairs in Brussels for there are now some 15 million people in the EC from Third World countries.[7] Generally, the EC maintains a low profile over race issues, fearful that any relaxation of the laws controlling immigrants will unleash racism in the Community. Such a fearful approach is bound to backfire; it will give encouragement to racists instead of controlling them, for racism is not an attitude that can be ignored; it is a disease that has to be tackled head-on by a government that knows what it wants and where it stands and is prepared to state its position and then defend it.

Despite expressions of horror from the leaders of Europe ethnic cleansing was pursued with unabated ferocity in the former Yugoslavia throughout 1992 so that it seemed far more likely that in the end Europe (and the world community) would come to accept ethnically cleansed successor states to the former Yugoslavia rather than intervene to prevent the cleansing process being continued. What was needed in mid-1992, and what was manifestly unforthcoming, was a statement from Europe, the United Nations and the United States that ethnic cleansing would not be permitted to succeed and that there would be no acceptance of permanent displacement of refugees whose right to return to their homes would be an automatic part of any eventual settlement. The Serbs, sensing western hesitation and its unwillingness to make firm commitments to restore to their rightful homes those who had been displaced, continued their policy of ethnic cleansing unabated. And while the ethnic cleansing continued the UNHCR was locked into a row with Britain, France and the United States over providing protection for convoys taking food and humanitarian relief to the starving. Indeed, a great deal of the ethnic cleansing tragedy was obfuscated by the priority given to humanitarian relief by the main western powers in lieu of any action to stop the conflict.

For years, in reaction to its Nazi past, West Germany leant over backwards to demonstrate its democratic credentials; its constitution made concessions to immigrants or refugees which put to shame the more stringent laws enforced by other European countries. There were, it is true, minority racist groups and periodic desecration of Jewish graves or monuments but it was possible to dismiss such activities as those of a tiny and unimportant fringe group. Then came the end of the Cold War, the reunification of the two Germanies and the subsequent, immense strains upon the economy while East Germans found that they, rather than the better off majority of West Germans, had to bear the full brunt of unemployment and the collapse of a lifestyle which, however restricted, had at least provided them with certainties. The resultant disillusionment has provided fertile ground for a growth in racism: partly the search for a scapegoat; and partly the release of deeply felt attitudes and convictions that communism had 'forbidden' or at any rate kept under strict control. German neo-Nazis represent a backlash that was inevitable: against the repression of nationalism that was central to the communist period; against incomers of all kinds who were seen to be usurping German rights; and against the mood of atonement that had been fostered in West Germany in relation to the holocaust and, more generally, the Nazi period. German 'skinheads' such as Leo who was interviewed for the British *Observer* are unashamed nationalists, regarding neo-Nazism as an acceptable creed, opposed to all foreigners on German soil, dismissive about the holocaust which he claims did not happen and wanting to see the greater Germany of the past restored despite his government's acceptance of its new national boundaries. The Leos of Germany may be only a tiny handful but they have the capacity to cause upheaval and sense that their government is afraid of them. This gives them enormous power and will continue to do so unless they are brought to heel.

At the beginning of December 1992 a quarter of a million Germans took to the streets of Munich in a demonstration against the new racism. They demonstrated under a banner which proclaimed: 'A city says No.' The giant demonstration was evidence of the mounting doubts and disquiet in a country whose economic performance has long been the envy of the world. The message of the rally was 'no' to xenophobia, 'no' to anti-Semitism and 'no' to the neo-Nazi thugs whose recent much-publicised activities had caused widespread concern. Josef Joffe, the foreign editor of the *Süddeutsche Zeitung* said of the rally: 'At last the silent majority is standing up for decency and democracy. People have begun to understand that attacks against foreigners are also attacks against us – against our whole way of life.'[8] The question which kept recurring was whether the developments of 1992 were similar to those of the 1920s which propelled Hitler to power, for the Hitler (or Nazi) bogey had come back to haunt the new Germany. And those who rallied were on the defensive, wanting to maintain the comfortable Germany of the post-war economic miracle years. By contrast the extremists of the right were on the offensive. One neo-Nazi, Michael Swierczek, who is the leader of the *Nationale Offensive* based in Augsburg, says: 'We won once and, for the first time since the war, we feel we could win again . . . The system is tottering. Destabilisation has set in. The boom years of the "economic miracle" are over. And in a crisis, Germans always turn to the far right.' The *Nationale Offensive* is one of 60 right-wing extremist organisations which between them boast 7,000 members nationwide.[9] This may be a tiny number and Michael Swierzcek may be wildly optimistic in his assessment of the German mood but the fact that he could make such claims at all is a chilling reminder of what might happen. During 1992 right-wing extremists carried out some 2,000 violent attacks in which 16 people died while more than 18,000 xenophobic or anti-Semitic incidents were recorded.

And fear of such developments was placed on record by the German President, Richard von Weizsäcker, at the anti-racist Berlin rally of November 1992 when he said: 'Let us entertain no illusions. What is happening this year has not occurred in this country since the war. Something evil is afoot.' It ought to be possible to contain the right-wing extremists without difficulty; it is the manifest nervousness of the government that is so disturbing. At least by mid-December 1992 tough action was being taken against extremists, with the neo-Nazi leader Thomas Dienel receiving a 32-month prison sentence for inciting racist violence. The Interior Minister, Rudolf Seiters, lodged an application with the country's constitutional court to restrict the civil liberties of Dienel and another neo-Nazi, Heinz Reisz, who had called for foreigners to be banned. The Nationalist Front was banned and the police raided the homes of scores of suspected neo-Nazis in a search for banned material and weapons. The minister's tough line came as a response to criticisms of the government's previous inaction in the face of extremist activities.

There are British German-watchers only too ready to condemn the rise of extremism there and to claim that it was to be expected; by doing so they divert attention from British racism and xenophobia which are every bit as virulent as anything to be found in Germany. The majority of the British people are opposed to immigrants and despite outcries in the liberal press the decision of the Home Secretary, Kenneth Clarke, to limit the number of Bosnian refugees to a mere handful was probably regarded as sensible and to be applauded. What the British are most opposed to, however, are large numbers of black or brown immigrants from the New Commonwealth, and during the 1970s and 1980s Britain steadily tightened her immigration procedures until by the 1990s, it had become harder for immigrants to enter Britain than any other part of the EC. As the *Independent* described the British racist phenomenon: 'In Britain, a special kind of euphemism has evolved to deal with black immigration: everyone knows, for instance, that when politicians are "concerned about the future of race relations in this country", they mean they are firmly anti-immigration. Otherwise, hardly anyone talks about it, except small numbers of racists so stupid they have failed (because of the silence) to notice their victory.'[10] Ironically, the crisis in former Yugoslavia has helped highlight British racism: sympathy for little white children shivering with cold in the snow contrasts with indifference towards black children dying under the sun of Somalia. It is, of course, a question of race solidarity. In London in November 1992 during Britain's presidency of the EC her Home Secretary, Kenneth Clarke, urged his EC counterparts to adopt Britain's tough stand towards asylum seekers and adopt a fast deportation process for those deemed to have a 'manifestly unfounded' claim for asylum. Mr Clarke told the BBC: 'We have to have a sensible, liberal system of controlling the numbers of people that can sensibly be absorbed by our economy and public services.'[11] That is the favourite approach of those who restrict entry and by 1992 Britain had been steadily restricting entry for 30 years. On the whole the British have been more adept – or more hypocritical – in playing down racism than have the Germans or French. Thus the British condemn the Germans for rising extremism even while the latter admit 200,000 Bosnian refugees as opposed to the grudging handful Britain allowed into the country. Partly it is a question of presentation and government willingness to face facts. Thus in Germany 14 racist murders over two years are cited as evidence of racism; 11 racist murders in Britain over 18 months are largely glossed over.

The problems in the United States have been highlighted by the separation of the races brought about by wealth disparities, with blacks and Hispanics living in the downtown ghetto areas and whites living in the out-of-town suburbs, the wealthier of them in increasingly fortified dwellings with guards and guard dogs and in the expectation that they will be mugged or robbed by the dispossessed of their society even if political correctness prevents them from calling such people blacks. It has become an accepted part of the modern American scene that young American blacks or Hispanics are at violent odds – war is sometimes not too strong a term – with prosperous white America. The new creed of political correctness prevents Americans from talking about poor blacks and thus acknowledging the existence of a racial problem; instead they speak of the economically disadvantaged of the inner cities, the euphemisms allowing the harsh truths about a racially divided society to be glossed over or ignored. The Los Angeles riots of April 1992 reminded the United States forcibly of the huge divides that exist in its society. As one commentator put it, the Los Angeles riot of 1992 was depressingly similar to the Watts riot of 30 years earlier yet in between the United States appeared to have learnt nothing at all.[12] In both cases the riots were sparked off by police brutality and black youths took to the streets, looted, burned and killed to remind white America of the volcano upon which its prosperity rests. The Watts riots of 1965 left a shattered Los Angeles and a white United States which believed the underclass was rising up *en masse*. Subsequently, vast sums of money were spent to assist the disadvantaged blacks with training, job opportunity schemes, investment in housing and positive discrimination, and the tactic worked. The black underclass became invisible once more and America turned its attention to other matters. 27 years later Los Angeles had turned into the greatest racial ghetto city in the world with 80 different languages taught in its schools and separate and large communities of Asians, Blacks, Hispanics, Central Americans, Eastern Europeans, Vietnamese and others while the Whites and Jews had become a minority in a city they once dominated and had retreated into protected areas. Even in the less than four months of 1992 prior to the April riots some 200 murders had taken place; most of these were either gang- or drugs-related killings. The clear divisions between racial groups, rich and poor, protected and underclass, make a nonsense of any claims that the United States has overcome its old racial problems. The divisions are there for all to see.

Any economically successful society is likely to depend to a greater or lesser degree upon an underclass and the success of a ruling elite (of whatever kind) depends upon its ability to defuse tensions between the two sides in this divide when these otherwise threaten to explode and destroy the position of the privileged or contented. During the present period this age-old division between haves and have-nots has been highlighted and made potentially even more explosive because a high proportion of the underclass can be identified with a different race – the *gastarbeiter* in Germany, the New Commonwealth immigrants in Britain, the Blacks and Hispanics in the United States – with the result that the guilt of the contented class whose wealth and lifestyle depends upon the existence of an underclass has been heightened by the fact that a large proportion of that underclass is of a different 'race' which, inevitably in the way of human beings, has come to be regarded as inferior. The more the underclass feels trapped the more dangerous and resentful it becomes. In Europe a high proportion of the underclass has recently arrived as migrants and, at least in theory, these may be sent home again if their presence becomes too threatening. In the United States the black underclass are American, the descendants of slaves, and have nowhere else to go.

The poor of the developing countries in the South might be seen as the world's underclass just as the poor of the inner cities in Europe and America are the underclass of the rich West, and it is yet another of the ironies surfacing at the end of the Cold War that just as the problems of the world's underclass – the South – had been clearly identified and quantified by such agencies as the World Bank in order that action to redress the balance might have seemed a real possibility, so the West has been forced to turn its attention to its own underclass of the inner cities. The despair and indifference that exist and were brought out by the Los Angeles riots are sufficient to divert attention from Third World problems at the very time that an end to the Cold War might have suggested it receive assistance on a scale that could have changed the imbalances for good.

Instead, race and class riots in the North will increase the fears and suspicions which already exist about the South and its potential hordes of migrants.

11 The Politics of Contentment

The function of governments in the past was the well-being of those they represented. Television has brought the world's problems into every living room in the North and this development, coupled with an outward-looking humanitarianism which is a form of *danegeld* paid to compensate for the wealth and power disparities between North and South, has distorted any sense of what governments can and ought to do. The huge demands placed upon the United Nations in the wake of the Cold War are a case in point. After a long period in which it was unable to act effectively because of the superpower constraints upon it the world body is now expected to solve every upheaval and crisis although none of the major powers has suggested giving it either more resources or more authority. The most likely outcome for this absurd expectation will be the collapse of the United Nations, which will simply become the scapegoat for the world's ills. Pressures upon the governments in the rich countries to take action are not supported by any willingness to pay higher taxes; in the long term such attitudes can only lead to policy failures whose most likely result will be a withdrawal of involvement in the troubled areas of the world except where action is seen to be essential to the well-being of the North. During the Cold War the global nature of the superpower confrontation meant that no crisis could be ignored for fear the other side would step in and obtain an advantage. Now, even if the North is tempted to intervene everywhere and police the world, it will be restrained by the politics of contentment.

In his book *The Culture of Contentment* Kenneth Galbraith argues that governments respond to those who have, the contented, rather than seeking to deal with the problems and needs of the weak and dispossessed; indeed, governments are

155

elected to do just this, for the marginalised no longer bother to vote: 'What is new in the so-called capitalist countries – and this is a vital point – is that the controlling contentment and resulting belief is now that of the many, not just of the few. It operates under the compelling cover of democracy, albeit a democracy not of all citizens but of those who, in defense of their social and economic advantage, actually go to the polls.'[1] This bleak assessment does not augur well for the poor and dispossessed whose state, increasingly, will only be seen and reacted to when unbearable pressures bring it to the point of explosion, as happened in the Los Angeles riots of April 1992. As Galbraith also argues: 'The result [of the contentment culture] is government that is accommodated not to reality or common need but to the beliefs of the contented, who are now the majority of those who vote.'

The contented, as Kenneth Galbraith points out, are a majority but not of all citizens, only of those citizens who vote, and the distinction is a crucial one. When a large number of its citizens, for whatever reason, do not bother to vote then a democracy is in trouble; nor is it enough to blame the leaders who in such circumstances are doing no more than respond to the voters. In the United States President Reagan was voted into power by the contented majority who did not want him to tackle awkward problems such as the plight of the inner cities since to do so would have cost the contented an increase in taxes. That was not the reason they voted Republican. Increased taxes to help the less fortunate are a cause of anger to the contented who have to find the money; they are not interested in funding massive programmes to change the status quo which, in any case, operates in their favour, and prefer inaction in the present to any long-term programmes which are designed to redress present inequalities but can only hope to do so at the expense of immediate contentment. Thus, as Galbraith tells us, Presidents Reagan and Bush responded to the contentment culture by not taxing the voters; and when Bush did raise taxes, if only marginally, he was bitterly attacked.

Contentment, however, depends upon an underclass, and economic progress will be more certain and take place faster if there is such a class and if it is constantly replenished as its more adventurous and progressive members move upwards and leave its ranks. If, for whatever reasons, it becomes impossible or at any rate far more difficult for members of the underclass to move upwards, as they could in the past, then a potentially explosive situation will be created. A frail or declining economy and the movement of industries out of the big cities (sometimes to relocations in the Third World) will produce a static underclass that sees no hope of changing the mould. In such circumstances it is likely to become totally disillusioned with the society to which in theory it belongs and opt out, as did many who failed to register to vote in the American and British elections of 1992. Explaining the new phenomenon of the inner cities of violence and despair Galbraith writes: 'There has been surprisingly little comment as to why parts of New York, Chicago and Los Angeles, once poor but benign and culturally engaging, are now centres of terror and despair. The reason is that what were once conditions for upward steps in economic life now spell a hopeless enthralment.' A phenomenon that is growing throughout the world is that of the protected enclave in the big city where members of the economic-power elites live surrounded by high walls, burglar alarms, guards and guard dogs with security firms patrolling the streets on their behalf. This has long been the norm in Third World cities, for example in Africa, where discrepancies of wealth and lifestyles between the African elites or the expatriates who come for a temporary sojourn in the country as businessmen or aid workers and the ordinary people are so great as to mark out these elites as natural targets for robbery, if nothing worse. The same phenomenon has become part of the United States: the well-to-do need protection and it is the business of government to see they get it – from the blacks or Hispanics or other members of ghetto society who regard the affluent as natural targets for their despair and rage and, of course, as people to be robbed.

When in April 1992 Britain yet again voted in a Tory government under John Major (after 13 years of Thatcherism and Tory rule) the electorate was voting for contentment and the status quo and ignoring the manifest problems that cried out for a different approach than that offered by a tired Tory Party which had already been too long in power. In part this result reflected the bankruptcy of the Labour opposition which was more concerned to demonstrate its appeal to the contented than to offer radical alternative policies. Contentment kept Margaret Thatcher in power throughout the 1980s even though large sections of the population felt themselves to be increasingly marginalised by her policies. When Bill Clinton and the Democrats won the American elections in November 1992 they did so by avoiding any commitment to change the imbalances in American society. Politicians who only seek the support of the contented because to do so offers them the safest road to power in fact invite decline. This approach now appears to be the accepted policy of all the major political parties in the West and though the problems to be tackled – unemployment, inner city decay, the run-down of educational and health services, increasing crime rates, the disaffection of the young – are well enough understood and have been exhaustively analysed politicians only pay lipservice to the needs while putting off action on the scale that the problems require.

By 1988 there were 32mn Americans living below the poverty line while one in every five children was born into poverty. At a time when there is much speculation as to whether the United States will become the world's 'policeman' the role of US servicemen is clearly of great importance. Most American servicemen are from the underclass for whom such service is an upward step; thus, the deployment of American forces in the Gulf was possible, despite publicly expressed fears of reactions to too many body bags returning home, because the contented class were largely exempt from military service. A generation earlier the war in Vietnam was brought to an end because of the revolt of the privileged from the contented classes who were not prepared to have their lifestyles put at risk by service in Vietnam.

Now if during the 1990s the underclasses of the United States and Europe are to be kept repressed because the contented refuse to vote for the taxes and political changes necessary to redress the huge imbalances which exist there would seem to be little likelihood that the North will behave in a different fashion in relation to the South. The politics of contentment in individual countries of the North will keep the underclass in its place; and the politics of contentment in the North as a whole will ensure that little is done – for example, by debt amelioration – to alter the underclass status of most Third World countries. Delay, indeed, is the key weapon of politicians voted into power by the contented. Further research, the device of the Royal Commission, Pearson or Brandt reports are all part of the armoury of delay in order to avoid commitments to action that would cost big money and put at risk the settled sense of security enjoyed by the contented. There is nothing unusual in this approach: those who have do not vote away their advantages although, as a gesture, they may concede a little to ameliorate the lot of the marginalised and dispossessed, partly in order to demonstrate their benevolent nature and partly (more importantly) to stave off the growth of revolutionary tendencies among the have-nots. In political terms a little benign charity goes a long way.

An immigrant underclass holds considerable political attraction for a rich, advanced economy. Immigrants are anxious to make good in their new society, they are therefore unlikely to be over-assertive about wages and will be less aggressive about their 'rights' than would local people; in many cases, moreover, because of the time needed to achieve citizenship qualifications or because they are illegal immigrants, they will not have or use the vote. The United States, Britain, Germany and France have each come to rely at least in part upon such immigrants to form the underclass. Perhaps their greatest advantage is their transient nature – they want to move up or, if they cause trouble, they can be deported; it is when the underclass becomes fixed that resentments build up to threaten the stability of the contented class above them.[2] Contentment also leads to deregulation, as the British discovered under Thatcher; the underclass seeks regulations which are generally seen to work to their advantage while the contented want maximum freedom to do as they will. The biggest deregulation, of course, is low taxation.

In Britain the new underclass is mainly white and young and consists of those who leave school to few or no prospects of employment. In July 1992, for example, some 400,000 young Britons came onto the labour market from school and it was estimated that a quarter of them would join the 100,000 youngsters from 1991 who had never had a job. They will swell the ranks of the permanently disaffected who engage in petty and not so petty crimes, steal cars for joyriding and riot. As Ron Hatfield, the Chief Constable of the West Midlands, argued in July 1992: 'These youngsters have no money and no jobs. We need to give them hope and security. We are talking about a small sub-class trying to survive. For them rioting is the most exciting event in their lives.'[3] The attitude of the government to such a group only forces them into a deeper sense of alienation. Thus, in 1992 more than 100,000 16/17 year olds had no jobs or income yet in 1988 the government stopped benefits for this age group while at the same time going back on its promise to provide training for all unemployed school-leavers, such provision having been the government's justification for curtailing the benefits. Here, indeed, was a government of the contented ruthlessly downgrading the underclass. This growing underclass has little education, few skills, is under-nourished and increasingly unemployable. Unsurprisingly its members turn to crime and the contented condemn them for their behaviour and demand more policing. Most riots are sparked off because the police take action against crime and the more the police attempt to enforce the law the more young people who are their principal targets become alienated. It is a vicious circle. What was distressing as well as damning about the politicians of the West during the 1980s was their apparent indifference to the growing alienation of these underclasses from the rest of society. Apart from repeated demands for more policing – so as to safeguard the contented – few political leaders or governments looked seriously at the problems of the growing underclass or came forward with any considered suggestions about how the ghetto cultures could be changed for the better. Any real as opposed to cosmetic changes will require money as well as imagination on a scale that, so far, has neither been forthcoming nor contemplated.

The politics of contentment, however, must almost certainly end in conflict and disaster, if only because of the changing nature of employment opportunities and the growing numbers of the underclass. It is now estimated by the Federal Census Bureau that whites in the USA could be outnumbered by blacks, Hispanics and other ethnic groups by the middle of the next century. Steep population increases are forecast for the 1990s and by 2050 the population will have reached the 380mn mark. The most important factor in this increasing population is the surge in immigration, legal and illegal. By 2050 the white American population will account for no more than 53% of the total; Hispanics will have passed blacks as the second largest group and will number approximately 80mn (just under 20% of the total); while blacks, at 62mn, will account for 16% of the population.[4] Such a change in the ethnic balance will turn upside down existing ideas of majority and minority groups. Against such predictions the contented ought to be thinking now about how to address the problems of the underclass, but there is little indication that they are either doing so or are inclined to do so.

In the environment debate that centred upon the Rio Earth Summit in mid-1992 the US stand in relation to global problems might as easily have been translated as pronouncements about the wishes of the contented as President Bush made plain he would attend the summit only if the declaration on global warming was shorn of all concrete commitments. Similarly, the White House overruled the environmentalists in favour of the timber industry and approved logging in huge

tracts of the Oregon forest which, among other things, provided
a home for the rare spotted owl. As the executive director of the
Council on Competitiveness, David McIntosh, said: 'The
President has always been in favour of protecting the environment in a way that is compatible with the economy . . . What
you are seeing is a series of decisions that focused on the
economic growth side of the balance.'[5] In fact, of course,
decisions about the environment are essentially long term; those
about the economy immediate, and it is the latter which always
come first.

Changing attitudes towards people from the Third World
reflect a growing harshness by the North in relation to the poor
of the world and an increasing impulse towards a laager
mentality. Thus, at London's Heathrow airport passengers
from Africa will be subjected to the humiliation of sniffer dogs
searching for drugs although such treatment is not meted out to
passengers from Europe or the United States. Britain, which
had the largest empire, now appears to have turned against the
Third World more than any other major country of the North
and treats people from the South with growing disdain. It was
hoped, briefly, when the Cold War came to an end, that the
huge energies and resources which had been deployed in the
arms race could be turned to the task of raising standards in the
Third World. Instead, it seems that a new division is taking
place: Russia and Ukraine will join the old First World as will a
few selected Third World countries such as Turkey and,
perhaps, South Africa; most of the rest including the former
Soviet republics such as Armenia or Tajikistan and almost all of
Africa and much of Asia and Latin America will remain
excluded. Thereafter, the rich nations of the North will be far
more likely to employ their surplus resources in assisting the
borderline states such as Russia than in assisting the bulk of the
old Third World. The principal relationship of the North with
the South now appears to be economic reform imposed by the
IMF and the World Bank to ensure, on the one hand, that the
North recoups its investments and, on the other, that Third
World economies are opened to unfettered market forces. The

idea of helping development has fallen by the wayside and even the rhetoric about development is disappearing.

Because of her past imperial involvement throughout the Third World it might reasonably be thought that Britain would have a wider understanding and greater sympathy for Third World problems than most other major states in the North except for France. This however is not the case. Ethnic cleansing in Bosnia produced hundreds of thousands of refugees yet in mid-1992 while Germany had taken in 200,000, Austria and Hungary 50,000 each, Sweden 44,000 and Switzerland 18,000 Britain had only accepted 1,300.[6] This miserable performance was justified by the Foreign Office on the grounds that it was better to help people on the spot or as near as possible to their former homes. But such an argument only makes sense if there also exists a clear commitment to ensure that the Bosnians regain their homes, and this was far from the case in July 1992. Now if Britain performs in such a manner in relation to a European country in distress she is unlikely to do any better in relation to a Third World country. In fact, even more than the rest of Europe, Britain is withdrawing into a 'laager'. British meanness, indeed, was emphasised at this time by the Home Secretary, Kenneth Clarke, who said that Britain did not want to encourage people 'to move further from Yugoslavia than they would be inclined to go'. Meanwhile, Britain was sending back 35 refugees from the former Yugoslavia to countries on the continent where they had passed on their way to Britain: 24 to Belgium, five to Germany, and two each to Italy, Austria and Turkey. Generosity of spirit was singularly lacking. By this time the war in Yugoslavia had created a total of 2.4mn refugees and Europe was dithering about the extent to which it should or should not intervene to stop the slaughter and ethnic cleansing.

A further complication that threatened the equilibrium of Europe was the turmoil into which the EC had been thrown by the end of the Cold War. The carefully calculated balance of the Community which had been created primarily as a western bastion against the Soviet threat and as a means of containing

Germany was once more in the melting pot. The reunification of Germany meant that the Franco–German balance which had been the dominant feature of the Community since the time of De Gaulle and Adenauer was now at an end, while the collapse of the Soviet empire also meant that a dozen newly 'freed' states wanted to join and, were they to do so, the EC balance would be still more profoundly altered. Arguments about the Maastricht Treaty dominated EC considerations through 1992 but the real argument should have been about how and to what extent the Community wished to embrace the states of eastern Europe. Germany, moreover, had not helped by its hasty recognition of Croatia in December 1991; rather, it had raised the fear (especially in France) that it wanted to embark upon an east European policy of its own. Further, the awkward possibility of a two-speed Europe now raised its head following Britain's withdrawal from the ERM while the four poorest members of the EC – Spain, Portugal, Ireland and Greece – expected to receive from the rest of the EC through the Cohesion Fund more aid per head for their combined 65mn population than any developing country of Africa or Asia. Europe, despite its squabbles, was looking after its own and the single Europe that supposedly came into being at the beginning of 1993 was yet another signal to the South that the North was drawing in its horns to concentrate upon its own affairs. Against this highly volatile background the North had discovered a new morality which it was busy applying to the South.

The publication of a *Human Development Index* by the UN Development Programme in 1991 and the failure of the 1992 UNDP report to repeat the exercise tells us a great deal about human behaviour: only those who are given a high rating are happy for such an index to appear regularly while those who receive a low rating are equally anxious to stop what, to them, is an obnoxious practice. During the Cold War more simplistic ratings were employed: communists and fellow-travellers; freedom-loving democracies and those who believed in the free enterprise (rather than capitalist) system. A statement of belief in one or other set of principles was enough to allow enrolment in one or other side in the Cold War until Nehru and other leaders of what became the Third World insisted upon non-alignment. Those three-way parameters have now disappeared and it is instructive that they are being replaced by a set of more complex – and almost certainly unworkable – moral attitudes. The new morality, needless to say, comes exclusively from the big powers of the North anxious, as always, to impose their precepts upon the lesser powers they would influence. Thus, in May 1992, for example, Britain and other Western governments blocked all but urgent humanitarian aid to Malawi until President Banda was prepared to respect basic freedoms and move towards ending one-party rule, and donors meeting in Paris blocked $74mn of aid. A statement from the World Bank which chaired the meeting said: 'Donors are seeking tangible and irreversible evidence of a basic transformation in the way Malawi approaches basic freedoms and human rights.'[7] President Banda (as well as a number of other Third World presidents) had been denying basic human rights for years without being taken to task, let alone having their aid cut off during the long years of the Cold War; the sudden shift makes sense only if it is seen as a prelude to the North cutting back on aid generally. Since the need for aid (at least in terms of past practice) is as great or greater today than during the years of the Cold War some kind of moral justification must be found for its retrenchment or curtailment.

But a policy half-based upon morality is bound to run into difficulties, as the British Overseas Development Minister, Baroness Chalker, discovered when she tried to balance moral outrage with British interests. Having given a pledge to cut aid to developing countries which violate human rights she then had to defend giving aid to countries that nonetheless did not meet her criteria. Thus, the publication of Amnesty International's 1992 report on human rights violations in India (a major recipient of British aid) faced her – and by implication all major donors who attempt to relate human rights to aid – with a political and moral dilemma. According to Amnesty torture is 'pervasive and a daily routine in every one of India's 25 states, irrespective of whether arrests are made by the police, the paramilitary forces or the army . . . It happens regardless of the political persuasion of the party in power. Many hundreds, if not thousands, have died because of torture during the last decade.' So Lady Chalker was at once faced with the necessity of prevaricating and making special exceptions. India, so the argument runs, is one of Asia's few genuine democracies, therefore . . . Meanwhile, during 1992 Britain also suspended aid to Sudan, Somalia, Burma and Sri Lanka and, along with the United States, suspended aid to Kenya for six months to increase pressures upon President Daniel arap Moi to hold multi-party elections.[8] What seems certain under the terms of this new morality is that principles relating to good governance or human rights will be readily enough waived when more important western interests are at stake.

But while the North applies its new morality to the South, its instrument the IMF continues to apply its structural adjustment programmes to debt-ridden countries of the South and, as Mr Donovan, a correspondent to the *Observer*, pointed out, its policies encouraged child slavery (for example, of children in the carpet industry in India). Thus the IMF stipulates deregulation and relaxation of the labour laws to make it easier for India to earn the foreign exchange needed to repay its debts to the West. Mr Donovan writes: 'Institutions such as the World Bank and IMF, while making fatuous statements about world poverty, refuse to accept their own active role in creating and perpetuating such conditions. When it comes to debt servicing, hard currency (normally US dollars) is what is required, few questions are asked as to how the funds were raised – the suffering of children is nowhere to be found on the balance sheet.'[9]

Back in Europe the new morality provides a convenient alternative to more difficult policies. After many months opposing any form of military intervention in Bosnia-Herzegovina Britain and the United States finally agreed with the French to support a UN resolution that would sanction the use of all necessary means (which includes force) to ensure that humanitarian aid got through to those who needed it. This aid was to assist the victims of 'ethnic cleansing' and, leaving aside the subsequent history of humanitarian convoys, the real question at issue was pinpointed accurately enough by the Bosnian UN ambassador, Muhamed Sacirbey, who accused the United States, Britain and France of salving public opinion (outraged by ethnic cleansing) by dealing with humanitarian aspects instead of facing up to the root cause of the conflict. Indeed, if the new morality is to have any value to its users this primarily will be as an excuse mechanism: not to give aid; not to take costly actions that will actually bring a conflict to an end; and so on.

In further pursuit of her new morality Britain decided to keep out the 'corrupt' as part of her immigration policy. In July 1992 the British Home Secretary, Kenneth Clarke, refused permission to remain in Britain to Abdulai Conteh, the former Vice-President of Sierra Leone (who had fled his country in April following a coup), on the grounds that he had been 'a member of a corrupt government'. When Mr Conteh asked for evidence he was told that there was no suggestion that he personally was corrupt although the government he had served had bankrupted his country. As the *Independent* suggested: 'Compared with the long list of crooks and butchers with whom British foreign secretaries have wined and dined, he [Mr Conteh] looks like an angel.'[10]

The switch in attitudes that has come with this new morality will land Britain, and any other country which pursues such hypocrisy, in situations which will make them look justly absurd. During the Cold War any regime was acceptable as long as it proclaimed its anti-communist credentials, and a western ambassador in Baghdad could say of Saddam Hussein that 'he is a bloody butcher but he's on our side'. Human rights and democratic values were largely ignored by western governments throughout the Cold War and left to the campaigning activities of minority groups. Now, suddenly, everything has changed: good governance, democracy and human rights are the new 'strings' the North attaches to its aid. Except, of course, where it is too costly to do so. Thus, although the West expressed justified outrage at the 1989 massacre in Tiananmen Square it was not long before it began to soft-pedal its criticisms and the reason is obvious enough: 1bn Chinese with the entrepreneurial capacities and potential productivity of Hong Kong. The West must come to terms with such a China but smaller fry who have long been in receipt of western aid can be suitably disciplined and, if they do not fall into line, dropped from the North's donor support list, which is probably the real object of the new morality.

At the beginning of 1993 as Britain was bound to discover, following the multi-party elections in Kenya, squaring the demands of the new morality with £1bn worth of British investment was not going to be easy. The Kenya elections were undoubtedly extensively rigged although Moi only held them when he was as certain as it is possible to be that the squabbling opposition groups would divide the anti-Moi votes between them and lose. He won 36% of the vote which was enough to keep him in power and allow him to argue that he had been democratic in the process. Here another aspect of the new morality came into play: the stationing of observer groups in Third World countries to pronounce on the fairness or otherwise of their elections. In Kenya the Commonwealth Observers' Group said of the results: 'In many instances [they] directly reflect, however imperfectly, the expression of the will of the people.' What, one might ask, of the other instances?[11] And if there is to be monitoring and the monitors decide that irregularities have taken place, what mechanism exists to force a new election? In Angola, where Jonas Savimbi was fairly defeated in monitored elections but nonetheless threatened to go back to the bush and resume the civil war, the monitors suggested that the winners should offer him a deal. Back in Kenya, despite massive evidence that the election was far from free and fair, both the United States and Britain urged the losers to accept the result. Perhaps the amazing thing in retrospect is that an election was ever held at all.

The new morality is only urged upon the weak. India and China will go their own ways and though they may occasionally be urged to be more democratic or to pay greater attention to human rights no other pressures will be exerted upon them because they are too important as would-be sources of investment and trade. Israel, which has treated every UN resolution about the Middle East with total contempt, is unlikely to have the new morality applied to its behaviour because of the powerful protective lobby that exists to support its cause in Washington. And other violators of western-proposed moralities will only be pressured according to their position on the scale of western interests. The concept of the new morality, perhaps peculiarly British, is fundamentally hypocritical: a new weapon to be used to discipline the weak and force them into adopting policies that suit the North; or, alternatively, a principle to be trotted out as an excuse for curtailing assistance that the North no longer has an interest in providing.

12 Policing the South

Keeping the peace or bringing law and order to a region of conflict was one of the many justifications advanced for European imperialism in the nineteenth century. Following World War II this peace-keeping function, supposedly, was to be discharged by the United Nations, except that Cold War rivalries often led instead to a prolongation of warfare as, for example, in Angola or Vietnam since, inevitably, one side was treated as an ally by the West and the other was supported by the Communist bloc. The end of the Cold War has presented the world with new alternatives: the first, that the United Nations really does become the world's peace-keeper, a role it can only discharge properly if it is given more resources and greater authority, and that decision must rest with the permanent members of the Security Council; the second, that the United States, assisted by the principal western powers, becomes the world's policeman. Either possibility raises huge problems and questions.

A number of arguments can be advanced to justify peace-keeping interventions: to stop aggression by one state against another (as in the Gulf when Iraq invaded Kuwait); to bring an end to total chaos in order to alleviate the suffering of the mass of the people (as in Somalia); to prevent crimes against humanity (which would be a justification for intervention in Bosnia), as opposed merely to guarding relief columns of supplies for the starving. Intervention can also be justified to stop a civil war if such a war threatens to spill over its frontiers and lead to a more general conflagration; or a peace-keeping operation may be justified if it is likely to prevent a delicately balanced political confrontation from degenerating into civil war (as in the case of the United Nations in Namibia in 1989–90). A good many other justifications will no doubt be forthcoming when the policing power or powers decide they are going to intervene anyway, and there is a danger that if early efforts at policing are successful the habit will grow since such interventions will be seen to confer prestige and influence upon the policing power (whether the United Nations or the United States). What became certain in the period 1989–92 was the expectation that the role of world policeman would be undertaken either by a strengthened United Nations or by the United States and its allies. That much requires policing is incontrovertible; whether the policing will be done correctly and without being distorted by big power policy considerations is another matter entirely.

However, the extent to which the powers with policing capacity can be expected to work together is at best limited, and the US-led alliance which intervened in the Gulf may turn out to be the exception rather than the rule. During the Cold War the West remained united – just – because it felt threatened; the lifting of the threat has revealed huge and potentially unbridgeable differences between the European powers, the United States and Japan so that, as the disintegration of Yugoslavia demonstrated, the chances of imposing a single European-American policy to stop the civil war are not high. Further, during 1992 the squabbling at the Rio Summit and the inability of the Group of Seven (G-7) to disguise their growing differences gave warning that the cohesion of the Group may not last very much longer. The greatest danger appears to lie in the growing antipathy (mainly over trade and protection) between Europe and the United States on the one hand and the United States and Japan on the other. Europe and the United States have in any case been in conflict for years though Cold War considerations and Washington's ability to play off one European power against another have dulled this perception. But increasingly, despite the set-backs of the Maastricht arguments, Britain, France, Germany and Italy (the four European members of G-7) have begun to act more in concert in relation to the United States. Between them the members of the G-7 possess overwhelming power, and it is from their ranks or with their resources that any system of world policing must be derived; but if they cannot agree upon an equitable world trading system they are unlikely – for long – to be able to work together over political issues either. And though the Cold War may have ended, Russia has not ceased to be a major power whose potential in terms of world influence will be ignored at Europe's peril.

There is another problem for G-7. In recent years, and notably in relation to the disintegration of the USSR, it has moved towards adopting foreign policy as opposed simply to economic decisions and in 1991, for example, it was suggested that a summit directory should be created to review the question of arms transfers; this initiative was killed off by France which opposes an increase in G-7 power since France would not be able to exercise a veto as she can in the Security Council, a consideration that may also apply to Britain.[1] A strengthened G-7 would be dominated by the United States (and, if Russia joins, increasingly by the two old superpowers); in the United Nations Britain and France still possess the veto and an illusion of power which is greater than the reality. The economic management role exercised by the G-7 during the 1980s in relation to Latin American debt, and at the end of the decade by easing the transition in Eastern Europe and Russia following the end of the Cold War, could be seen as successes. But a new role is now required if the Group is not to lose its influence; whether the strains in the old Western Alliance of the Cold War period will allow this to happen is doubtful.

Crucial to the way the 'new world order' develops is American power. In December 1989 American armed forces landed in Panama to replace General Noriega, who was subsequently taken to the United States for trial as a drug trafficker, and see installed a government more amenable to Washington. This American intervention could be seen as policing – drug trafficking is certainly a major world problem – or it could be seen as outrageous imperial-style bullying, but either way Washington had succeeded in its objective and the rest of the world was unable to do anything to stop it. In 1991 the display of American military might in the Gulf, overshadowing the contributions of all its allies, created an image of immense and unrivalled power, unchecked, as it might have been in the Cold War, by any comparable Soviet military display. On the whole, the State Department was cautious in its reaction to the Soviet Union's retreat from foreign entanglements; for example, it negotiated orderly withdrawals in Africa (Angola and Ethiopia) and, following the Gulf War, brokered a regional peace conference effort in the Middle East. But a clear pattern began to emerge: Russia was encouraged to play a part where it could be useful as the retreating power; Britain, where she could, dutifully produced troops and support in her old, revived special relationship role; the United Nations was given the task of providing legitimacy for intervention (as in the Gulf or Somalia) or taking responsibility for monitoring as in Angola. But everywhere the new driving force for these police actions, if and when they took place, was the United States. The problem which the rest of the world must face is that of a United States which believes it won both the Cold War and the Gulf War and, with the disintegration of the USSR, has no rival. The danger that now faces the world community is of a single superpower deciding if, when and how intervention will take place; either ignoring the United Nations as ineffective or using it to provide legitimacy for what essentially are American interventions; using a relatively willing Britain and France as small-scale military allies; and treating Germany and Japan as sources of finance for such interventionist policies. Should this indeed become the pattern the South will find that it faces a new form of imperialism.

Old habits die hard, however, and American interventions in Africa over 30 years were dictated solely by Cold War considerations or, as in Liberia, myopic calculations of American interest. In Zaire the CIA helped bring Mobutu to power and subsequently supported him in power no matter what he did to his benighted country; in Angola American support for Savimbi, because he was anti-communist, encouraged one of Africa's most brutal civil wars; in Somalia during the 1980s (having lost their foothold in Ethiopia to the Soviets) the

Americans backed an increasingly dictatorial and brutal Siyad Barre because they wanted the Berbera base facilities. In Latin America Washington's interventions were more overtly imperialist – controlling its 'backyard' – though the communist threat (in Cuba, or Nicaragua or Grenada) always provided the *raison d'être*. In Asia, following the traumatic defeat in Vietnam, the United States has adopted a more wary role with no further attempts at direct intervention. The fact that the Cold War is over is unlikely to mean that American interventions will change much in terms of objective – safeguarding, in one way or another, US interests – even if the removal of the Soviet superpower rival now means there is no one to offer any countervailing restraint.

In 1991 President Bush indicated that he wanted a revitalised United Nations to act as the centre of his 'New World Order'; this came as a major surprise in the G-7's London communiqué because throughout the Reagan years the United States had either ignored the United Nations or treated it with contempt and Washington had withdrawn virtually all its funding from the world body in 1986. It was the collapse of the USSR which had been able to sustain a coalition of non-aligned states against US dominance that made the United Nations attractive again as an instrument for US policy; any US intervention backed by the United Nations would be able to avoid accusations of big power bullying or neo-colonialism and enjoy legitimacy instead. Thus, following the liberation of Kuwait, President Bush was able to say: 'This is a victory for the United Nations, for all mankind, for the rule of law and for what is right.'[2] Just over a year later President Bush offered to put US military resources at the disposal of the United Nations for peace-keeping operations. Speaking to the General Assembly he said: 'I want to draw on our extensive experience in winning wars and keeping the peace to support UN peace-keeping,' and he went on to say that he had ordered the US Defense Department to place 'a new emphasis on peace-keeping' which he described 'as a mission for the United States military'. However, the President did not make any

commitment to assign troops to a standby UN fighting force;
nor did he offer to pay the arrears of American dues of $757mn.
In the same speech, and much more ominously, President Bush
tackled the question of foreign aid, saying that 'the notion of
the handout to less-developed countries' should be abolished
and replaced by policies which promoted the private sector and
the free market in developing countries. Much of this speech
was aimed at the US electorate in an election year and as one
commentator noted 'The Bush speech was simply Bill Clinton's
foreign policy by another name.'[3] For the South, however, it
did not matter whether the sentiments were those of Republican Bush or Democrat Clinton: they amounted to the same
thing – a new American approach to both the United Nations
and the South.

Aid, supported by the humanitarian lobby, changed its
nature during the 1980s to become the harbinger of the
North's new policeman role. World Bank and IMF insistence
upon conditionalities, donor insistence upon an IMF 'seal of
approval' before providing new aid, the sudden adoption of the
new morality by the North as it has come increasingly to tie aid
to political and human rights performances between them add
up to a powerful coercive weapon in the hands of the North:
'act as we dictate or forgo aid'. Except, of course, for
humanitarian aid: governments which are now threatening to
withhold aid until a recipient government reforms nonetheless
say they except humanitarian aid and in hard political terms
there are very good reasons for making such an exception. In
the first place donors need to placate their powerful humanitarian lobbies; in the second place they need to ensure that a
foothold of influence is maintained in the recipient country
even when it is being disciplined. Aid may thus be seen as the
'soft arm' of the North's new policing policy. In any case, by
the beginning of the 1990s the sheer volume of organisations –
both government and private – concerned with aid in all its
forms added up to a formidable establishment in the North; 40
years of aid-giving has created a major vested interest and
growth industry of experts and university departments and aid

lobbies and non-government organisations (NGOs) that have no intention of relinquishing their interests in the South. In the changing climate of the 1990s they are likely to provide the North with an insidious fifth column in the South whose business, whatever their original motives, will be to stay there and ensure an ongoing presence of influence.

The new imperialism or, perhaps, the old imperialism in a new guise, has come increasingly into the open since the end of the Cold War. In August 1991, for example, Britain's Foreign Secretary, Douglas Hurd, suggested that the British government's desire to link overseas aid with good government ought to be discussed at the forthcoming Commonwealth summit to be held in Harare, Zimbabwe, later in the year. He had also written to Jacques Delors, the president of the European Commission, making similar suggestions about EC aid. At the same time the Minister for Overseas Development, Lynda Chalker, said: 'Many people who understand the economic and moral case for development aid became profoundly disillusioned during the 1960s and 1970s. They were rightly repelled by taxpayers' money being spent to reinforce brutish and self-serving regimes.' She followed this hard statement with what was becoming almost *de rigueur* in such speeches when she added: 'It would be quite wrong to punish those existing on the very edge of survival for the failings of their governments.'[4] Subsequently, Lynda Chalker made another contribution to the new morality in an article in The *Sunday Times*: 'I hope the Harare [Commonwealth] meeting will focus on how we can work together on a new "good government" agenda rather than re-running the battles of the past. For 20 years, smart opinion dubbed any criticism by Western countries of the political systems of developing countries as "neocolonialism". Like much of the conventional wisdom of the period, this was claptrap.' Clearly the new conventional wisdom was to be maximum interference.

When Prime Minister John Major attended the Harare Commonwealth summit in October 1991 he scored a diplomatic success by having a British declaration on promoting

democratic government and human rights in the Commonwealth accepted by the summit although Britain's favourite
phrase 'good governance' was deleted from the declaration.
This declaration, however, was unaccompanied by any mechanisms to enforce its precepts; these, if they come at all, will
be applied by the aid donors in the Commonwealth, which
means primarily Britain. In essence it was an exercise in big
power diplomacy in the one area where British economic
strength gives her a major role to play.

The desire of the old colonial powers along with the United
States to launch a new era of disciplining the South gathered
momentum during 1992 so that at the end of the year Mr Willy
Claes, the Foreign Minister of Belgium, announced that his
government was considering all options to try to resolve the
chronic political crisis in Zaire, its former colony, including
military intervention. The chaos Belgium left behind in 1960
when the Congo became independent was hardly a recom-
mendation for any intervention by Belgium in 1992 whether
military or otherwise but the suggestion was accepted almost as
though it was reasonable. North–South relations had indeed
come full circle.

In its increasing determination to dominate the South the
North has been canvassing a number of different approaches.
Britain's Foreign Secretary, Douglas Hurd, who clearly
hankers after an earlier age, suggested in September 1992
that the UN should adopt an 'imperial role', an unfortunate
phrase to say the least but one that acurately enough reflected
thinking among the politicians of the North. Mr Hurd talked of
'putting blue on the map'.[5] The UN Secretary-General, Mr
Boutros Boutros-Ghali, though not using such language, was
pushing the idea of a UN 'foreign legion' of standby forces able
to be moved at 48 hours' notice to prevent international
explosions taking place. But many in the South viewed
statements such as that by Hurd with misgivings, seeing the
UN Security Council as being under the control of the western
big three – the United States, Britain and France – while the
South is increasingly marginalised. What must give the South

further cause for suspicion is the fact that the major powers in the North who suggest a greater role for the United Nations do not at the same time argue for more power or offer more money so that it can actually carry out efficiently the functions they so readily put upon it. The possibility that the North will institute a new age of 'imperialism' – that is, constant interference and policing in the South – is considerable and growing at the present time. All the prevailing political circumstances make this new approach to the world's problems increasingly attractive: poverty and aid dependence, civil wars and other conflicts on the one hand; and the collapse of Soviet power and end of the Cold War on the other. At no time since the beginning of the 1960s when the end of the European empires at last seemed a permanent fact has the independence of the South – or at least large areas of it – been so much at risk.

At least some of this new fervour to police the South might be more readily accepted if the North refused as a matter of policy and principle to arm warring factions in the South; instead, the major powers compete ruthlessly to sell all the arms they possibly can, ensuring among other results the ongoing indebtedness of many developing countries. In its *World Development Report* of 1991 the World Bank floated the idea of a lending embargo against countries that spend too much on arms, although the idea is unlikely to attract much real support from the principal arms exporting nations which always find justifications for selling arms no matter who the recipient may be. The Bank asks: 'Aid and finance agencies are entitled to ask whether it makes sense to help governments whose first priority is not to develop but to add to their military strength.'[6] Plenty of countries fall into such a category: Iraq, Angola, Chad, North Korea, Uganda and Zaire, for example, spend more on the military than on education and health combined. In 1991 military spending had reached a global figure of $1,000bn of which $170bn was spent by the developing world. Moreover, in the period since 1949 all but 11,000 out of more than 19mn war deaths had occurred in developing countries. A meeting of international aid agencies at Atlanta, Georgia, in December

1992 concluded that most efforts to develop Third World countries would remain ineffective unless the rich nations stopped selling and supplying them with arms. Such a conclusion was hardly sensational; the chances of arms control working when offset against the huge profits involved are not great. In 1992 the arms business was the largest and most profitable activity in the world (followed by the international drugs trade).

Even so, periodic attempts are made to limit the trade. At the end of August 1992 a new foreign affairs think-tank, Safer-world, called on Britain to use its presidency of the EC to restrict the international arms trade; it published an eight-point code of conduct which stated that arms should not be sold to any country or group at war unless it is recognised by the United Nations as defending itself against aggression; to any party which refuses international mediation; to countries which threaten the security of their own people; to sponsors of international terrorism; and to countries which re-export to third countries in violation of end-user certificates.[7] This formidable list of prohibitions, if put into effect, would halt half the arms sales world-wide. Nonetheless, in September 1992 the European parliament adopted a resolution calling for an EC code of conduct on arms exports though there was little possibility that the resolution would be adopted. The one area where the North will take action to limit the sale and spread of arms is in the nuclear field: not for moral reasons but because nuclear proliferation represents a threat to the interests of the North which far outweighs the commercial advantages of spreading and selling such know-how. Thus, in 1991 President Bush tried to persuade India and Pakistan to dismantle their nuclear weapons programmes, but without success. However, as always in the arms business, political considerations complicate what otherwise might seem straightforward. Thus, in November 1992 the International Atomic Energy Agency (IAEA) in Vienna told the United States not to use its power to isolate or destabilise Iran. It told Washington either to produce proof that Iran was making an atomic bomb or to stop pressuring Teheran. The Agency had suddenly moved into the limelight as the instrument to spearhead efforts to contain nuclear proliferation. Iran is believed to be spending about $800mn a year outside its conventional military budget and there is western concern that it may obtain the help of scientists from the former soviet republics.[8] The West, meanwhile, has tried to tighten controls on the export of nuclear technology. Given that apart from the major nuclear powers at least a dozen countries in the world, including Israel, are believed to have nuclear capacity the American concern with Iran was seen as being at least as much to do with demonising a fundamentalist state generally seen as antithetical to the West than about limiting its nuclear capacity. And while the United States was concerned about Iran's nuclear arms programme – real or imagined – a scandal surfaced in Britain about a company that had breached the government's embargo on arms sales to Iran and had done so with the connivance of the Ministry of Defence. The company, Allivane, was involved in a complex international operation to circumvent trade restrictions so that arms could be exported to Iran and Iraq. Both the Ministry of Defence (MoD) and the Department of Trade and Industry (DTI) appear to have connived at this and other companies breaking the embargo on arms to Iran and Iraq. A sufficient number of revelations about arms embargo evasions in Britain led Sir Anthony Parsons (a former British ambassador to the United Nations) to call for a UN Security Council veto on arms sales to the Middle East even as the Labour opposition called for an investigation into the roles of the MoD and DTI in British arms embargo evasions.[9] In August 1992 a report by the think-tank Saferworld accused Britain and the United States of fuelling a Middle East arms race, and that between £18bn and £23bn worth of arms had been sold to the Gulf states since Iraq invaded Kuwait in August 1990. No major arms producing country is going to hold back when money on this scale is on offer while governments as a matter of policy turn a blind eye to arms embargo evasions because of the value of the sales and because, as they always argue, if their country does not obtain the sales a rival country will do so. But while the possibility of a general embargo on arms sales to the South is unrealistic simply because the trade is too lucrative, particular countries may well be selected to suffer embargos because their behaviour is deemed antithetical to western interests. Thus, in November 1992 the United States called a meeting of the G-7 in order to persuade the richest nations to resist arms orders from Iran, a major bogeyman for Washington. As an official reported: 'There is a common appreciation that Iran is an unpredictable and possibly threatening power. . . and a common assessment of the need to watch closely arms deliveries to Iran. Where opinions differ is over supplies of equipment which could be civilian as well as military.'[10] It was on the question of equipment which could have both civilian and military use that British companies such as Matrix-Churchill argued for export licences even though they must have known that the equipment was intended for military use. The hypocrisy surrounding the arms business is monumental. President Bush promised to make the Gulf region secure in the aftermath of Kuwait's liberation; the United States then sold $17bn worth of arms to Saudi Arabia and a total of $28.5bn worth of arms to the region as a whole. Iran, castigated by Washington, was busy over the same period acquiring arms from Russia, North Korea and China. As a matter of policy the United States may stop or at least curtail sales of arms to a particular country but the overall arms business is so important to the economies of the rich nations that no moral considerations or concepts of policing the South and maintaining peace will be allowed to interfere with the trade as a whole. Britain appears to be one of the most dishonest of all the major arms selling powers; revelations at the end of 1992 showed how Britain secretly collaborated with the Pinochet regime in Chile to sell arms to Iraq through the offices of a Chilean company in London, Cardoen International Marketing SA (Cimsa).

Justifications for such murky activities are always forthcoming: that despite official embargoes Iran is a major regional power and needs to be courted for the future; that if Britain or France or another power does not supply the arms someone else will do so anyway and it would therefore be absurd to lose a profitable market; and so on. If the North is serious about policing the South it should halt all arms sales; of course it will do nothing of the sort. Instead, periodically and discriminately depending upon the interests involved, it will intervene in a country which has become awash with arms as the United States decided to do in Somalia. The Somali case, indeed, is likely to provide a good many lessons for the future.

Early in December 1992 some 28,000 American troops were landed in Somalia in what was described as 'Operation Restore Hope'; their object, according to a White House spokesman, Marlin Fitzwater, was to support the UN peace-keeping efforts and help create a new government. A portion of the group would remain as part of the continuing UN peace-keeping force to be joined by others. The purpose of keeping American forces in Somalia after humanitarian relief routes had been secured would, according to Mr Fitzwater, be to maintain: 'the control or the law and order that is established by virtue of the initial thrust and providing a climate where, hopefully, the UN can be working with whoever they can – other countries as well as the factions there – in terms of political settlement'.[11] That statement was sufficiently vague as to suggest that the Americans themselves did not know what they intended to achieve; nor did the spokesman dispel the impression that the United States might subsequently seek to influence the long-term political reconstruction of the country. The original suggestion by President Bush that a US force could go into Somalia in December and be out by 20 January simply did not make any kind of military or relief sense in a country where the ongoing civil war had resulted in anarchy and famine and an estimated 500,000 deaths. France, which had already deployed a small force under UN auspices, managed nonetheless to achieve a high profile and joined with the United States in trying to engineer a meeting between the leaders of the two main warring factions led by General

Mohamed Farah Aideed and interim president Ali Mahdi Mohamed. The potential pitfalls of policing operations were highlighted by a senior Somali source close to General Aideed who confirmed that the Americans, who had equipped the Siyad Barre government with $600mn of military supplies, were determined not to allow France to steal the negotiating initiative. At the beginning of the US operation sharp differences of opinion emerged with the United Nations which warned that a 'quick fix' operation by the Americans could make matters worse for the starving. The United States began by declaring it had no intention of disarming the warring clans and that its troops would only be sent to the most troublesome spots such as Mogadishu, Bardera and Baidoa. And a pattern which had emerged in the Gulf reappeared, with the United States seeking contributions to the cost of its operation from Britain, Japan, Germany and other countries. As one diplomat pointed out: 'The US does not see its mandate as stabilising the country by removing arms, and since the UN is not paying for the operation or running it in any meaningful way there is little it can do about it.'[12] Thus the seeds of a bitter US–UN row were sown right at the beginning with the United Nations demanding a long-term stay by the Americans if anything worthwhile was to be achieved and the United States clearly not certain at the beginning just what it had come to do.

A Somali aid worker voiced local doubts when he said: 'The general feeling is that the Americans will be welcome but I am unsure about their overall objective. Why are they coming only now? If the scheme works Mr Bush goes out looking good and America gets nice pictures of starving kids being fed at Christmas. If it doesn't work, Mr Clinton inherits a problem.'[13] There was, in any case, something grotesque about the American troops landing in Somalia to be greeted by hordes of reporters tipped off by Washington so that they walked up the beaches straight into the glare of television lights and popping cameras. No matter what disaster is occurring in the South or what the world is doing about it the media is likely to be there in force.

As the Americans rapidly discovered, the problem of policing Somalia was infinitely more complex than the quick media-conscious fix that Washington had seemed to imagine would take place. There were the independent agencies who feared a 'shoot-to-feed' policy and had to be placated or otherwise managed. There was the question of choice between escorting a convoy of supplies to a given destination and then leaving it (in which case armed gangs at once appeared to plunder the food) or staying to supervise the distribution of food and seeing that those who received it could actually eat it. There was the problem of disarming the clan gangs. Before the Americans arrived aid agencies operating in Somalia said that imposing troops on the country would be a disaster and the British government said it would not support the militarisation of food aid. As the Americans soon found, the role of peace-keepers can quickly escalate into that of peace-enforcers but in a country of countless small clans and groups the enemy is almost impossible to pinpoint and groups can melt into the bush at will. On the eve of the US landing in Somalia when for all practical purposes the American commander had overall control of the UN operation the US Defence Secretary, Dick Cheney, went on record saying: 'We are not going to wait for people to shoot at us.'[14] Once shooting takes place acceptance of the American presence would be likely to evaporate very quickly. Contradictory statements from American politicians and military demonstrated how little thought had gone into the operation. Shortly after landing, while American Cobras swooped above General Aideed's house in Mogadishu in an apparent show of strength, US Marine Colonel Ted Peck said: 'We have no plans to go into any of the towns and become an occupying force. We are not going to do any street searches or house-to-house searches.' Yet, as a Somali said when the Americans arrived: 'If this had happened six months ago, 30,000 lives could have been saved.'[15]

Three days after the American landing the two principal Somali warlords, Ali Mahdi Mohamed and General Mohamed Farah Aideed, agreed under US pressure to talk peace and

General Aideed said: 'We ask the Americans and the United Nations to disarm the Somali people because if you do not disarm, peace will not come back to this country.'[16] Three weeks after the American arrival it was plain Somali expectations that peace would follow had not been met. At the United Nations Secretary-General Boutros-Ghali called for a wider and longer involvement of US troops which would include disarming the warlords and gangs. And in classic colonial style an outraged Marine colonel said: 'We are not going to let planeloads of khat [the essential drug for all Somalis] come into Mogadishu and if that isn't exactly the letter of the law well so be it.' The Americans, it might be said, were getting dug into their new colonial task and inevitably in the process they found themselves increasingly at odds with both the Somalis they had come to feed, and especially the Fundamentalists who did not want them there at all, and the United Nations in whose name they were acting. Ten days after the Americans had landed in Somalia, adding to the surreal colonial aspect of the entire operation, Chancellor Helmut Kohl of Germany announced his intention of despatching German troops to assist in the relief operation: 'This is hugely important for Germany's image in the world', he said, 'Germany cannot stand on the sidelines.'[17]

It was soon possible to see the American policing operation in Somalia as a test case: if it worked perhaps the United States would graduate to more difficult interventions, possibly in Bosnia. If it did not work they might think again. Clearly the outcome of 'Operation Restore Hope' would have a crucial bearing upon future American interventions. Already by Christmas one aspect of the operation was, sadly, to spread the violence and looting; as the Americans moved into an area the armed gangs simply withdrew taking their operations elsewhere in the country. And though, as was to be expected, the Americans were drawn inexorably into the business of disarming the gangs many of these crossed over into Ethiopia to regroup and wait for the Americans to go. In fact there is only one way for an external force to solve the kind of problem presented by Somalia: effective occupation of the entire country with enough forces to hold it down followed by systematic disarming of the population. The old imperial powers knew this, as did those they came to police. In 1882 the British occupied Egypt in a 'policing exercise' and insisted that their stay was to be temporary; 40 years later in 1922 an Egyptian wag pointed out that on no less than 78 occasions during the intervening years the British had stated their intention of leaving. 'When', he asked, 'are you actually going to go?' Not until the trauma of the Suez debacle in 1956 did the British finally give up their pretentions to police Egypt.

The question of policing became increasingly more urgent as the crisis in Bosnia developed during 1992. Official policy of the main European powers and the United States was to make it appear that their governments were doing something, by backing UN observer forces and humanitarian convoys, as the unfolding horror of the civil war became daily more apparent, while evading the real question: that only full-scale military intervention could prevent the devastation of the civil war. But there was no common policy. Britain does not see the Balkans as a vital issue, the United States is unwilling to commit itself in notoriously difficult terrain, Germany shies away from any military commitment and France objects to an independent NATO role while in the background hovers the uneasy thought that at some point Russia might back her traditional allies, the Serbs. Rescuing the Bosnian Moslems (or failing to do so) is a fraught political task but its evasion is likely to cause even greater damage to the North's image than would some form of military intervention. However, at the very end of 1992 President Bush, who in both Somalia and Bosnia was burnishing his image before final political departure from office, sent a letter to Serbian President, Slobodan Milosevic, in which he said that in the event of: 'any military action in the Kosovo caused by Serbian action, the United States will be prepared to employ military force against the Serbians in the Kosovo and in Serbia proper'.[18] Slowly but surely the West was brought closer to contemplating full military intervention in the former Yugoslavia as a less dangerous course than inaction.

The shooting of the Bosnian deputy prime minister, Hakija Turaljic, by a Serbian soldier while he was actually in a UN vehicle (9 January 1993) demonstrated the ineffectiveness of the United Nations in Bosnia; still more did it illustrate the dangers of indecisiveness. Either the West (whether the United States, the EC, NATO or a combination of the three) should intervene in the Balkans and stop the slaughter or it should put a ring fence round the area and leave it alone. Policing to make any sense has to be effective and that means the deployment of overwhelming force. As yet the West, which really means the United States, has not made up its mind on this score and may only do so when its success or failure in Somalia has become a matter of record, but by then it may well be too late for the Balkans.

A study for the Pentagon conducted by the Rand Corporation suggests that threats to US interests from the Third World are now seen by the American military as their principal preoccupation and both the US air force and navy see the post-Cold War world as one dominated by small wars throughout the Third World which threaten US interests. The United States is developing new tactics to deal with North–South confrontations and with the disappearance of the Soviet threat the new approach appears to be one that says that the United States and its allies must be prepared to maintain their wealth by force in a world of increasing pressures upon the environment and its resources.

13 The United Nations Alternative

During the 1980s the United Nations touched the nadir of its fortunes: the big powers treated it with indifference and sometimes contempt while the United States and others withheld the bulk of their dues; corruption scandals from the Waldheim years and an overpaid bureaucracy whose greed for place and money far outdid its competence in performance tarnished its image; and its inability to resolve problems because the permanent members of the Security Council would not provide it with the means or authority to do so threatened to destroy it in much the same way as its predecessor, the League of Nations, had been destroyed. In 1985 the fact that the United Nations was still in being to celebrate 40 years of existence was itself seen as something of a triumph. Then came the end of the Cold War and the United Nations was fashionable again. The constant threat of a Soviet or Western veto was removed and President Bush suddenly saw the world body as a useful ally in promoting American global policies. By 1989 the United Nations had a presence in Nicaragua where its mandate was to ensure fair elections in February 1990, and a military mission in Central America to monitor the commitment of those countries not to aid the 11,000 Nicaraguan Contra rebels; in Namibia (1989–90) it achieved one of its few but well-deserved triumphs after many painstaking years when it deployed 4,650 troops to supervise elections that would bring an end to South African control and usher in a black government to lead the country to independence on 21 March 1990. The UN force in Namibia was the largest to be deployed since the Congo crisis of 1960–4. Also in 1989 a UN fact-finding mission went to Cambodia to examine the possibility of the United Nations monitoring elections there.

189

The UN role expanded again during 1990 at a time of unparalleled cooperation between the United States and the USSR with the Gulf crisis taking centre stage. Cambodia was placed under a UN Transitional Authority including a military force of 16,000 men for a year until elections under its auspices could be held while in Nicaragua the UN monitors were able to pronounce the elections free and fair. During 1991 the Gulf War and its aftermath, and the civil wars in Angola, El Salvador, Cambodia and Yugoslavia each required and obtained a growing commitment from United Nations. By the beginning of 1992 when the new Secretary-General, Boutros Boutros-Ghali (who could claim the distinction of being both the first African and first Arab in the post) took over from Javier Perez de Cuellar, the prospects for the United Nations at last fulfilling the role for which it had been created looked brighter than at any time since the commencement of the Cold War. But then the strains began to tell.

There had always been a conflict of interest in the United Nations between the big powers on the one hand and the newly enfranchised states of what came to be called the Third World on the other. In any case, the world of 1945 was a very different place from what it had become at the beginning of the 1990s: only 51 nations made up the United Nations at its inception whereas by 1992 there were 166 members and the great majority of these belonged to the Third World. The big powers always regarded the United Nations as an instrument which they could control and use as and when it suited them to maintain the status quo which they dominated. The countries of the Third World, however, early recognised the value to them of the United Nations and proceeded to manipulate its structures for all they were worth despite big power attempts to downgrade the world body whenever it failed to work to their advantage. During the Cold War, when the permanent members of the Security Council were prepared to block UN measures by using their vetoes, the Third World countries nonetheless discovered how persistent lobbying could produce results in their favour. Now that the Cold War is over the prime question for Third World members is whether such lobbying can still produce results when the United Nations is dominated by the United States and the other western powers without benefit of a rival communist bloc to hold the balance. The UN agencies have always been of particular importance to the Third World. These include the financial institutions such as the World Bank and the IMF, the development agencies like UNDP and FAO and those agencies concerned with social and living standards such as the ILO, UNESCO and WHO. As far as the Third World is concerned the problem has always been that while its members had the numbers and the needs the rich minority of nations possessed the wealth required to finance the programmes whose benefits, overwhelmingly, would go to the South. Now, quite suddenly, the United Nations has once more moved centre stage; if it can obtain both the finances and the mandate from the Security Council to operate with genuine independence (and not be constantly circumscribed by big power interests and jealousies) then it represents the best hope for the Third World in what in any case is going to be a particularly turbulent era.

The dilemma in which the world body is likely to find itself for the balance of the century was aptly illustrated by the Gulf crisis precipitated by Iraq's invasion of Kuwait on 2 August 1990. The alliance formed to force Saddam Hussein out of Kuwait was an American achievement: it was made possible, it is true, by the acquiescence of the USSR which would have been inconceivable a few years earlier and it was given legitimacy by the United Nations which, after a decade of appalling difficulties, saw and grasped the chance to move centre stage again. But the subsequent story of Iraq and the United Nations has simply served to demonstrate how weak the organisation remains. Iraq's defiance of the United Nations over the issue of the Marsh Arabs, over its refusal to sell oil under UN terms or its obstruction of UN weapons inspectors has simply highlighted the fact that only if and when the big powers – in this case the United States – insist can something actually be accomplished. Thus, in August 1992 the United

States, Britain and France did not consult the United Nations before declaring a 'no fly' zone over southern Iraq and in fact there is no UN resolution authorising such action. The point is that the United Nations remains both dependent upon the big powers and their prisoner: it is dependent upon them (quite apart from the authority they exercise in the Security Council) because only they have the capacity in terms of either money or troops to apply the financial or military sanctions needed to force Saddam Hussein (or any other recalcitrant ruler) into line; and it is their prisoner in the sense that they control the Security Council and ultimately make the decisions about intervention or non-intervention. These decisions, moreover, are not made in a detached sense of determining what is good for world peace and then acting accordingly; but in terms of what suits the self-interest of the big powers.

The civil war in Somalia went on for more than a year before it attracted UN intervention and though this was subsequently subject to many criticisms it was Boutros-Ghali's accusation that the West was blind to war and starvation in Somalia as opposed to Yugoslavia (the rich man's war) which finally produced action. But if he can take credit for that the UN performance in Somalia thereafter was abysmally weak and its very hesitations led to the American offer to send 28,000 troops to protect the delivery of food, which it did in December 1992. With unconscious irony a western relief worker in Mogadishu put his finger on the problem when he said: 'While they are talking in New York, children here are dying. If the US can move, why can't the UN?'[1] The short answer to that criticism is simply that the United States is a single state whose President and Congress can take a decision and act upon it; the United Nations is the sum of all its squabbling parts.

In August 1992 the United Nations Security Council authorised the use of force, if necessary, to ensure the delivery of humanitarian aid to the starving and besieged in Bosnia-Herzegovina. That resolution went through because the major western powers were slowly coming to accept the need to intervene, and if force is used in the former Yugoslavia only the western powers have the capacity to deploy what would be required. By January 1993, after a year of western agonising, the question of whether or not to intervene in order to stop the fighting in Bosnia had moved much closer to being answered with a 'yes' on the grounds that this, as opposed to standing by and doing nothing except send in humanitarian aid, would be the lesser evil. Hesitations about intervention are more than justified by history: when big powers do intervene, for whatever reasons, it is rare that the end state is any better than the one which prompted the intervention in the first place. Intervention in a civil war should not be undertaken lightly: if it appears that the fighting can be confined to the country of origin outsiders would do well to remain outside; on the other hand, if it seems probable that the civil war will spread to involve neighbouring countries then there is a case for intervention in order to contain what otherwise might become a general conflagration. That, heartless as it may seem, should form the basic guideline for UN interventions. Since the war in what was Yugoslavia shows every possibility of spreading to involve Albania, Greece, Bulgaria, Hungary and Turkey with Russian support for the Serbs and Islamic support for the Bosnian Moslems also likely to come at a later stage, a powerful case can be made for massive intervention before this happens. Thus, the disintegration of Yugoslavia ought to be a principal concern of the United Nations since keeping the peace was the reason for the creation of the world body in the first place. Unfortunately, it has spent its entire existence keeping the peace between the superpowers and is not geared to solving smaller, regional conflicts. These, however, are likely to be the main questions it will face for the balance of the century and it should start looking seriously at the creation of regional structures. During the Cold War Washington and Moscow acted as global stabilisers. The world now expects the United Nations to fill this role but it will be able to do so only if it is given far greater authority and resources than it enjoys at present; however, the sheer extent of western disarray over the Balkans issue does not make this seem very likely.

Moreover, despite the readiness of governments and aid agencies alike to criticise UN performance in the field this does not prevent them from constantly calling upon it to undertake further tasks. During 1992 the South African government and the ANC agreed to allow UN observers to be stationed at flashpoints and to the appointment of a special envoy, Cyrus Vance. A month later when the ANC march on the black homeland of the Ciskei led to bloodshed in which 200 people were wounded and 28 killed there was still no UN presence in South Africa and complaints were duly forthcoming that it was too slow and cautious in taking on responsibilities, the accusation which had also been advanced in relation to Somalia and Yugoslavia. Yet in December 1992, despite the range of its burdens and its continuing financial crisis, the Secretary-General, Boutros-Ghali, nonetheless proposed the establishment of a big new peace-keeping operation in Mozambique to monitor the agreement which had been signed in Rome the previous October ending the civil war in that country. This would involve a UN peacekeeping force of about 7,500 troops, police and civilians. There is thus an expectation that the United Nations will somehow be able to undertake any new commitment which is put to it.

The growing number of crises arising in the wake of the Cold War and the insistent demands made for action will almost certainly force the United Nations to change the ground rules which cover intervention. In the first place, it has to take into account the new American hegemony which has replaced the Cold War balance; instead of the United States sulking in its tent and virtually boycotting the United Nations it is now calling for actions which it proposes to lead. Second, following the mass move of Kurds into the mountains of northern Iraq in the spring of 1991 and the establishment of 'safe havens' from Saddam Hussein's forces, the United Nations discovered that, *de facto*, it had intervened for the first time in the affairs of a member state without its consent. This signalled a significant turning point, which growing involvement in the former Yugoslavia later emphasised, as the beginning of a new phase in the history of the United Nations. Bernard Kouchner, the French secretary of state for humanitarian action, was able to say in relation to the Kurdish development: 'We are entering the twenty-first century, when it will no longer be possible to exterminate in the shadow of national boundaries.'[2] The disintegration of Yugoslavia and the USSR has created about 20 new states, most of them beset by problems of minority rights which sooner or later could involve the United Nations. Yet, even as it is expected to undertake an ever-increasing burden of commitments, the United Nations faces growing debts and a peace-keeping bill that reached $220mn a month at the end of 1992. Boutros-Ghali unveiled his own Agenda for Peace in June 1992 but found little support for his reforms in the Security Council apart from France and faced two kinds of opposition to any reforms: his own, bloated UN bureaucracy is likely to fight fiercely to protect its position against any moves either to slim it down or make it more efficient; while the Security Council is seen to be out of tune with the needs of the great majority of members in the General Assembly as the old Cold War is replaced by a new North–South divide with the major western powers who control the Security Council representing the rich minority in what may turn into an even more damaging world confrontation than that between East and West.

The basic problem is the grip exercised by the Security Council which alone has the power to decide what actions the United Nations will take. Created in the closing days of World War II and delicately geared to ensure that a suspicious USSR would join the organisation, the UN Security Council has become ossified in the mechanisms that operated throughout the Cold War while at least two of its permanent members, Britain and France, should no longer be on it; not at least if Japan, Germany and India are excluded. But Britain and France will support domination of the system by the United States in return for their own continued Security Council status and possession of the veto which gives them more influence than their real power warrants. That is the kind of self-interest the Secretary-General must contend with and the likelihood of Britain and France voting themselves off the Security Council in an act of statemanship designed to make the United Nations more truly representative of the world in which we live seems remote. In broad terms, the Security Council takes action when a particular crisis embarrasses the interests of one or more of its members, which is why it was moved to act over the Kurds (though only following domestic criticisms of government cynicism), and over Yugoslavia which threatens the peace of Europe, but ignored Somalia (until the Secretary-General shamed the big powers into activity by his famous remark) which did not. At the same time the international community is ready enough to dump any problem on the United Nations and claim that it alone has authority.

One of the most respected men to have worked in the United Nations, Britain's former Under-Secretary-General Sir Brian Urquhart, claims that Boutros-Ghali's new blueprint, Agenda for Peace, represents a very good programme; in particular its concept of peace-enforcement units drawn from standing national armies to be available to the UN on 48 hours' notice and his call for regional organisations to play a stronger role so as to lighten the UN burden. As Sir Brian Urquhart said: 'The Security Council should take much more trouble to consult the other members. Sooner or later they also have to address the problem of permanent membership. They don't want to, because nobody has an answer.'[3] Sir Brian was being diplomatic; he should have said 'they don't want to because the obvious answers are anathema to the present members'. Other problems facing the United Nations concern its reading of international law: the brutalities of ethnic cleansing in former Yugoslavia or the Iraqi genocide activities against the Kurds or the endless slaughter in Somalia add up to gross violations of international law yet it is far from clear whether international law permits interventions to prevent such violations. Up to the present time the United Nations has only become involved in internal conflicts when invited to do so by the government of the state concerned. This now appears to be changing. Thus

Security Council Resolution 688 condemned 'the repression of the Iraqi civilian population in many parts of Iraq . . . the consequences of which threaten international peace and security'.[4] When Iraq ignored this resolution Britain, the United States and other members of the coalition deployed forces in northern Iraq. Then, in August 1992, the same countries established a 'no fly' zone over southern Iraq to protect the Shia population with Britain defending the action on the grounds that 'international law recognises extreme humanitarian need'. France, meanwhile, called for a new recognition of the right of humanitarian 'interference'. As Britain's Foreign Secretry, Douglas Hurd, said in this context: 'Not every action that a British government or an American government or a French government takes has to be underwritten by a specific provision in a UN resolution, provided we comply with international law.'[5] It is one thing for the big powers to take such a line when they are involved in a crisis that, nonetheless, comes under an overall UN mandate for intervention; the basic issue, however, is one of control, and the United Nations should be provided with the capability of acting as the world's policeman in place of the powers merely obtaining UN approval to act as policemen themselves. Only if the big powers are prepared to trust the Secretary-General with far greater authority than at present will the United Nations be able to perform the roles which are now being thrust upon it. The Secretary-General, therefore, must carry the major powers with him. But in the summer of 1992 this looked far from certain. Boutros-Ghali, for example, spoke of 'turning the Security Council', a phrase which was interpreted as meaning the five permanent members who regard the United Nations as their own property; what the new Secretary-General tried to do in his first year was emphasise how the United Nations was an entity in its own right rather than an instrument of the big powers, an approach which ought to be welcomed by the great majority of its members though one that is clearly resented by the big powers. An unseemly row then erupted between Britain and Boutros-Ghali who claimed he had come under particular criticism in the British press and suggested that it was 'maybe because I am a wog'. The British Foreign Secretary then said publicly that 'I think he is going to be a very effective Secretary-General', although he went on to say 'The Secretary-General . . . finds that the queue of trouble outside his door grows all the time.'[6] It was clear from these and other exchanges that substantial antagonism had been generated between Boutros-Ghali and Britain which was hardly an auspicious prelude to reforms. The row highlighted the need to reform and reshape the Security Council and it is possible that British antagonism to the new Secretary-General arose precisely because he was seen to challenge – in his desire to reform the organisation – Britain's continued place as a permanent member of the Security Council. With the passing of the Cold War the need for the veto has also passed and the Security Council should become more representative; the five permanent members should relinquish their veto powers and acknowledge that modern problems require solutions based upon consensus. A permanent membership of the Security Council, without vetoes, would be far more representative of the world in which we now live if it consisted of the United States, Brazil, the EC, Nigeria, Russia, China, India and Japan. If something along these lines is not attempted in the near future the United Nations is in danger of being destroyed by big power quarrels much as was the League of Nations.

As Boutros-Ghali described his problem in 1992, the United Nations faced a 'crisis of too much credibility': 'In the Cold War', he argued, 'the problem of the UN was in maintaining any credibility at all. Now that the Cold War is over, the problem is that we have too much credibility. People expect us to be supermen.'[7] As a result the world was piling tasks upon the organisation but failing to pay the increased costs. In the four-year period 1989–92 the United Nations had undertaken more peace-keeping than in the previous 40 years of its existence and by the middle of the latter year was maintaining 12 peace-keeping operations round the world at an annual cost of about $3bn. The early post-Cold War hope that the major powers would finally give the United Nations the authority it had always been supposed to have was briefly encouraged by the events of the Gulf War when President Bush said the United States would act as a global policeman with the authority of the United Nations. In the two years that followed Iraq's withdrawal from Kuwait, however, these hopes were largely dashed: the disintegration of the USSR and the growth of mistrust among the powers and their reactions to the escalating problems of the post-Cold War world were more reminiscent of the pre-1914 world of great power management than of a new order in which the United Nations could wield real authority. And yet, at the same time, more and more problems have been referred to the United Nations: partly because no one knows what else to do with the problems; partly because no one wants openly to admit that they are unprepared to work through the world body; and partly because it can subsequently be blamed if the problem becomes worse. In today's world an increasing number of problems – such as the international traffic in drugs – require an international response and so, in theory at least, only the United Nations is seen as having both the resources and the legitimacy to override national sovereignty when that is necessary. But such reasoning can only make sense in the wake of real reforms that include a big power willingness to finance the United Nations on a scale appropriate to the problems it is being asked to resolve. The indications, unfortunately, point in the other direction: that the major powers, led by the United States, will not be prepared to give the United Nations the backing it requires and are determined to keep all the decision-making in relation to a world policing role in their own hands.

As an increasing number of people have come to recognise, the Cold War confrontation is now being replaced by a North–South confrontation, and political leaders in the South have not been slow to voice their fears that a new-style imperialism is emerging whose essential object is to police the South for the greater comfort of the North. The United Nations ought to be the champion of the South, a role it often played during the

Cold War, but this now seems less and less likely, for in the absence of Cold War balances the world body may well find that it is wholly at the mercy of American and, more generally, western dictation. Only if the United Nations can be reformed in a way that will not be possible except with the willing agreement of the permanent members of the Security Council will it be able to meet the crisis of too much credibility to which the Secretary-General has referred. Such reforms would include: the restructuring of the Security Council and removal of veto powers; the creation of a UN task force able and authorised to intervene to maintain law and order; and a recognition that there are international laws which are more important than, and override, the integrity of individual states. The alternative is a return to an older 'dog-eat-dog' world of squabbling great powers, dominated by the United States in which the United Nations is used as a principal scapegoat for crises which the powers cannot or will not control. By the beginning of 1993 the latter scenario appeared more likely to become the international norm.

14 The New Imperialism

One of the few absolute certainties in international affairs is the abiding determination of the strong to interfere in the affairs of the weak. The justifications for such interference are endless though fashions change. Straightforward imperialism is not yet back in favour although in a country like Britain, where nostalgia for empire is far from dead, there are not lacking those who look back to a past in which the great powers controlled most of the rest of the world. In the troubled aftermath of the Cold War an increasing number of voices are likely to be raised in favour of a system of world policing that brings law and order to areas of conflict and, for example, the suggestion has already been mooted that some kind of UN mandate should be imposed on Somalia until peace has been restored in that unhappy land and thereafter for a period until it is deemed once more able to rule itself. Imperialism through the agency of the United Nations, as opposed to the big powers of the past, is not as impossible as the history of the world body over its first 45 years might suggest. The aid age is now passing, although there will certainly be more aid on offer, and instead we appear to be on the threshhold of a new missionary age which, like its nineteenth century Christian model, could well be the harbinger of the new imperialism. This time, however, the missionaries are the humanitarians.

The idea of development, which is what aid was supposed to promote, really dominated North–South relations for the 30 years from 1950 to 1980; it was greatly assisted by the Cold War whose rivalries drove both sides to seek allies in the Third World by offering them economic assistance. By the beginning of the 1990s, however, it had become plain that development in its various manifestations had not worked and that a large number of Frantz Fanon's 'wretched of the earth' remained wretched.[1] Over the years the aid 'business' has grown very substantial indeed and in the process has created a self-justifying mechanism. Thus, when one approach to development fails there is a switch to another which, in its turn, is promoted to become the new fashion; when that also fails to produce the required development another switch is made and so on. These changes are presented as the product of sophisticated thought about development problems: 'we are learning from experience' is the justification for the switch but when, after a few years, the new approach has achieved no more than its predecessors the same process is repeated. What no one ever does is question whether development as such or, even more important, development imposed from without can ever work or provide the answer to the problems of poor countries whose economies in any case are being controlled and 'managed' by an ever-larger bureaucracy of international experts. Even the designations keep changing – developing, less-developed, under-developed – but no matter what rhetoric is employed the poor remain poor. Moreover, when it is pointed out (as happens from time to time) that the poor are no better off than they were despite 20 or 30 years of so-called aid-induced development this is never interpreted, as it should be, to suggest that the development process itself is at fault and that development imposed from outside is neither working nor likely to work; instead, with a shrug of understanding at *their* incompetence or corruption or lack of sufficient education or drive the aid lobby resigns itself to the fact that it must battle on for another decade or two before the magic goal of development is achieved.

In the post-war world of the late 1940s the Americans helped Europe back on its feet with the Marshall Plan and President Truman promised to bring an end to 'under-development' in the 'free world'; thereafter aid became the panacea for all the problems of the South (as well as promoting the interests of the North) and in over 30 years we passed through a number of phases: if sufficient aid was provided economic take-off would follow; if a country could feed itself it would be that much easier to promote industrialisation or other developments so 'back-to-the-land' and 'green revolutions' were proclaimed; if the standard of living of the world's poorest 800mn could be raised they would become a new force for development because they would go to market and purchase goods that they could afford for the first time. Basic needs, small is beautiful, import substitution, participation, sustainable development – each new theory had its day, did not – quite – produce the appropriate answers and so was superseded by something else. Always the emphasis was upon economic development for that was the one value the West clearly understood – or thought it did. The end of the Cold War has removed the political need to provide aid; and the growth of the environmental lobby has called in question the endless pursuit of growth since this destroys the environment. The result of these changes must be a search for yet another approach to development. More than half the problems of the South have been created by the North, for the concept of development that has been so assiduously promoted by the North assumes overtly or at any rate implicitly that much of the lifestyle of the South – the countries which need to be developed – is backward, faulty, requires modernisation, is not capable of answering the needs of the people or, in other words, is only semi-civilised. And the moment a poor country accepts aid it also, by implication, accepts this judgement that it is poor and needs to catch up and imitate the lifestyles of the rich donors so that at once an unequal relationship has been created which in the end is the one clear achievement of the aid age.

The large output of books and critiques on aid, the number of universities which have courses and departments that deal with it as an academic subject, the consultancy firms specialising in development, the plethora of experts on the subject, the huge range of non-government agencies (NGOs) concerned with development and disaster whose representatives turn up by the planeload in the wake of every hurricane or flood testify to the importance of aid to the North, where it has long been a growth industry. The minister responsible for aid in Upper Volta (before it changed its name to Burkina Faso) once complained that he had to deal with a different visiting group of aid experts, either government or private, on every day of the year except for four so that he never had time himself to look at his country's problems. Entire government departments in the North are devoted to the subject of aid and both governments and NGOs via with one another to give press conferences and show that they are active in the wake of every disaster, while the publication of the World Bank's or the UNDP's reports has now become an annual event. In the South a number of countries – Bangladesh is an excellent example – have become so dependent upon aid that they have all but lost the practice of doing things for themselves (and it is now many years since those in the aid business actually argued that one of its principal objects was to train the local people – as soon as possible – to take over so as to make the aid worker redundant). And now, quite suddenly, in one of those political changes that sweep away a particular fashion it looks as if the North is really going to cut back aid rather than simply trim aid budgets because of bad times.

Britain and other countries of the North made various pledges of more aid when their leaders attended the Rio Earth Summit in June 1992, yet by October of that year Britain was threatening to scrap its pledges and was leading moves by western countries to cut back on their aid. Various Rio agreements – to tackle global warming and protect the world's threatened biodiversity or the wide-ranging global action programme – each depended upon increased aid from the North and this was promised at the time. However, using the recession as its excuse Britain argued for drastic cutbacks in aid that would not only kill off these Rio commitments but seriously affect existing programmes as well. In Washington during September 1992 Britain, France, Japan and the United States claimed they were unable to meet the new targets. Sweden and Spain, among others, announced aid cuts and it really did appear that a genuine aid fatigue was setting in. If in fact this turns out to be the case, and most political omens point this way, the entire aid business may be facing terminal decline which, the cynics will argue, is not before time. However, the World Bank and other principal agencies concerned with aid represent very big business indeed and will not permit their empires to collapse without a struggle.

It was therefore worthy of particular note, amidst the general North–South distrust that the Rio Summit had generated and the subsequent gloom which followed the North's cuts in aid, that the United Nations Secretary-General, Boutros Boutros-Ghali, published a top-level UN report to show how the number of hungry people in the world is falling despite the appalling picture emerging from Africa and despite the repeated fears of rapid population growth so often voiced in the North. The sub-committee on nutrition of the United Nations 'Cabinet' chaired by the Secretary-General had prepared the report for the heads of 22 UN agencies. The report speaks of a 'turning point in world history', suggests that famine has been 'virtually eradicated' outside Africa and demonstrates that there were 200mn fewer hungry people in 1990 than 15 years earlier and that whereas in 1975 one-third of people in developing countries were hungry, by 1990 the figure had dropped to one-fifth. Speaking at the UN International Conference on Nutrition in Rome, Dr John Mason (one of the authors of the report) said optimistically: 'We seem to have passed the point in history where the earth has the maximum number of underfed people.'[2]

Another up-beat report from the World Bank suggested that the transfer of resources from rich to poor countries increased substantially to more than $56bn in 1992, although this included much higher rates of private investment in Latin America as well as credits to the former USSR. The tenor of the report, that the worst of the debt crisis was over, no doubt came as a comfort to the North. Figures showed that the net transfer of long-term resources jumped from $8.1bn in 1989 to $37.7bn in 1991 to $56.5bn in 1992. The sting was in the tail, however, for the report was also obliged to admit that the overall stock of debt owed by the Third World had grown sharply to $1,703bn in 1992 (up $100bn in a year). In the light of these figures it is difficult to accept the report's contention that the worst of the debt crisis had passed.[3]

Coming at a time of overall gloom which has been fuelled by recession, aid cutbacks and post-Rio suspicions between North and South, the timely appearance of these reports was no doubt designed to show that all was well with the aid business, but they are unlikely to produce many converts. The aid business and the relationship between North and South which it links are in deep trouble.

The NGOs insisting that humanitarian aid must be taken to the starving in war situations, whatever governments may do, have become the conscience of the North, the new missionaries. By publicising disasters in their appeals to the general public they are able to exert pressure upon reluctant governments, forcing these to become involved in situations which they would prefer to ignore. Britain's Prime Minister, John Major, having dismissed the revolt of the Kurds in the aftermath of the Gulf War with the remark that he could not recall their having been asked to take part, was obliged within days to execute a U-turn and propose safe havens for the Kurds largely as a result of a public outcry on their behalf. This growing power of the new humanitarian lobbies may answer the needs of many in the North who want to 'do something' about conditions in the South, yet the end result of such lobbying in international affairs is highly dangerous on two counts. In the first place providing humanitarian assistance in a war situation such as that in Somalia may have the opposite result to the one intended and actually prolong both the fighting and the suffering. If, no matter what atrocities the warlords carry out, the humanitarians continue to bring in food and other supplies they actually make it easier for those who wish to do so to continue fighting, for as long as such supplies keep arriving there is an additional reason for fighting, as the Americans learnt very quickly after they had arrived in Somalia. On the other hand, if no supplies are provided then in the end even the warlords will be forced to sit down and talk and a conclusion to hostilities may be achieved sooner rather than later. In any case, as some of the more perspicacious aid workers in Somalia realised, there is something grotesque about sending a large military force to see people are fed even if this is only possible by shooting other people. And in the later perspective of history a humanitarian exercise whose end result is a military occupation may not be seen as humanitarian at all. Secondly, this humanitarian insistence upon providing aid leads, sooner or later, to greater and more dangerous involvements. The British government may yet rue the day that it committed British troops to guarding relief columns in Bosnia. In the nineteenth century Christian missionaries went to Africa, unasked, to convert the heathen and succeeded in turning existing social patterns upside down. Then, when their own positions were threatened not least because many of those they had come to convert preferred to be left alone, they began to call for protection leading ultimately to the Scramble for Africa. By the end of the present century we may well find that the humanitarians have created a new set of conditions for interference in the South.

The Canadian General Lewis Mackenzie who commanded the United Nations peace-keeping operations in Sarajevo argued in mid-1992 that further western military intervention in Bosnia-Herzegovina would prolong the fighting. He said, for example, that the mere possibility of intervention, especially by the United States, encouraged the Bosnian Moslems to continue fighting. And of relief measures he said: 'In my opinion, it is certainly feasible to escort humanitarian convoys if you throw adequate resources at it. But you shouldn't start thinking you can limit involvement to just that because very quickly the potential exists for these convoys to be engaged [by the local forces] so that pressure is brought to bear to expand the fighting.' The result is to increase the size of the escorts so that even more force is made available to get supplies through and the escalation of military involvement increases the likelihood that they will become engaged in the civil war. The General also made the point (equally applicable to Somalia for example) that another dangerous situation is created when such protecting forces are withdrawn: 'My concern is that if you pacify Bosnia and Herzegovina and you leave without these hatreds being resolved by some constitutional resolution, it will start all over again.' The logic of General Mackenzie's thinking was to 'rip the rug of intervention out' and force people to sit down and talk.[4] (The general's reasoning should be greatly reinforced by events in Iraq following the freeing of Kuwait. Mainly humanitarian considerations led the allies to proclaim protected havens for the Kurds and a 'no fly' zone in the south to protect the Marsh Arabs from Saddam Hussein although no long-term strategy has been worked out in relation to either group: do the allies intend indefinitely to protect these two areas of Iraq? Or are they merely waiting for the assassination of Hussein? Or will they relinquish their protection at some convenient time in the future without first having ensured that a permanent constitutional solution is in place and guaranteed by the international community?) The general's logic is likely to be ignored, however, as humanitarians insist upon the duty of the international community to intervene. Calls for intervention whether in disasters or civil wars or for monitoring 'returns to democracy' as in Kenya became a feature of the early 1990s and look set to become the new 'politically correct' activity of the North for the balance of the present century.

The humanitarian lobby exercises great appeal in the countries of the North where a growing feature of modern society is political frustration: many people feel marginalised by the sheer size of modern governments and though they may participate in elections every few years, in between they see themselves being manipulated by bureaucracies and large corporations or ignored. Disasters in the South provide them with a cause, a human problem to which they can contribute in some small but concrete fashion and this makes them feel good for they are encouraged to believe that they have done something which will alleviate suffering and make a difference. It is no accident that in disaster situations like that in Somalia it is often NGOs rather than governments which make the most impact upon the public at large. In August 1992, for example, *The Observer* and *Save the Children* launched an emergency appeal for Somalia immediately after the United Nations had pledged to step up supplies to that country and President Bush had announced a US airlift of 145,000 tonnes of additional food. Nicholas Hinton, the director-general of *Save the Children*, took it upon himself to urge the EC to match the American donation: 'Throughout this crisis there has been a disastrous lack of political will. The only way to ensure that we alleviate the worst human catastrophe facing the world is to flood Somalia with food.'[5] Here was the authentic voice of the humanitarians who would obtain a large response from the British people. Yet his formula, to flood Somalia with food, was not one that would end the fighting; on the contrary, it would help prolong the fighting since it would provide something extra to fight over and subsequently – as turned out to be the case – lead to an influx of troops to protect the flood of food and, if necessary, fight those who were already fighting. Whatever the end result in Somalia *Save the Children*, no matter how good its intentions, will have to bear some of the responsibility. But at the time of this appeal, correctly judging the public mood, another spokesman for *Save the Children* said: 'We don't believe that compassion fatigue affects the public; perhaps it only affects governments.'[6] There is a particular irony in this statement, for the relief activities of NGOs are often welcome to governments since they provide them with an excuse not to take action themselves. The British decision to protect aid convoys in Bosnia reflected the power of the humanitarian lobby on the one hand and the reluctance of the British – and other governments – to adopt more realistic policies on the other. The real problem facing the recipients of the aid convoys was that they were being relentlessly fired upon day and night by the Serbs and the help they most needed was action to bring the firing to an end. The British commitment to protect the aid convoys did nothing about this problem and as one doctor in Gorazde said: 'We will all die with full bellies.'[7] As politicians of all persuasions know only too well they must be seen to be doing something and the humanitarians often provide them with something to do which is easier and cheaper than addressing the root cause of the disaster. If western governments are not prepared to send massive military forces into former Yugoslavia in order to stop the fighting altogether should they send small forces into the country to safeguard the delivery of food which ensures that the fighting continues?

Easy humanitarian options exercise much attraction in a West that is in great danger of losing its way, and a British government initiative to help couples adopt Bosnian orphans was fully in keeping with the new conscience. The British Under-Secretary of State for Health, Tim Yeo, asked local authorities to speed up adoption procedures so that babies born to Moslem women who had been raped by Serbian soldiers could be adopted by British families without bureaucratic delay. Needless to say, the baby issue had its humanitarian supporters and 'campaigners for inter-country adoption' welcomed the minister's initiative which they contrasted with previous 'failure to encourage' couples to adopt Romanian orphans after the overthrow of the Communist regime in that country three years earlier. They were talking about babies who had not yet been born. Since there are plenty of unwanted babies already requiring adoption in Britain it is legitimate to ask how much the desire to adopt Bosnian babies was no more than a temporary 'bleeding hearts' reaction by a particular section of the humanitarian lobby?

Against a deeply troubled background of disasters headed by Somalia and Yugoslavia attempts were made to define a doctrine of humanitarian intervention. If the North is about to adopt a policy of humanitarian interventions the need for an acceptable doctrine to justify them immediately becomes apparent and here two contrary approaches are liable to clash: on the one hand hard-headed politicians will argue that intervention in another state should only be undertaken on the rarest of occasions when such a state is acting in breach of international law and represents a threat to its neighbours or world peace; on the other hand the humanitarians will reply that where whole populations are at risk of starvation or atrocities in a civil war the international community then has an overriding moral obligation to intervene. Some sound arguments may be adduced on either side but it was already clear by the end of 1992 that the principle of non-intervention in the internal affairs of member states which had been sacrosanct during the first 45 years of the UN's existence had now been breached and that humanitarian need had emerged as a new criterion for action. Whichever way the argument develops the first consideration that ought always to be satisfied before intervention takes place must surely be that – insofar as it is ever possible to judge such things – the intervention will reduce suffering and not provide an excuse for continuing civil war. Such a judgement will always be exceptionally difficult to make.

The humanitarians, it would seem, are about to have their day but another strand of western thinking is emerging after a long period in which its voice has remained muted and its proponents have been dismissed as racists or something worse. Speaking in mid-1991, the British Tory MP, Sir Nicholas Fairbairn, said that the sum of £167mn emergency food aid which Britain had contributed to Africa since 1989 would have been better spent on condoms and he rebuked the Overseas Development Minister, Mrs Lynda Chalker: 'She is the face of the weeper. All she is doing is giving these poor people the chance to breed more children who will suffer the same horrible fate as their parents: death by starvation.' Now Sir Nicholas might be seen to represent the unacceptable face of harsh self-interest in a West that is increasingly concerned with the growing pressures upon its resources by the poor majority in the South, yet he did, in a quite literal sense, go to the root of the problem. Humanitarians are essentially curative in their approach to the problems of the South, reacting with emotion to disasters but rarely dealing with the causes; Sir Nicholas, harshly and selfishly perhaps, was going to the nub of the problem.[8]

The problems of the South have produced a series of dilemmas for the North which, essentially, wants to be humanitarian, wants to maintain law and order so that its interests are not threatened and wants to do these things on the cheap. These dilemmas can best be illustrated by reference to the questions of body bags and the international trade in drugs. When the United States decided upon military intervention in the Gulf to force Saddam Hussein to retreat from Kuwait the issue of body bags dictated the military approach. There was a deep fear in Washington of the political consequences if too many American casualties were to result from a war in the Gulf in which American soldiers took part, and frequent reference was made to Vietnam and not wishing to repeat the level of casualties which that war had produced. As a result the military adopted a strategy of massive and lengthy aerial bombardment before the ground forces attacked and in the event the number of casualties was kept very small, leading to a victory at minimum cost in lives to the allies (the number of deaths in Iraq was another question entirely). Sensitivity over the number of body bags, it might be argued, does any government credit and yet there is more involved. Soldiers are trained to kill, that is their business, and the most obvious occupational hazard of being a soldier is to be killed in turn, yet it has become part of the politics of contentment in the West that we expect or at least hope that soldiers can be deployed on a military mission without having to pay this awkward price of being killed. The first British military casualty in Bosnia in Janury 1993 led at once to questions among MPs about bringing the soldiers back home for if the price of taking supplies to the Bosnians is to be British casualties then many Britons are likely to say 'no'. The attitude to body bags is one that must be considered if the North is about to embark upon an era of military policing of the South.

The international traffic in drugs is now second only to the arms trade in profitability and was worth more than $500,000bn in 1991. The traffic is symbolic of all that is worst in North–South relations. In broad terms the South produces the drugs and the North consumes them. Latin America – Bolivia, Colombia and Peru – produces the cocaine while the golden crescent – Pakistan, Iran, Afghanistan – and the golden triangle – Burma, Thailand and Laos – produce the heroin, and the drugs are then despatched by a variety of routes to the principal drug using countries of the United States, Europe and, increasingly, Russia. The market forces so beloved of the West dictate that as long as a market exists the drugs will be produced and the biggest market of all is to be found in the ghetto cultures of the United States. In recent years the United States has spent an increasing amount of effort and money assisting the governments in Latin America fight the powerful drug producing cartels. One apparently sensible approach to the problem has been to provide aid for peasants who grow coca to persuade them instead to grow ordinary agricultural crops such as wheat; the peasants duly comply and then grow the coca as well in another area since this is far more valuable than any food crop. American aid thus gives the peasants a double income without bringing an end to the cultivation of the coca, which was hardly the object of the exercise. In any case, tackling the drugs problem this way round will not work. As far as the United States is concerned the traffic in drugs will continue until the social conditions which give rise to its ghetto culture have been eradicated. But to remove those conditions would be far more expensive and potentially politically dangerous to the contented society that elects an American government than to tackle the external problem of drug production in the Third World. By addressing the problem in the producing countries instead of at home Washington is evading the fundamental issue which is not Latin American peasants growing the coca plant nor even General Noriega acting as a middleman-distributor but the social hopelessness of an American generation that sees no future for itself. As long as this and other generations demand drugs it is unrealistic to imagine that in the free enterprise world which the United States has done so much to encourage the drugs will not be forthcoming. If the United States really wants to end the drug problem it should turn its attention to the social conditions at home which at present marginalise a fifth of its population. Instead, by adopting programmes to eliminate drug production in poor countries where the trade may be the most important earner of foreign exchange Washington is implying both psychologically and by its actions that the South rather than the North is responsible for the problem.

The break-up of the Soviet Union was seen at least in some quarters in the West as a triumph for capitalism: the stronger, the more enduring, and morally superior of the rival systems had outlasted its opponent and there was an immediate readiness to welcome the newly freed states of eastern Europe into the capitalist fold. Perhaps of all these countries Czecho-Slovakia deserved a special welcome. Founded in 1918 out of the dissolving Austro–Hungarian Empire it was betrayed by the great powers in 1938–9 and fell under Hitler's yoke; its plight was largely ignored by the West in 1948 and it was absorbed into Stalin's empire; it was greatly admired in the West for the Prague Spring of 1968 when it attempted to break out of the communist grip but no help was forthcoming when Russian tanks came to break the revolution. Finally, in 1989 it achieved its 'velvet revolution'. This was presided over by Vaclav Havel, a Czech, and Alexander Dubcek, a Slovak, and communism collapsed. It was one of the most encouraging outcomes of the dissolving Soviet empire yet three years later the country went through a 'velvet divorce' and split into Czechland and Slovakia to demonstrate that even one of the most sophisticated peoples of Europe were unable to rise above the narrow demands of nationalism. The split, which came into effect at the beginning of 1993, augurs ill for eastern Europe as a whole or the world more generally. If the removal of the constraints of Soviet imperialism means break-up in a small country like Czecho-Slovakia what does the removal of a common enemy mean to the West as a whole?

The demise of communism was interpreted in the West as the triumph of capitalism and at once, or almost at once, everyone wanted to get on the capitalist bandwagon. In China Deng

Xiaoping was carrying out a quiet capitalist revolution while proclaiming continuing adherence to communist principles; in Russia and other successor states to the USSR governments attempted to go too fast and invited counter-revolutions which are likely to occupy the remainder of the century; elsewhere centrally planned socialist economic systems were in retreat and the IMF was enjoying a field day providing prescriptions for new economic programmes. And then, in the midst of this capitalist euphoria, came the realisation that there were almost as many approaches to capitalism as there were countries and that differences which had been papered over during the Cold War were everywhere surfacing to reveal a capitalist world, including its new adherents, which was far more divided than it had ever been during the era of Cold War confrontation. Communism may have failed but capitalism has in no sense succeeded and though the USSR finally gave up the economic struggle, its system quite unable to compete with that of the capitalist West, it subsequently found that the system it wanted to embrace was riven with contradictions and that the divisions which were always inherent in the western system but had been held in check as long as the Cold War lasted were now coming into the open.

The principal western powers did not find themselves united as the Soviet empire collapsed but in growing disarray. The United States which for 45 years had provided leadership for the anti-communist coalition found itself poised between deepening social problems at home which its contented society did not want to face, let alone try to solve, while abroad it began to turn the problems of the South into a new threat that could replace communism. The main powers of Europe – Germany, Britain, France and Italy – were in disarray over the future of the EC and over how they would cope with applications for membership from eastern Europe. Germany, having achieved its dream of reunification, was becoming schizophrenic over its desire to remain a good member of the EC and the temptation to exercise its greater power in new policies. Britain and France were equally determined to demonstrate through the United Nations or in disintegrating Yugoslavia that they remained great powers, while a growing proportion of western citizens as a whole demonstrated increasing cynicism about their much vaunted 'free' political systems. Japan which had raised itself to second place in the capitalist hierarchy was both distrusted and feared by the United States and regarded with unease by the rest of the West. Three years after its end the Cold War was revealed as the cement which held the western world together and despite President Bush's confident proclamation of a 'New World Order' what has appeared instead seems much closer to the old order of disparate and squabbling nation states, each pursuing its own interests without the cement of Cold War fears to keep antagonisms in check. In such a world the weak, including the countries of the South, are far more likely to be pushed to the wall than was ever the case when the Cold War dominated international politics. We may yet discover that the USSR won the final battle of the Cold War for, by disintegrating, the Soviet Union has done more to destabilise the West, with all the consequences which will flow from this, than it managed in over 45 years of Cold War confrontation.

Notes and References

1 Introduction

1. Independent, 6 June 1992.
2. Ibid., 3 March, 1992.
3. Ibid., 28 February 1992.
4. Ibid., 8 April 1992.
5. Ibid., 23 April 1992.
6. Ibid., 28 April 1992.
7. Ibid., 25 May 1992.
8. Ibid., 4 June 1992.
9. Ibid., 13 June 1992.

2 Origins and History

1. Arnold, Guy, *The Third World Handbook*, Cassell, 1989, p.47.
2. *Independent*, 2 September 1992.
3. Ibid.
4. *Guardian*, 2 September 1992.
5. Arnold, *The Third World Handbook*, p.162.
6. Ibid., p.169
7. *North–South: A Programme for Survival*, The Report of the Independent Commission on International Issues under the Chairmanship of Willy Brandt, Pan Books, 1980.
8. *What kind of Africa by the Year 2000?*, Final report of the Monrovia Symposium on the future development prospects of Africa towards the year 2000, OAU, 1979, p.21.
9. For The Arusha Declaration, see J. Nyerere, *Freedom and Socialism*, Oxford University Press, 1968, p.385 *et seq.*

3 Aid

1. Bauer, P.T., *Equality, the Third World and Economic Delusion*, Weidenfeld & Nicolson, 1981.
2. Rostow, W.W., *The Stages of Economic Growth A Non-Communist Manifesto*, Cambridge University Press, 1960.

3.   Ward, Barbara, *The Rich Nations and the Poor Nations*, The Massey Lectures Inaugural Series, CBC, Toronto, 1961.
4.   United Nations Development Programme (UNDP), *Human Development Report 1992*, Oxford University Press, 1992.
5.   World Bank, *World Development Report 1991*, Oxford University Press, 1991.
6.   *Independent*, 7 March 1992.
7.   *Independent*, 23 April 1992.
8.   *Independent*, 18 June 1992.
9.   Overseas Development Institute (ODI), Special Report, *The GATT Uruguay Round: Effects on Developing Countries*, Sheila Page, Michael Davenport, Adrian Hewitt, 1991.
10. *Observer*, 1 March 1992.
11. *Independent*, 19 August 1991.
12. *Observer*, 14 June 1992.
13. *Observer*, 27 September 1992.
14. *Deutsches Allgemeines Sonntagsblatt*, Hamburg, 14 August 1992.

4   The Poor of the World

1.   United Nations Economic and Social Commission for Asia and the Pacific (ESCAP), New York, 1991.
2.   World Bank, *World Development Report 1991*, Oxford University Press, 1991.
3.   United Nations Development Programme (UNDP), *Human Development Report 1992*, Oxford University Press, 1992.
4.   Ibid., pp.34–40.
5.   *The Amex Bank Review*, 28 January 1992, vol. 19, no. 1.
6.   *Independent*, 13 August 1992.
7.   *Independent* (Ms Rakiya Omaar), 21 August 1992.
8.   *Independent*, 13 May 1992.

5   Pressures on the Third World

1.   United Nations Development Programme (UNDP), *Human Development Report 1991*, Oxford University Press, 1991.
2.   *Financial Times*, 11 November 1991.
3.   Independent, 28 April 1992.

4. *Independent*, 12 July 1991.
5. *Observer*, 19 April 1992.

6 Special Cases

1. Young, Hugo, *One of Us*, Macmillan, 1989, p.475.
2. *Independent*, 27 November 1991.
3. *Independent*, 29 November 1991.
4. Rowland, R. W. ('Tiny'), *Observer*, 28 June 1992.
5. *Independent*, 3 August 1992.
6. *Independent*, 7 August 1992.
7. *Observer*, 16 August 1992.
8. *Independent*, 6 August 1992.
9. *Independent*, 12 August 1992.
10. *Independent*, 22 August 1992.
11. *Independent*, 5 September 1992.
12. *Independent*, 16 July 1992.

7 The Question of Debt

1. *Independent*, 15 February 1992.
2. United Nations Development Programme (UNDP), *Human Development Report 1992*, Oxford University Press, 1992.
3. Figures for country GNPs, etc. throughout this chapter have been extracted from the *World Development Report 1991* of the World Bank, Oxford University Press 1991.

8 Resources

1. *Standard*, 1 June 1992.
2. *Independent*, 2 March 1992.
3. *Financial Times*, 29 May 1992.
4. *Independent*, 10 June 1992.
5. *Independent*, 5 June 1992.
6. See *The World Trade System*, ed. Robert Fraser, Longman Current Affairs, 1991, for a guide to international commodities.

9 The Turn to the East

1. *Independent*, 19 February 1992.
2. *Independent*, 25 April 1992.

3. *Independent*, 4 March 1992.
4. *Independent*, 29 April 1992.
5. *Independent*, 22 September 1992.
6. *Observer*, 9 November 1992.
7. Ibid., 9 November 1992.
8. *Independent*, 26 September 1992.
9. *Independent*, 19 August 1992.
10. Overseas Development Institute (ODI), Briefing Paper, *The European Bank for Reconstruction and Development*, September 1990.

10 Western Racism

1. Galbraith, John Kenneth, *The Culture of Contentment*, Sinclair-Stevenson, 1992.
2. *Independent*, 7 December 1992.
3. Ibid., 7 December 1992.
4. *Independent*, 11 April 1992.
5. *Independent*, 22 October 1992.
6. *Independent*, 28 November 1992.
7. *Independent*, 18 July 1992.
8. *Observer*, 22 November 1992.
9. *Independent*, 7 December 1992.
10. *Independent*, 20 November 1992.
11. *Independent*, 28 November 1992.
12. *Observer* (Adrian Hamilton), 3 May 1992.

11 The Politics of Contentment

1. Galbraith, John Kenneth, *The Culture of Contentment*, Sinclair-Stevenson, 1992, p.10
2. Ibid., p.40
3. *Observer*, 20 July 1992.
4. *Independent*, 7 December 1992.
5. *Independent*, 28 May 1992.
6. *Independent*, 30 July 1992.
7. *Independent*, 14 May 1992.
8. *Independent*, 21 May 1992.
9. *Observer*, 3 January 1993.
10. *Independent*, 28 July 1992.
11. *Independent*, 4 January 1993.

12 Policing the South

1. *Independent*, 3 June 1992.
2. *Independent*, 18 July 1991.
3. *Independent*, 22 September 1992.
4. *Independent*, 19 August 1991.
5. *Independent*, 21 September 1992.
6. World Bank, *World Development Report 1991*, Oxford University Press, 1991.
7. *Independent*, 1 September 1992.
8. *Independent*, 30 November 1992.
9. *Independent*, 31 August 1992.
10. *Independent*, 30 November 1992.
11. *Guardian*, 8 December 1992.
12. *Independent*, 8 December 1992.
13. *Independent*, 8 December 1992.
14. *Independent*, 7 December 1992.
15. *Independent*, 10 December 1992.
16. *Independent*, 12 December 1992.
17. *Independent*, 18 December 1992.
18. *Independent*, 30 December 1992.

13 The United Nations

1. *Observer*, 23 August 1992.
2. *Observer*, 2 August 1992.
3. Ibid., 2 August 1992.
4. *Independent*, 26 November 1992.
5. *Independent*, 21 August 1992.
6. *Independent*, 5 August 1992.
7. *Observer*, 5 July 1992.

14 The New Imperialism

1. Fanon, Frantz, *The Wretched of the Earth*, MacGibbon & Kee, 1965.
2. *Observer*, 13 December 1992.
3. *Independent*, 17 December 1992.
4. *Independent*, 13 August 1992.
5. *Observer*, 16 August 1992.

6. *Independent*, 26 August 1992.
7. *Independent*, 19 August 1992.
8. *Standard*, 10 May 1992.

Index

Index

Aaronson, Mike 80
Adenauer, Konrad 164
Aeronautics 109, 110
Afghanistan 43, 118, 125, 213
Africa 3, 14, 16, 18, 24, 25, 32, 34,
   35, 36, 38, 43, 52, 53, 54, 55, 59,
   60, 61, 63, 64, 65, 66, 67, 68, 78,
   81, 90, 91, 93, 98, 107, 112, 113,
   115, 116, 117, 127, 157, 162,
   164, 173, 174, 205, 207, 211
Africa 2000 23, 24
Africa Watch 52
African, Caribbean, Pacific (ACP)
   countries 1, 25
African Goundnut Council 115
African National Congress
   (ANC) 83, 85, 86, 87, 194
Aid vii, 1, 2, 5, 15, 19, 24, 25,
   27–41, 44, 46, 48, 57, 59, 62, 64,
   66, 67, 71, 80, 81, 92, 103, 130,
   132, 133, 136, 139, 157, 164,
   165, 167, 168, 176, 177, 179,
   201, 202, 203, 204, 205, 206,
   207, 213
Aideed, Mohamed Farah 79, 184,
   185, 186
Aids 35
Airbus-Industrie 110
Albania 193
Algeria 53, 54, 113, 118
Algiers 17, 20, 22
All-Party Parliamentary Group on
   Somalia 81
Allivane 181
Aluminium 109, 111, 112
Amazon 4, 40
Amnesty International 78, 165
Anderson, Holger 39
Angola 2, 59, 60, 63, 65, 67, 112,
   168, 171, 174, 179, 190
Anti-Defamation League of B'nai
   B'rith 140

Apartheid 83, 84, 85, 86, 88
Arab League 52, 75
Argentina 47, 90
Armenia 125, 162
Arms industry (trade) 111, 118,
   180, 212
Arusha Declaration 18, 24, 25
Asia vii, 14, 15, 18, 43, 45, 98, 106,
   107, 122, 162, 164, 166, 175
Aswan High Dam 27
Atlanta (Georgia) 179
Atlantic 106
Australia 105, 112, 113, 115, 116,
   117, 118
Austria 41, 141, 143, 163
Aven, Piotr 130
Azerbaijan 125

Baden-Württemberg 142
Baghdad 167
Baidoa 184
Balkans 133, 187, 188, 193
Baltic 123, 124
Bananas 114
Banda, Hastings 38, 165
Bandung Conference 16, 18
Bangladesh 115, 116, 204
Bank of Credit and Commerce
   International (BCCI) 110
Bardera 184
Barre, Siyad 51, 77, 78, 175, 184
Barroso, Dura 82
Bauer, P.T. 27
Bauxite 111, 112
Belarus 125
Belgium 41, 163, 178
Belgrade 16, 17
Berbera 175
Berlin 73, 149
Berlin Wall 122
Black, Timothy 62
Boipatong 83, 85, 86

Bolivia 113, 118, 213
Bonn 39, 40
Bosnia 17, 132, 133, 134, 135, 163, 166, 171, 187, 188, 192, 193, 207, 208, 209, 212
Botha, role of 'Pik' 87
Botswana 59, 66, 67, 112, 116
Boutros-Ghali, Boutros 8, 10, 18, 51, 78, 87, 178, 186, 190, 192, 194, 195, 197, 198, 205
Brady Plan 93
Brandt Report vii, 23, 28, 29, 159
Brazil 4, 39, 40, 46, 90, 97, 106, 111, 112, 113, 114, 115, 116, 117, 198
Bretton Woods 112
Britain 6, 22, 25, 27, 37, 38, 39, 41, 46, 49, 63, 71, 72, 73, 74, 75, 76, 77, 80, 82, 84, 85, 86, 87, 88, 92, 98, 109, 110, 113, 115, 117, 132, 140, 141, 142, 144, 145, 146, 149, 150, 152, 158, 159, 160, 162, 163, 164, 165, 166, 167, 168, 172, 173, 174, 177, 178, 181, 182, 183, 184, 187, 192, 195, 196, 197, 198, 201, 204, 206, 210, 215
British Broadcasting Corporation (BBC) 150
British Somaliland n81
Brundtland Commission 6
Brussels 127, 134, 142, 146
Bulgaria 122, 193
Burma *see* Myanma
Burundi 115
Bush, George vii, 5, 9, 11, 104, 135, 137, 156, 161, 175, 176, 180, 182, 183, 184, 187, 189, 199, 209, 216

Cairo 17
California 104
Cambodia 189, 190
Cameroon 114, 115
Canada 41, 49, 50, 60, 98, 105, 112, 113, 116, 117, 118
Cardoen International Marketing SA (CIMSA) 182

Caribbean 14, 114, 144
Castro, Fidel 10, 11, 71
Caucasus 123
Ceauçescus 122
Central African Republic (CAR) 112
Central America 107, 189
Central Intelligence Agency (CIA) 174
Cesarani, Dr David 141
Chad 179
Chalker, Lynda (Baroness) 36, 37, 38, 62, 165, 166, 177, 211
Charter of Economic Rights and Duties of States 22
Cheney, Dick 185
Chernomyrdin, Vktor 129
Chicago 157
Chile 111, 112, 113, 182
Chiluba, Frederick 34, 92
China 14, 15, 43, 46, 61, 98, 110, 112, 113, 114, 115, 116, 117, 118, 123, 125, 168, 169, 182, 198, 214
Chinese Communist Party 15
Chromium 59, 113
CIPEC 112, 119
Ciskei 87, 194
Claes, Willy 178
Clarke, Kenneth 149, 150, 163, 167
Clinton, Bill 158, 176, 184
Coal 111
Cocoa 109, 114, 119
Coconuts 115
Coffee 109, 114, 115
Cold War vii, viii, 1, 2, 10, 13, 14, 15, 16, 17, 18, 19, 25, 27, 28, 29, 32, 33, 34, 63, 77, 92, 95, 105, 121, 123, 124, 127, 131, 136, 137, 139, 140, 147, 152, 155, 162, 163, 164, 165, 167, 171, 172, 173, 174, 175, 177, 179, 188, 189, 190, 193, 194, 195, 198, 199, 200, 201, 203, 215, 216
Collor, President 106
Colombia 115, 118, 213

Colombo 17
Colonial Development and Welfare
  Act 1940 27
Commonwealth 2, 36, 149, 152,
  168, 177, 178
Commonwealth of Independent
  States (CIS) 32, 124, 126,
  127, 128, 129, 130, 135
Communism 28, 102, 122, 140,
  214, 215
Comoros 116
Computers 110
Conference on Human Environment
  1972 104
Conference on International
  Economic Cooperation and
  Development (CIEC) 20, 22,
  23
Congo 178, 189
Congress of People's Deputies 129,
  130
Conteh, Abdulai 167
Contra rebels 189
Convention for a Democratic South
  Africa (CODESA) 85
Copper 59, 112, 119
Côte d'Ivoire 16, 114, 115
Cotton 115
Council of Europe 134
Council of Competitiveness 162
Croatia 132, 134, 164
Cuba 16, 113, 116, 117, 130, 175
Culture of Contentment, The 155
Czechland 135, 214
Czecho-Slovakia 117, 122, 131,
  135, 214

Debt 18, 24, 44, 46, 50, 53, 89–102,
  159, 166, 173, 205, 206
De Cuellar, Perez 190
De Gaulle, Charles 61, 164
De Klerk, F.W. 83, 85, 86, 87
Delors, Jacques 177
Denmark 41
Department of Trade and Industry
  (DTI) 181
Dhlakama, Afonso 66
Diamonds 59, 83, 112

Dienel, Thomas 149
Di Meana, Ripa 7, 107
Djibouti 79
Dominican Republic 115
Dubcek, Alexander 214

East 2, 14, 16, 137
East Germany (DDR) 55, 122,
  123, 140
Eastern Europe 2, 34, 55, 84, 85,
  112, 121, 123, 125, 129, 130,
  131, 135, 136, 137, 173
Economic and Social Commission
  for Asia and the Pacific
  (ESCAP) 43
Economist, The 36
Ecuador 114, 118
Egypt 13, 46, 54, 74, 90, 115, 117,
  187
El Salvador 115, 190
Electronics 110
Ellemann-Jensen, Uffe 82
Estonia 124, 125
Ethiopa 46, 63, 65, 66, 79, 102,
  174, 186
Europe 2, 26, 32, 40, 55, 68, 79,
  97, 104, 106, 109, 110, 111, 113,
  114, 116, 118, 125, 131, 134,
  135, 136, 137, 140, 141, 142,
  143, 144, 145, 146, 152, 159,
  162, 163, 164, 166, 172, 173,
  196, 202, 213, 214, 215
European Bank for Reconstruction
  and Development
  (EBRD) 135, 136
European Commission 7, 36, 38,
  68, 177
European Community (EC) 25,
  68, 75, 80, 82, 84, 86, 88, 105,
  107, 110, 111, 114, 115, 116,
  121, 127, 131, 133, 134, 135,
  137, 140, 142, 144, 146, 149,
  150, 163, 164, 177, 180, 188,
  198, 209, 215

Fairbairn, Sir Nicholas 211
Famine 63–8, 78
Fanon, Frantz 201

Faul, Erwin 142
Federal Census Bureau (USA) 161
Financial services 51, 110
Finland 41
Fisheries 117
Fitzwater, Marlin 183
Food and Agriculture Organization (FAO) 107, 191
Forests 105, 106, 107, 109, 119
Forsythe, Robert 81
France 39, 41, 46, 49, 61, 74, 75, 76, 77, 80, 81, 82, 98, 109, 116, 118, 125, 141, 142, 143, 146, 159, 163, 164, 167, 172, 173, 174, 178, 183, 184, 187, 192, 195, 196, 197, 204, 215
Free Officers 71
Friends of the Earth 30, 106

Gabon 20, 113
Gaddafi, Muammar al- 71, 72, 73, 74, 77
Gaider, Yegor 129
Galbraith, Kenneth 139, 155, 156, 157
gastarbeiter 144, 152
General Agreement on Tariffs and Trade (GATT) 35, 50
Georgia 125
Germany 2, 39, 40, 41, 46, 49, 55, 61, 82, 98, 110, 112, 113, 115, 116, 117, 123, 124, 130, 131, 134, 135, 137, 140, 141, 142, 143, 147, 148, 150, 152, 159, 163, 164, 172, 174, 184, 186, 187, 195, 215
Ghana 112, 114, 115
glasnost 124
Global Forum 4
Global Partnership '92 conference 144
Goenez, Arpad 131
Gold 59, 83, 112
Goldemberg, Jose 106
Gorazde 209
Gorbachev, Mikhail 2, 85, 121, 122, 124, 126
Greece 47, 118, 132, 164, 193

Grenada 116, 175
Groundnuts 115
Group of Seven (G–7) 31, 32, 33, 48, 97, 98, 106, 126, 172, 173, 175, 182
Guadalajara 60
Guatemala 115, 118
Guinea 112
Gulf War (crisis) 4, 26, 158, 171, 172, 173, 174, 184, 185, 191, 199, 206, 212

Haddam, Anwar 53
Haider Jörg 141, 143
Haiti 43
Harare 17, 36, 177
Hatfield, Ron 160
Havana 17
Havel, Vaclav 122, 214
Herzegovina 133, 134, 166, 192, 207, 208
Hinton, Nicholas 209
Hitler, Adolf 75, 144, 148, 214
Holland *see* Netherlands
Honduras 114
Honecker, Erich 122
Hong Kong 43, 110, 115, 116, 168
Hopkinson, Nicholas 145
Human Development Index 58, 164
Human Development Reports (1991 and 1992) 3, 29, 31, 33, 44, 46, 57, 58, 93
Hungary 61, 122, 130, 131, 163, 193
Hurd, Douglas 36, 53, 82, 86, 127, 132, 177, 178, 197
Hussein, Saddam 4, 71, 74, 75, 135, 167, 192, 194, 208, 212

Idriss, King 71
Independent 52, 75, 81, 135, 149, 167
India vii, 1, 2, 13, 15, 43, 46, 61, 90, 97, 98, 113, 115, 116, 117, 125, 130, 165, 166, 169, 180, 195, 1298
Indonesia 17, 112, 113, 114, 115, 116, 117

Inkatha Freedom Party   83
Intergovernmental Panel on
    Climate Change   106
International Atomic Energy
    Agency (IAEA)   180, 181
International Bank for
    Reconstruction and
    Development (IBRD) (World
    Bank)   2, 3, 23, 27, 30, 31, 33,
    36, 43, 44, 48, 53, 64, 68, 85, 91,
    93, 97, 98, 106, 127, 129, 130,
    152, 162, 165, 166, 176, 179,
    191, 204, 205
International Labour Organization
    (ILO)   191
International Monetary Fund
    (IMF)   vii, 2, 3, 23, 30, 31, 32,
    33, 34, 35, 44, 48, 53, 59, 85, 91,
    97, 98, 126, 127, 128, 129, 130,
    162, 166, 176, 191, 215
Iran   17, 54, 71, 73, 74, 76, 113,
    114, 116, 118, 125, 180, 182, 213
Iraq   17, 46, 71, 75, 111, 114, 116,
    117, 130, 135, 171, 179, 181,
    182, 191, 192, 194, 197, 199,
    208, 212
Ireland   41, 164
Iron ore   112
Islam   53, 54, 126
Islamic Conference (IC)   52
Islamic Salvation Front (FIS)
    (Algeria)   53, 54
Israel   72, 76, 111, 169, 181
Italy   41, 49, 98, 110, 116, 117, 118,
    143, 163, 172, 215

Jamaica   112
Japan   3, 10, 41, 46, 49, 98, 108,
    110, 111, 112, 113, 114, 116,
    117, 172, 174, 184, 195, 198,
    204, 216
Joffe, Josef   148
Johnson, Lyndon B.   61
Jordan   113
Jute   115

Kampuchea   43
Kaunda, Kenneth   34

Kazakstan   125
Kennedy, John F.   16, 28
Kenya   16, 37, 38, 65, 79, 110, 117,
    166, 168, 208
Khartoum   66
Khomeini, Ayatollah   71
Khrushchev, Nikita   16
Kohl, Helmut   11, 186
Korea   47
Kosovo   187
Kouchner, Bernard   80, 195
Krenz, Egon   122
Kuala Lumpur   107
Ku Klux Klan   141
Kurds   17, 74, 194, 196, 206, 208
Kuwait   52, 75, 123, 171, 175, 181,
    182, 191, 199, 208, 212
KwaZulu   87
Kyrgyzstan   125

Lamont, Norman   38
Laos   118, 213
Latin America   14, 16, 43, 90, 98,
    107, 113, 116, 127, 162, 175,
    205, 213
Latvia   124, 125
Lawrence, T.E.   83
League of Nations   77, 104, 189,
    198
Lebanon   76, 118
Lenin, V.I.   124
Leo   147
Lesotho   67
Liberia   65, 112, 174
Libya   71–77
Lithuania   124
Lockerbie   74, 75, 76, 77
Lomé Conventions   1
Lomé III   25
London   6, 34, 72, 82, 107, 126,
    131, 1341, 144, 150, 162, 175,
    182
Los Angeles   44, 151, 152, 156, 157
Lusaka   17

Maastricht Treaty   26, 121, 137,
    164, 172
Macedonia   132, 133

Machine tools   110
Mackenzie, Lewis (General)   207, 208
Madagascar   116
Major, John   11, 36, 38, 158, 177, 206
Malawi   38, 66, 67, 165
Malaysia   7, 17, 49, 107, 108, 109, 110, 113, 114, 115, 116
Mandela, Nelson   83, 86
Mao Zedong (Mao Tse-tung)   15
Marie Stopes International Foundation   62
Marsh Arabs   135, 191, 208
Marshall Plan   27, 85, 97, 202
Mason, John   205
Matrix-Churchill   182
Mauritania   46
McIntosh, David   162
Meat   116
Médécins sans Frontiéres   80
Mestrinho, Gilberto (Governor Amazonas, Brazil)   4
Mexico   50, 51, 54, 60, 61, 89, 90, 96, 113, 114, 115, 118
Michael, Alun (MP)   81
Migrants' Forum of the European Community   146
Milosevic, Slobodan   187
Ministry of Defence (MOD) (UK)   181
Minty, Abdul   86
Mobutu, Sese Seko   174
Mogadishu   65, 79, 80, 82, 184, 185, 186, 192
Mohamad, Mahathir   7, 8, 17, 107, 109
Mohamed, Ali Mahdi   79, 183, 185
Moi, Daniel arap   38, 166, 168
Moldova   125
Mombasa   82
Monrovia   23
Montreal Convention   76
Morocco   113, 118
Moscow   33, 48, 122, 127, 131, 193
Motor vehicles   110
Mozambique   35, 59, 60, 63, 65, 66, 67, 100, 101, 117, 194

Mukerjee, Tara   146
Munich   148
Myanma   37, 118, 166, 213

Namibia   59, 66, 67, 112, 117, 171, 189
Narcotics   118, 213
Nasser, Gamal Abdel   13, 16, 27, 71, 74
Nationale Offensive   148
National Front (France)   140, 143
Nationalist Front   149
Natural gas   113
Nehru, Pandit   vii, 2, 13, 15, 16, 165
Neo-Nazis   140, 141, 143, 147, 148, 149
Netherlands   41, 49, 113, 115, 116, 117, 117, 143
New Delhi   15, 16, 17
New International Economic Order (NIEO)   19, 20, 21, 22, 23, 24, 25, 28, 103
New World Order   137, 139, 173, 175, 216
New York   6, 8, 140, 157, 192
Newly Industrialising Countries (NICs)   43, 110
Nicaragua   46, 175, 189, 190
Nigeria   46, 47, 89, 98, 110, 111, 114, 115, 198
Nkrumah, Kwame   18
Non-Aligned Movement (NAM)   vii, 1, 2, 13, 15, 16, 17, 18, 74
Non-Government Organizations (NGOs)   37, 38, 51, 79, 80, 83, 177, 203, 204, 206, 208, 209
Noriega, Manuel   173, 213
North   viii, 1, 2, 3, 4, 5, 6, 7, 8, 9, 10, 13, 14, 15, 17, 18, 19, 21, 21, 23, 24, 25, 26, 27, 28, 29, 31, 32, 44, 45, 46, 47, 48, 50, 51, 52, 53, 54, 55, 57, 58, 59, 60, 61, 62, 63, 64, 65, 66, 67, 68, 69, 71, 84, 88, 89, 90, 91, 92, 93, 94, 95, 96, 97, 99, 100, 101, 103, 104, 105, 106, 107, 108, 109, 110, 111, 112,

113, 114, 116, 117, 118, 119,
136, 152, 155, 159, 162, 163,
164, 165, 168, 169, 176, 177,
178, 179, 180, 183, 187, 188,
195, 199, 201, 202, 203, 204,
205, 206, 208, 210, 212, 213,
214
North Africa 142, 143
North America 2, 51, 110
North American Free Trade
Agreement (NAFTA) 50
North Atlantic Treaty Organization
(NATO) 18, 73, 133, 134,
137, 142, 187, 188
North Korea 111, 179, 182
Norway 4, 41, 112, 113, 114
Nyerere, Julius K. 17, 25

Observer 76, 147, 166, 209
olive oil 118
Olzewski, Jan 128
Omar, Rakiya 52
Operation Restore Hope 183, 186
Organization of African Unity
(OAU) 15, 23, 52, 53
Organization for Economic
Cooperation and Development
(OECD) 8, 40, 41, 47, 48, 49,
98, 99
Organization of Petroleum
Exporting Countries
(OPEC) 19, 20, 21, 22, 23,
25, 28, 49, 71, 89, 103
Overseas Development Institute
(ODI) 35

Pacific 14, 43
Pakistan 47, 115, 116, 117, 118,
125, 180, 213
Pan-Africanist Congress (PAC) 87
Panama 173
Pan-American (flight 103) 74
Panshila 15, 16
Paper 118
Paris 20, 23, 165
Paris Club 53, 59
Parsons, Sir Anthony 181
Peace Appeal 16

Peace Corps 28
Peaceful co-existence 15
Pearson Report 28, 29, 159
Peck, Ted 185
Pentagon 188
Pepper 116
perestroika 2, 124
Peru 112, 113, 118, 213
Petroleum 114, 119
Pharmaceuticals 110
Philippines 113, 114
Phosphorites 113
Pinochet Ugarte, Augusto 111,
182
Platinum 59, 113
Poland 3, 122, 127, 128, 129, 131
Population 61–3
Population Concern 62
Portugal 39, 47, 164
Prague Spring 214
Preston, Lewis 127
Pretoria 86, 87
Prince Charles 6

Rainforest Pilot Project
(Brazil) 106
Rand Corporation 188
Reagan, Ronald 73, 156, 175
Reisz, Heinz 149
Republic of Somaliland 81
Resistencia Nacional Mocambicana
(Renamo) 66
Rhodesa *see* Zimbabwe
Rice 116
Rifkind, Malcolm 132
Rio Earth Summit 5, 6, 7, 8–11,
58, 61, 91, 103, 104, 105, 107,
161, 172, 204, 205, 206
Rio de Janeiro 4, 38
Rio São Francisco (Brazil) 39
Riyadh 20
Roman Catholic Church 62
Romania 122
Rome 194
Rostow, W.W. 28, 29
Rowland, R.W. ('Tiny') 76
Rubber 116
Rushdie, Salman 74, 142

Russia   32, 33, 34, 46, 48, 101, 105,
    110, 112, 113, 114, 115, 116,
    117, 121, 124, 125, 126, 127,
    128, 129, 130, 131, 136, 162,
    173, 174, 182, 187, 198, 213,
    215
Rwanda   115

Sacirbey, Muhamed   167
Saferworld   180, 181
Sahnoun, Mohammed   79
Salinas, Carlos   50, 60
Sarajevo   52, 207
Saudi Arabia   114, 116, 182
Save the Children   67, 79, 80, 209
Savimbi, Jonas   63, 168, 174
Schönhuber, Franz   141, 142
Scotland   76
Scramble for Africa   207
Security Council   *see* United
    Nations
Seiters, Rudolf   149
semi-conductors   110
Senegal   113
Serbia   132, 133, 187
Shearer, David   79
Shia Moslems (Iraq)   135, 197
Siemens   39
Sierra Leone   112, 167
Silver   113
Singapore   110, 115, 116
Sixth Special Session of UN   22
Slovakia   135, 214
Slovenia   132, 134
Somalia   37, 46, 51, 52, 65, 66, 71,
    77–83, 150, 166, 171, 174,
    183–7, 192, 194, 196, 201, 206,
    207, 208, 209, 210
South   vii, 1, 2, 3, 4, 5, 6, 7, 8, 9, 10,
    13, 14, 17, 18, 19, 20, 21, 23, 24,
    25, 26, 27, 28, 29, 44, 45, 46, 47,
    48, 50, 51, 52, 54, 55, 57, 58, 59,
    62, 63, 64, 65, 68, 69, 71, 76, 77,
    89, 90, 91, 92, 93, 94, 95, 96, 97,
    98, 99, 101, 102, 103, 104, 105,
    106, 107, 108, 109, 110, 111,
    112, 113, 114, 115, 116, 117,
    118, 126, 127, 128, 135, 136,

    138, 139, 140, 152, 153, 155,
    159, 162, 164, 166, 174, 176,
    177, 178, 179, 182, 183, 184,
    188, 191, 195, 199, 201, 202,
    203, 204, 205, 206, 207, 208,
    211, 212, 214, 215, 216
South Africa   59, 60, 66, 67, 71,
    83–8, 111, 112, 113, 116, 117,
    118, 162, 189, 194
South Africa Defence Force
    (SADF)   87
Southern African Development
    Coordination Conference
    (SADCC)   68
South Korea   43, 110, 111, 113,
    116, 117
Spain   7, 49, 118, 164, 204
Spices   116
Sri Lanka   115, 116, 117, 166
Stages of Economic Growth, The   28
Stalin, J.V.   214
Stockholm   7
Strong, Maurice   5
Suall, Irwin   140
Sub-Saharan Africa   33, 35, 45, 90,
    145
Sudan   37, 54, 63, 65, 66, 115, 166
Sudan People's Liberation Army
    (SPLA)   66
Suddeutsche Zeitung   148
Suez Canal   27
Suez crisis   27, 74, 187
Sugar   116
Suharto, President   17
Summers, Lawrence   36
Sunday Times   36, 37, 177
Surinam   112
Swaziland   67, 117
Sweden   41, 163, 204
Swierczek, Michael   148
Switzerland   41, 110, 163
Syria   46, 73, 74, 76, 113

Taiwan   43, 47, 110, 111
Tajikistan   125, 162
Tanzania   25, 112
Tea   117

Teheran 181

Telecommunications 111

Textiles 117

Thailand 47, 113, 114, 115, 116, 117, 118, 213

Thatcher, Margaret 59, 73, 158, 160

Third Development Decade 22

Third Force 2, 13, 16

Third World vii, viii, 1, 2, 3, 5, 6, 7, 9, 10, 11, 13, 14, 15, 16, 17, 18, 19, 20, 21, 22, 23, 24, 25, 27, 28, 30, 31, 32, 33, 34, 36, 38, 39, 40, 48, 49, 51, 57, 58, 59, 60, 61, 62, 64, 68, 71, 77, 78, 82, 84, 88, 91, 110, 112, 114, 116, 121, 125, 126, 127, 130, 135, 136, 140, 144, 145, 146, 152, 157, 159, 162, 163, 165, 168, 180, 188, 190, 191, 201, 205, 213

Tiananmen Square 123, 168

Timber 118

Tin 113

Tito, Josip Broz 13, 16

Tobacco 117

Togo 113

Tory Party 158

Tourism 118

Tripoli 73

Tropical fruits 114, 117, 119

Truman, Harry S. 202

Tunisia 54, 113, 118

Turaljic, Hakija 188

Turkey 117, 125, 137, 143, 162, 163, 193

Turkmenistan 125

Uganda 49, 50, 66, 179

Ukraine 114, 125, 137, 162

Uniao Nacional para la Independencia Total de Angola (UNITA) 63

Union of Soviet Socialist Republics (USSR) viii, 2, 16, 20, 27, 47, 85, 92, 109, 110, 112, 114, 121, 123, 124, 125, 126, 130, 131, 133, 137, 173, 174, 175, 190, 191, 195, 199, 205, 214, 215, 216

United Arab Emirates (UAE) 114, 116, 118

United Nations (UN) 2, 5, 13, 22, 28, 30, 38, 39, 41, 44, 53, 65, 75, 76, 77, 78, 79, 80, 81, 82, 83, 86, 87, 88, 104, 132, 133, 134, 135, 146, 155, 166, 169, 171, 172, 173, 174, 175, 176, 178, 179, 180, 181, 183, 184, 185, 186, 187, 188, 189–200, 201, 205, 207, 209, 211, 216

United Nations Conference on Environment and Development (UNCED) 4, 7, 38

United Nations Conference on Trade and Development (UNCTAD) 2

United Nations Development Programme (UNDP) 3, 44, 50, 57, 58, 80, 93, 164, 191, 204

United Nations Educational, Cultural and Scientific Organization (UNESCO) 25, 191

United Nations High Commissioner for Refugees (UNHCR) 146

United Nations International Conference on Nutrition 205

United Nations Population Fund 61

United Nations World Food Programme (WFP) 65

United States of America (USA) viii, 3, 4, 5, 6, 7, 8, 9, 10, 16, 17, 22, 25, 27, 41, 44, 45, 46, 49, 50, 51, 54, 60, 61, 63, 64, 71, 72, 73, 74, 75, 76, 77, 80, 84, 85, 88, 97, 98, 105, 106, 109, 110, 111, 112, 113, 114, 115, 116, 117, 118, 121, 133, 135, 139, 140, 142, 146, 150, 151, 152, 156, 157, 158, 159, 161, 162, 166, 167, 168, 171, 172, 173, 174, 175, 176, 177, 178, 180, 181, 182, 183, 184, 185, 186, 187, 188, 189, 190, 191, 192, 194, 195, 197, 198, 199, 200, 204, 207, 209, 212, 213, 215

232 *Index*

Upper Volta (Burkina Faso) 203
Urals 106
Urquhart, Sir Brian 196
US News and World Report 29
Uzbekistan 125

Vance, Cyrus 87, 194
Vanilla 116
Vatican 7
Venezuela 47, 113
Vienna 180
Vietnam 46, 116, 158, 159, 171,
     175, 212

Waldheim, Kurt 189
Ward, Barbara 29
Warsaw 128
Warsaw Pact 137
Washington 3, 28, 33, 48, 122,
     130, 169, 172, 173, 175, 180,
     182, 184, 185, 193, 204, 212,
     213, 214
Washington Post 132
Watts riot 151
Weizsäcker, Richard von 149
West, the 1, 2, 3, 4, 14, 16, 19, 20,
     27, 34, 35, 36, 52, 54, 64, 71, 73,
     74, 77, 80, 82, 85, 88, 118, 121,
     122, 124, 126, 127, 128, 130,
     131, 132, 133, 134, 135, 136,
     137, 139, 140, 141, 145, 152,
     158, 160, 166, 168, 171, 172,
     181, 187, 188, 192, 203, 210,
     211, 212, 213, 214, 216
West Germany 22, 109, 144, 147
Wheat 118
Wheelus base 72
White goods 111

White House 5, 161
Wierner Library 141
Wilton Park 145
Wine 118
Wood 108, 118
Wool 118
World Bank *see* International Bank
     for Reconstruction and
     Development
World Development Report
     (1991) 179
World Economic Outlook (1991)
     (IMF) 32
World Health Organization
     (WHO) 191
World War I 77, 104
World War II 28, 104, 124, 171,
     195
Wretched of the Earth 201

Xiaoping, Deng 215

Yeltsin, Boris 129, 130
Yemen 52, 79
Yeo, Tim 210
Yugoslavia 4, 13, 17, 26, 52, 68,
     78, 81, 121, 131, 132, 133, 134,
     135, 140, 144, 145, 146, 150,
     163, 172, 187, 190, 192, 193,
     194, 195, 196, 210, 216

Zagreb 133
Zaire 112, 174, 178, 179
Zambia 34, 59, 67, 92, 112
Zanzibar 116
Zhou En-lai (Chou En-lai) 15
Zimbabwe 59, 64, 66, 67, 74, 89,
     111, 113, 116, 117, 177
Zinc 59, 113